THE CHURCH INFILTRATED

THE CHURCH INFILTRATED

Alexander Seibel

CHAPTER TWO
Plumstead, London

ISBN 1 85307 011 4

Bible quotations taken from the Authorized Version
(Crown copyright)

Distributors:
Australia & New Zealand: Geelong Christian Literature,
110 Barwon Blvd., Highton, Victoria 3216, Australia.
Canada: Believers Bookshelf Inc., 430 Victoria Street,
Niagara on the Lake, Ontario LOS 1JO, Canada.
Eire & Northern Ireland: Words of Truth, PO Box 147,
Belfast BT8 4TT, Northern Ireland.
India: Christian Truth Bookroom, Paddisonpet,
Tenali 522 201, Andhra Pradesh.
Ronny Fernandes, 3 Chuim Village, Khar, Bombay 400 052
United States of America: Believers Bookshelf Inc., Box 261,
Sunbury, Pennsylvania 17801, USA.

Production and Printing in England for
CHAPTER TWO
199 Plumstead Common Road, London SE18 2UJ by
Nuprint Ltd, Station Road, Harpenden, Herts AL5 4SE.

CONTENTS

CHAPTER TWO

The Question of Spiritual Darkness in Relation to God's Children

CHAPTER THREE

Considerations Concerning the Laying on of Hands

PUBLISHERS NOTE

The editorial work on this translation has not eliminated all the Germanisms. We considered it of greater importance to have the book published as soon as possible. At every step we were hindered. We learnt something of the spiritual conflict referred to by Paul in Ephesians 6:10–18. With the Lord's help we reached this point and are grateful for His sustaining grace and protection.

We commit this book to the Lord Who is able to make us understand, enjoy and walk in the power of His Spirit.

E.N.C.
Plumstead 1991.

PREFACE

My initial contact with the author of this book represents one of the most striking encounters of my Christian service. Obviously Evangelist Seibel has experienced considerable distress concerning the undermining of the Church in these last days. As Christians many of us share this same distress.

After one of our early conversations I took from Alexander Seibel a set of duplicated manuscripts which I studied thoroughly. After this I prepared a first draft of the work. In spite of heavy commitments at the Bible School it became both a commission from the Lord and a privilege for me to re-edit this draft and to prepare it for printing. Since then the author himself has revised and extended his subject. We now rejoice together in the fact that the word is at last ready for printing.

The subject is one of pressing importance. Several times the New Testament makes reference to the danger of a Christian being undermined by the powers of darkness in the last days. Now this is contrary to the widespread opinion of many believers, that such a thing is not written in the Bible anywhere. The Apostle warns his hearers at Corinth that

Satan could deceive them. In 2 Corinthians 11:4 Paul highlights the danger that believers can in fact 'receive another
spirit, which ye have not received'. According to 1 Timothy 4
the influence of evil spirits in the Church itself and among
believers will increase in the latter times. That these things
will in fact occur is revealed by the Lord Himself in His open
letter to the church at Thyatira.

In the light of these warnings from the Word of God it will
be necessary to test especially those much-praised Pentecostal and Charismatic movements of this century. Alexander Seibel clearly sees this as part of his special
commission. His warning call is alarming and at times pro-
vocative. It would certainly have been easier for him to write
against obvious heresies, modernistic Bible criticism etc.
However, he has set out in this work to bring to light some of
the evangelically-disguised movements of the adversary of
God. The undermining work of the enemy in the end times is
so commonly confused with the edifying work of our Lord
Jesus Christ. Christians must learn to detect these things and
take care to avoid them. It is our desire and our prayer that
this new publication will be used of God to this end.

Peter Mayer, Beatenberg

FOREWORD

I have found Mr Seibel's book very enlightening on questions like: 'Is it actually possible for Christians to *receive* "another spirit"?' (2 Cor 11:4) or 'Could a Christian be *filled* with the devil?' (Acts 5:3).

Too long have we been inhibited in considering these questions for fear of committing the sin of blasphemy against the Holy Spirit, but we must not ascribe the work of deceiving spirits to the Holy Spirit.

'Believe not every spirit but try (test) the spirits' (1 John 4:2) is the injunction we have in the Word. And the discerning of the spirits is the gift of the Holy Spirit. It is very possible for us to mistake an evil spirit for the Holy Spirit. It is to the believers the devil masquerades as an 'angel of light'. He does not really need to do this to the unbelievers.

This book would be helpful to anyone who has been exposed to the charismatic problem and controversy. The subject is as relevant in India as in the USA or Europe. We are not total strangers to the charismatic debate. But unfortunately many of our churches and Christian institutions have already been undermined by either easy-believism or sensationalism or indifferentism. It is in this context I believe the present book renders an invaluable service to the Church of our Lord Jesus Christ.

Mr Seibel's work is scholarly and forthright. His desire evidently is to see confused Christians helped and liberated. I have no doubt this will be accomplished by God's grace in the lives of many Christians through this book.

Dr J. Buraga, M.A., B.D., D.LITT.

INTRODUCTION

Today perhaps as never before the Church of our Lord Jesus Christ finds itself both undermined and assaulted by the deceiving powers of evil. The Bible declares that in the latter times 'some shall depart from the faith, giving heed to seducing spirits' (1 Timothy 4:1). The adversary of God, the Scriptures tell us, takes great pleasure in manifesting himself as an 'angel of light'. Today it would appear the devil is particularly active in this disguise.

One example of this might briefly be cited. Through the clear proclamation of the Gospel by an evangelist a young girl makes a decision for the Lord Jesus Christ. After her surrender to the Lord the preacher lays hands on her. And approximately one year after this it turns out that a false spirit has been transferred to the girl in this way.

Is something like this actually possible? Surely nothing of this kind could really happen! A child of God can surely not have a demon! Is this not unthinkable? How could God possibly allow something like this to occur? Views of this kind are expressed by many today, even sincere Christians.

What is the truth concerning this matter? Is the notion

that a Christian can be affected by demonic forces an extreme, exaggerated or even dangerous one? This book will try to examine and show certain teachings from the Bible which have hardly been noticed by many Christians until now. The resulting exposition is intended to find in Scripture the truth concerning this problem.

Recently I came across a spiritistic book entitled *Communication with the Spirit World* by Greber. This book describes how Greber, having held weekly meetings of prayer and Bible study with the people of his church, saw the occurrence of 'wonderful' and somewhat peculiar manifestations. The comment on these manifestations which is noted on page 31 of his book is quoted below:

> Similar happenings had also occurred in the gatherings of the first Christians. And as evidence I read to them the 14th Chapter of 1 Corinthians and explained it to them as well as I could.

This letter of the Apostle Paul to the Corinthians has been much referred to of late and will now be examined in a different manner; this will involve a partly synoptical and partly detailed approach.

Steinkreuzstr 2,
D-6331 Schöffengrund 2,
West Germany.

September, 1984.   Alexander Seibel

PLEASE NOTE: not all the quotations are verbatim, but have been translated from German books. 'Translated' in the table of references denotes quotations which are translated from the German text. In a few cases this also refers to books that are available in English.

1

THE FIRST LETTER TO THE CORINTHIANS
SOME NEW PERSPECTIVES

A Church in Need

The first Letter to the Corinthians has as its basic theme regulations and instructions to the local churches. According to Ralph Shallis the letter was written 'to bring order out of chaos'.

After the very polite introduction in Chapter 1, verses 1–9 where Paul clearly brings out their relationship as children of God, he goes on to warn those in this church about divisions in verse 10, and then gives strong exhortations right to the end of the letter. 'Now I beseech you...' (1 Corinthians 1:10). Verse 11 reveals the contentions among them. Verses 12–23 disclose the divisions.

A short description of the historical background throws some light on the context of this letter. Like Athens (Acts 17:16) Corinth was also 'wholly given to idolatry'. Sexual perversion and a strong emphasis on philosophy and worldly wisdom were its characteristics. As in Athens, there was in Corinth a large number of schools of philosophy. A very strong emphasis upon worldly wisdom was evident there as one sees in verses 18 and 19 of chapter 3. Paul warns his readers about the 'wisdom of words' (1:17) and in contrast declares the foolishness of the Cross as the true wisdom of the Church. From verse 18 to the end of the second chapter, Paul shows that the Church is not founded on worldly wisdom, philosophy or the much-praised Gnosis of the Greek, but on the message of the Cross.

Many of the Corinthians preferred 'excellency of speech

and of wisdom' (2:1) to the foolishness and offensiveness of the Cross. Chapter 3:1–3 shows clearly just how immature many believers were at that time. Paul describes them as 'carnal' and 'babes' (3:1). These people obviously believed themselves to be highly educated, but were in fact quite ignorant of spiritual things. No less than ten times does the Apostle Paul ask them in his letter, 'Know ye not...' The immaturity and inexperience of their condition are clearly indicated in these words. (The verses where Paul asks this question are: 1 Corinthians 3:16; 5:6; 6:2,3,9,15,16,19; 9:13,24.) From a spiritual point of view these believers were unlearned and 'disobedient' children. In Chapter 15:34 the Apostle writes with a certain sharpness:

> Awake to righteousness, and sin not: for some have not the knowledge of God: I speak this to your shame.

In Chapter 3:11 Paul teaches that the foundation of every church is the Lord Jesus Christ—a foundation which all believers have in common, whether carnal or spiritual. However, Paul points out that while the spiritual Christians shall receive a reward, the others shall suffer loss (3:14–15).

In Chapter 3:17 Paul engages in some very serious teaching about the corruption of the temple of God. We shall return to this subject a little later. Verse 18 reveals that the Corinthians through their worldly wisdom were in danger of self-deception, a danger caused especially by pride (Chapter 4).

Another negative characteristic of the Corinthians is revealed in verses 6, 18, and 19 of Chapter 4 as well as in Chapter 5:2. This is their arrogance ('being puffed up'). In reference to the life of the church, in Chapter 4:6 Paul gives a warning never to go beyond or 'exceed that which is written'.

As a result of their spiritual pride these believers were

tempted to believe that they already had attained a certain spiritual position, perhaps a higher form of Christian life (verse 8). In verse 7 Paul highlights the danger that spiritual gifts may often lead the believer into pride and self-edification along with the conviction of being 'someone special'. He goes on to show, however, that apostleship, seemingly the special and important thing, does not bring fame but sometimes great degradation and contempt from the world (verses 9–13).

In Chapter 5 some more serious facts concerning relationships and sins are brought to light. Verses 1–5 reveal that someone had committed incest and that to such a degree that 'he was delivered unto Satan for the destruction of the flesh' (5:5). This had occurred despite the fact that he was a child of God. This very difficult verse will be examined more closely later. However, it should be pointed out at this juncture that the actual word 'destruction' or 'destroy' is used here and also in Chapter 3:17. This passage reveals, too, that Satan can have a hold on the flesh or body of a believer although the spirit is saved.

Verses 6–18 of Chapter 5 indicate that very serious sin was being committed by a number of people in church. This sin was of such a degree that the church had to be disciplined and some of its members 'put away from among them' (verse 13). In verse 11 six serious transgressions are actually named. To continue in these transgressions meant separation from the church. Such people had to be 'put away' (verse 13). The leaven (verses 6–7) had to be removed.

It is interesting to note that strife in the Corinthian church was so great that some of its members were actually bringing legal charges against each other and having them heard before secular judges. Concerning this Paul asks in Chapter 6:5:

Is it so, that there is not a wise man among you? no, not one that shall be able to judge between brethren?

From verses 12–19 the Apostle warns of the danger of involvement in sexual sins. It is obvious that when a believer makes himself one with an unbeliever (verse 16) this act involves the mixing of light and darkness. The commandment of God concerning this great danger of 'intermixture' is to 'flee' (verse 18).

In Chapter 7 Paul reveals nothing negative in principle, but deals with the matter of marriage and abstinence.

Chapter 8 indicates that the Corinthians were still eating 'things offered unto idols'. The danger in such cases was that their arrogance could prove fatal for others (verse 11).

Lack of consideration is shown in verse 12. According to verse 10 some had obviously 'sat at meat in the idol's temple'. The danger of mixing with the ungodly is of course highlighted here.

In Chapter 9 one finds a passionate justification of Paul's apostleship. The unspiritual Corinthians had accused him of being carnal and 'not free' (9:1) and had questioned his apostleship (9:2). As his spiritual children they had in fact practically sat in judgement over him (verse 3). Paul's words in verse 16 involve an exhortation to all Christians:

Woe is unto me, if I preach not the gospel.

A Strong Warning

Chapter 10 reveals some interesting circumstances. Again ignorance must be dealt with (verse 1). In verses 1–4 the word 'all' is repeated five times.

Looking back into the Old Testament Paul stresses the clear relationship of the Israelites to God. Such a relationship when viewed in the light of the New Covenant reveals that the sonship of the Corinthians, their being part of

Christ's body, was never questioned at all. In fact, one finds a special emphasis upon it. Verse 3 indicates in fact that there were signs of real spiritual life. If someone is eating and drinking he is undoubtedly not only alive but growing also. Although these provisions were made, one reads in verse 5 the very stern comment:

> But with many of them God was not well pleased: for they were overthrown in the wilderness.

In verse 6 Paul relates this strongly emphasised warning to himself (think about Chapter 9:27) and to the Corinthians.

In verses 7–10 one learns of a number of incidents where Israelites of the Old Covenant died under the judgement of God. Verse 11 shows clearly that 'these things happened unto them for ensamples; and were written for our admonition'.

There is no doubt that in his letters, Paul was giving counsel on actual spiritual problems which existed within the particular church to whom he was writing. His explanations are actually related to specific problems and questions as evidenced in his comments on the subject of 'circumcision' in his letter to the Galatians. We could almost say that Paul, as a thorough man, presented comprehensive 'Bible studies' on current problems. Why, one might ask, would the Apostle mention the dead of the Old Covenant? Why would he point out that so many died at this time under the Law?

I would venture to suggest that in connection with this question a new aspect of the Corinthian Epistle became clear to me. This question constituted a problem also for the Corinthians. There were people among them who with God's permission were stricken dead. That is, they died physically. This is revealed in verses 29 and 30 of Chapter 11. The expression 'sleep' (verse 30) means in Greek the same as dead. It is obvious from a reading of these verses that one is not to interpret this spiritually. In understanding this, the meaning of verse 5 of Chapter 5 already quoted became clear to me also. The person in question had to die under the severest penalty (not under the judgement of condemnation), even though he was a child of God, and the text specifically states: 'that the spirit may be saved'. The possibility of this man's repenting before he died cannot be discounted. Many commentators are convinced that the verses in 2 Corinthians 2:5–11 referred in fact to this. If this is the case then physical punishment is hardly necessary. These things have nothing to do with eternal life as such (1 Corinthians 11:32) but have a primary bearing on rewards (2 John 7–8). It is no coincidence, as has already been stated, that the Letter to the Corinthians in Chapter 3 deals with the subject of rewards. Such people are saved as by fire (3:15). This is also indicated in verse 17 of the same chapter in connection with chapter 5:5 and 11:29–30. One reads here that in judgement God can destroy our temple, that is our body (1 Corinthians 6:19), and allow us to die. This is strong meat not only hard to grasp for some but very hard to digest.

Now the question is, when did God let His people (Old Covenant) and His children (New Covenant) die in judgement? I deliberately formulate this question in the past tense because I believe that at the beginning of every dispensation God would rather intervene with signs. The New Testament as such was not in existence at that time (only parts of it) and the Lord sometimes made up for that deficiency with visible signs and wonders and by so doing often confirmed the spoken Word (Mark 16:20). It is my conviction that generally speaking, in the case of similar transgressions, the Lord no longer intervenes in this way.

Now when did these people expose themselves to such a judgement of God? It is clear that one would not be stricken dead for some small transgressions. As one considers the examples above and also other facts in Scripture, then one comes to the conclusion that God would let His people (Old

Covenant) and His children (New Covenant) die in judgement if they were unrepentant in the grip of Satan and in fellowship with demons. If they through severe transgressions opened themselves to the adversary and were involved in the practice of sin, that would cause the enemy of God to fill their hearts. This was probably the case with Ananias and Sapphira (Acts 5:1-5). Satan had filled Ananias's heart (verse 3) and although a child of God, he 'fell down and gave up the ghost' (verse 5). He had lied to the Holy Spirit (verse 3) which as far as I can ascertain can only be done by a believer. Since an unbeliever does not have the Holy Spirit (Romans 8:9) he cannot lie to Him.

The possibility of the intermingling of light and darkness, of the Holy Spirit and the Spirit of Satan, of godliness and ungodliness in one person, is actually strong meat (1 Corinthians 3:2; Hebrews 5:13-14). (Naturally such an intermixture does not exist in the invisible world, for the Holy Spirit never has fellowship with darkness.) Many a believer considers this to be impossible and can hardly even comprehend it. As this question represents a fairly complex subject it will be deferred until it can be examined in more detail in the next chapter.

Paul is unable to discuss this directly with the carnal Corinthians although he clearly tells them in an indirect way. In Chapter 10, beginning in verse 14, he makes reference to the invisible spiritual mingling through idolatry, in contrast to the visible mixing through fornication (carnal) referred to in Chapter 6. God's answer to this again is 'flee'. In other words one must completely and utterly separate oneself from anything that leads into fellowship with darkness.

In verses 16-20 of Chapter 10 the Apostle mentions the word 'fellowship' or 'communion' three times and states very clearly in the second part of verse 20: 'and I would not, that ye should have fellowship with demons.' This statement shows that it is possible for God's children to have fellowship with demons. One can only warn against something, when it lies within the realm of possibility. The following verses also show that it is indeed possible and how much the Corinthians were in fact already involved in it:

> Ye cannot drink the cup of the Lord and the cup of demons; ye cannot be partakers of the Lord's table, and of the table of demons. Do we provoke the Lord to jealousy? are we stronger than He? (10:21–22).

The answer to these rhetorical questions is of course, *no*. The proof of this was to be seen in the dead in that church. God allowed them to die, for their physical strength to cease. He is the stronger One. What Paul is endeavouring to say in these verses could be formulated thus: 'You are in fellowship with demons. You drink of the cup of the Lord and also of the cup of demons.' (In Chapter 11:20 he tells the Corinthians that it is not the Lord's Supper for which they come together.) 'You are partakers of the table of demons. But this is an impossible situation, contrary to God, and your unrepentant behaviour almost seems as though you want to defy God. One could almost believe you imagine yourselves to be stronger than God. But why do you have so many weak and sick and dead among you? Because it is God who is the stronger One, as you can see it in yourselves.'

It is surely not a coincidence that this letter brings out the principle of the transference of the powers of the invisible world, through intense relationships, from one person to another. This is the law of identification, for example:

'What? know ye not that he which is joined to an harlot is one body? for the two, saith He, shall be one flesh. But he that is joined unto the Lord is one spirit.' (1 Corinthians 6:16–17).

Anyone who makes himself one with the Lord Jesus identifies himself with Him, which again is only possible at the Cross. In doing so, he receives the Holy Spirit, and as he dies to self and grows in the Lord, may be filled more and more. However, anyone who is joined to an harlot can receive unclean spirits and sins against his own body. According to verse 19, the body is 'the temple of the Holy Ghost' and is in danger through sins like these of becoming the dwelling-place of Satan (2 Corinthians 6:16a). This does not only mean the worst kind of intermingling, but also this fellow-ship with demons is completely against God. Such a person is in great danger of destroying the temple of God and there-fore to come under the visible judgement of God, that is physical death (1 Corinthians 5:5; 10:8 for carnal fornication; 1 Corinthians 10:7; 11:30,32 for spiritual fornication).

'If any man defile the temple of God, him shall God destroy; for the temple of God is holy, which temple ye are.' (1 Corinthians 3:17).

Again it might be mentioned: in 1 Corinthians 10:7-8 Paul first warns of idolatry and fornication. The passages quoted earlier show without any doubt the penalty to be physical death. The Apostle does not mention this by chance, as these were precisely the two main problems of intermixture which were prevalent in that church. They are literally unclean. We find an Old Testament parallel of this situation in Leviticus 7:20-21, as the Lord's supper is, among other things, in a certain sense a sacrifice of peace within the New Testament situation.

But the soul that eateth of the flesh of the sacrifice of peace offerings, that pertain unto the Lord, having his uncleanness upon him, that soul shall be cut off from his people. Moreover, the soul that shall touch any unclean thing, as the uncleanness of man...(let us just think of all the possibilities of spiritual defilement we have today)...and eat of the flesh of the sacrifice of peace offerings, which pertain unto the Lord, even that soul, shall be cut off from his people. (Leviticus 7:20,21).

During the time of the Old Testament and in Corinth, destruction, that is, judgement, followed, which obviously meant physical death. Today, as we do not live in the dispensation of visible signs, this means strong or definite invasion by the powers of darkness, who are in a certain sense, portraying the judgement of God.

Returning to 1 Corinthians 6:16–17, as already stated, one finds in these two verses the law of transference. On the one side we have the carnal relationship with darkness and on the other side we have the Spirit of the Lord—one negative, one positive. As mentioned before, this is strong meat. Had the Apostle told the carnal Corinthians directly it would have been too much for them in their spiritual immaturity.

The fact is that many an immature believer gets really confused and upset when speaking about this subject. He either shuts himself away completely or torments himself day and night with the thought that he too perhaps could be 'possessed'.

In his second Letter to the Corinthians, the Apostle Paul practically tells this to them directly, as they have become more mature and partly repented (2 Corinthians 2:6–7). In 2 Corinthians 11:4 we read the not very flattering words: '...or if ye receive another spirit...ye might well bear with him...' Also the verses 14–16 of 2 Corinthians 6 refer to this possible complete intermixture, and therefore the commandment follows 'not to be unequally yoked together'—but to 'separate themselves' (6:17; 7:1). Especially those believers whose bodies (fornication: 1 Corinthians 6) or spirits (passive meditation, Yoga, sins of sorcery, witchcraft, etc or idolatry: 1 Corinthians 10) are defiled, are prone to mix according to 2 Corinthians 6:14–16. One could also say that they are believers who are still under subjection because of sins of the occult or flesh—especially if holiness is not pursued (2 Corinthians 7:1b).

Vestiges of Paganism

Here again we must look at the pagan background of the Corinthians. The widespread teaching of the Gnosis of that time contained salvation by human reasoning, not by obedience in relation to the truth. Sin was considered to be neutralised to a certain degree through knowledge and understanding. Once one had recognised Jesus it was thought that everything was now settled.

There are still Christian denominations today which are inclined to believe in perfectionism. They say a believer cannot commit sin any more. This opinion that a child of God is not able to have fellowship with demons or could not have a false spirit is indeed very common. For the Corinthians who were influenced also by Gnosticism this idea was completely impossible. Therefore any supernatural as well as physical manifestations had to be 'from God' no matter how peculiar and contradictory to the teaching of the apostles. This is a very dangerous attitude, as through this complete ignorance and carelessness—though based upon honest convictions—doors could be opened to the enemy (Acts 20:28–31).

The Corinthians believed that through new understanding they could go on living the same old way, and Christian concepts were mixed with pagan ideas.

In Greece, the cult of Dionysus, the god of life and gaity, of wine and fertility, was widely known at that time. Those who drank from the cup of this god during the so-called 'Bacchanalia' became intoxicated (1 Corinthians 11:21), indulged in sexual activities (1 Corinthians 5,6)—such as fornication—and very often fell into ecstatic states and trances.

We also find these same elements in the church presented to us here. They were partly mixed with pagan elements, cults and therefore very strongly mixed with demons. The pagan festivities were chaotic and disorderly and it is not mere coincidence that the Apostle stresses the fact that God is not a God of confusion but of peace (1 Corinthians 14:33). In fact a false spirit can cause an intoxicating condition (Isaiah 19:14; 29:9–10) and even prophecy (1 Samuel 18:10; 1 Kings 18:29).

Something of that life of gaity in Greece was supposed to be reflected in the 'gatherings of the Christians'. Especially the believers were to have life and joy. Instead of drawing the fulness from the only true Fountain, that is the Lord Jesus and His Cross, many tried to increase their bliss by other means (that is, wine).

Today we also increasingly observe the tendency towards creating the 'right mood' through various emotional and worldly actions and techniques (rhythm, hard beat, clapping, shouting, sighing and so on) to prove life and 'fulness of the spirit'. Particularly to members of dead churches such 'lively meetings' have a special appeal and unfortunately emotional excitement is confused with the work of the Holy Spirit. Those who are involved in such confusion may well be 'jumping out of the frying-pan into the fire'. Paul however wrote this letter which primarily contains instruction and correction for a church situation which was marked by a terrible mixture of light and darkness.

Perhaps we ought to mention here that the 'Oracle of Delphi' was the most famous cultic centre at that time. No Greek state agreed on any undertaking without having first asked the Oracle. Women served in this place; the priestess was called 'Pythoness'. (The name comes from Python, the monstrous snake which was killed by Apollo. Later the city of Pytho or Delphi was founded there.). The Oracle of Delphi was therefore dedicated to Apollo the Greek god of prophecy and poetry. As practically every great event was directed from there, we can also expect that this whole area was more or less 'leavened thoroughly' and marked by that spirit of divination and prophecy. Therefore it is not surprising when we read that in Philippi the Apostle Paul had cast a 'spirit of Python' (as we read in the original text) out of the damsel (Acts 16:16). When the Oracle was consulted, Pytho-ness would sometimes go into ecstacy. The result was a 'speaking in tongues', about which Plato expressed a rather sarcastic opinion. Every time this happened people thought the godhead was speaking directly through the priestess and every word was recorded. The man who wrote down and passed out those words that were babbled in a trance was called 'Prophetes'.[1]

Both the cities of Corinth and Delphi were situated on the Gulf of Corinth. The close location of the two cities itself explains the special influence, inasmuch as it was nothing unusual in the church for women to speak in tongues or even to lead the worship service. It is not by chance that the Apostle emphasises in Chapter 11:1–16 the secondary posi-tion of the woman to her husband in the church. In Chapter 14:34 it is prohibited for women to speak in tongues in the church. Later we shall have a closer look at this very contro-versial point.

Without wanting to be dogmatic, perhaps the above-men-tioned background explains something else. We have already seen how carnal and puffed up the Corinthians were. Because they now spoke in tongues they thought perhaps that they would therefore be the better and greater Chris-tians. But pride is the root of all intemperance and decep-tion. When we think of the reputation of Pythoness and the world wide fame of the place of the Oracle, the gift of speaking in tongues must have seemed to them to be the greatest and most desirable thing. For that reason alone the practising of that gift could put them into an egoistical state of trance and emotional rapture. Possibly they had the idea that now they were not inferior to any of the most famous places of the religious world of that day. This desire for fame, honour and importance is sometimes very strong in carnal Christians. Perhaps that is why the Apostle says:

'...for greater is he that prophesies than he that speaketh with tongues' (1 Corinthians 14:5). In any case, Paul upholds prophecy as a more desirable gift in Chapter 14.

Deceived Believers

Having made this brief excursion into the past, let us now return to the systematic study of these chapters. After the explanation of a woman's position in the church, the Apostle relentlessly declares: '...that ye come together not for the better, but for the worse' (1 Corinthians 11:17). This is a strong statement! But after all the things we have heard so far this is certainly no exaggeration. If we find weak, sick and even dead believers as the consequence of a worship service, then we can hardly speak of anything good or of edification at all. That already means a judgement of God, and in the last verse of this chapter the Apostle speaks very clearly of this possibility. It can literally happen, unless a change of mind and behaviour does occur (Chapter 11:31–34).

In verse 18 Paul mentions divisions. He writes: 'For first of all, when ye come together...' and picks up this train of thought again in verse 20, where he expresses his view about the Lord's Supper and categorically declares: 'When ye come together therefore into one place, this is not to eat the Lord's supper.' Truly this is devastating criticism. Such verses are usually very quietly ignored.

Paul practically declares here that the Corinthians were not celebrating a Christian supper but rather pagan idolatry, as we have seen above. Let us imagine a Christian community who were told that they were not celebrating the Lord's Supper together but some kind of pagan feast. What kind of edification can you expect from such a church? sometimes this is intentionally concealed or just overlooked in order to be able to bring certain 'charismata' as wisdom's highest aim amongst the believers.

As we study the whole letter thoroughly we can have

serious doubts about the alleged uniqueness of the gifts of the Corinthians. But once we have allowed ourselves to be 'pro' programmed then experience shows that afterwards, the 'con' will scarcely be accepted. One usually clings to three or four verses which are only too often taken out of context. In this area we find an alarming blindness and deception prevalent. Verse 21 of chapter 11 even shows that some were drunken during this 'feast'.

Then with verse 23, the Apostle commences to explain the correct way to celebrate the Lord's Supper. The disgraceful condition of some members of this church (resulting from their contact with idolatry and demons and committing adultery) had resulted in death for some (verses 29–30), as we have already shown above. To be quite honest: could there be anything worse for God than to have to let His children die in judgement? Let me explain: rather than have them separated eternally from Him, God allows them to die physically so they 'should not be condemned with the world' (Chapter 11:32). To return to Chapter 3 once more—such persons shall be 'saved yet so as by fire' (3:15). Immediately following, in verses 16–17 of this third chapter, Paul mentions the 'destruction of the temple' (death) and thereby gives the proper answer of how to understand this 'salvation by fire'. Death should not be thought of as a 'refining process', which is completely unbiblical, but this intervention is to prevent a still greater yielding of self to the enemy or a total 'turning aside after Satan' (1 Timothy 5:15).

For the sake of truth and the entirety of the Word of God, this aspect of the assembly in Corinth should also be mentioned, as we find in these last days that this kind of church is being introduced to us as the ideal Christian fellowship just because its members were supposedly enjoying all the gifts.

Sometimes I have been reproached for looking at these things too negatively. Yet I fear, in the light of the Apostle Paul's writings, that the viewpoint I am criticising is based upon emotional rather than objective factors. According to the Apostle Paul this church was threatened with condemnation (1 Corinthians 11:34).

At this point I would like to explain once more that I do not doubt the sonship of the Corinthians. This is undeniable. Furthermore, Paul emphasises this by means of the examples given of the redeemed people of Israel; again and again he emphasises the word 'all' at the beginning of the 10th Chapter (also 1 Corinthians Chapter 12:13). But then comes the big 'but...' in Chapter 10:5.

It was pointed out above that Paul uses the expression 'for first of all' or 'firstly' in Chapter 11:18. This really requires the expression 'and secondly' or 'in the second place' following later. But the fact is that we do not find this precise wording until the end of the letter. Nevertheless, after the Apostle deals with the Lord's Supper he turns to the gifts and in my opinion this paragraph should also be seen under the heading of 'ye come together for the worse' (11:17).[2] After all that this letter has shown about this church so far, one can hardly expect anything positive in regard to the new subject.

Passivity

After Paul chooses a similar definition in Chapter 12:1 as in Chapter 10:1, we perhaps still remember what was shown to us there. We are now not surprised to find the Apostle explaining to the Corinthians already in the next two verses (2–3), how to discern the false gifts. That proves that to some extent they had false 'charisma'. (This is precisely the fact that will not be acknowledged by so many under any circumstances.) Otherwise the Apostle would hardly have had to show these criteria. As already mentioned, the Apostle Paul writes concerning the specific spiritual conditions of churches, and it should be unnecessary for him to explain how to discern the counterfeit if that particular problem did not exist.

In chapter 12:2 we find a verse that is overlooked or wrongly interpreted by many and we shall also examine it more closely in the next chapter.

Ye know that ye were Gentiles, carried away unto these dumb idols, even as ye were led.

Translated from the Zürich Bible it states: 'you allowed yourself to be pulled irresistibly to the dumb idols, as you were drawn' (passive form). As a matter of fact, one hears from certain people who testify of their experiences of 'baptism in the Spirit' that they felt an inner 'slipping-away' or 'being carried away'; or else they were actually 'pulled away' and the new experience simply came over them in such a way that they could not resist at all. Let us consider the clear warning of the Bible on this subject: 'Resist the devil...' (James 4:7; 1 Peter 5:9).

The Scriptures do not speak of a passive 'letting yourself go', slipping away, emptying or opening-of-self, as is being practised more and more today. The words and commands in the Bible about prayer and discipleship are usually in the active form and are also meant to be active: pursue after, flee, draw nigh to God, test, fight, seek, ask, stand, watch, strive, run, etc. The biblical command to 'seek after' gifts excludes passivity.

I hope this is not misunderstood. We are called to have a 'quiet time', to be silent before the Lord, but this is never with a passive mind. For instance, in Joshua 1:7−8 or Psalm 1 we are to memorise the Word. This is the way to fruitful service and discipleship and the very opposite of a passive mind.

Because these things are so important and crucial to a right understanding I would like to quote a short passage from the book mentioned in my introduction, *Communica-*

tion with the Spirit World. Under the title 'The Training of Mediums' it says:

> He starts with a short prayer, then has a reading from the Holy Scriptures and meditates on this reading. Then he holds in his hand a pencil over a piece of writing paper in front of him and keeps himself in an attitude of expectation 'without any kind of mental strain'. Should he be urged to the writing down of thoughts which are with certainty given to him by inspiration he writes them down. Should his hand be moved by a strange power he submits to it.[3]

This unbelievable biblical camouflage ought to frighten us. Perhaps more so because Frank Buchman the founder of 'Moral Rearmament' gave almost exactly the same instructions to his associates for their personal quiet time. And through Frank Buchman, several Christian circles were infected. Today we find many groups who propagate such 'dynamic tranquility'. Here again the critical factor emerges—the principle of passivity. Watchman Nee to that end writes in his book, *The Spiritual Man*:

> The particular sin of omission which gives ground to the evil spirits is the believer's passivity.... For a person to cease engaging any part of his talent but to allow it to sink into inertia is to provide occasion for the devil and his army to exercise it for him. This is the ground for their sinister operations.... The primary cause of deception...in surrendered believers may be condensed into one word: Passivity, that is, a cessation of the active exercise of the will in control over spirit, soul and body, or either, as may be the case.... The passivity of a saint arises out of the non-use of his various talents. He has a mouth but refuses to talk because he hopes the Holy Spirit

will speak through it. He has hands but will not engage them since he expects God to do it. He considers himself fully surrendered to God; so he no longer will use any element of his being. Thus he falls into an inertia which opens the way for deception and invasion.[4]

Today one can read increasingly of how one is to meditate passively, to withdraw oneself into 'inner quietness'. Sometimes one is to exercise continuous meditation on pictures or objects. Yes, even certain breathing, speaking or 'keeping-quiet' exercises are recommended to enable a deeper working of the 'Holy Spirit'. Without mental strain one should simply surrender oneself to anything that comes along. But it is in this way one fulfils the law of passivity and thus lays the foundation of deception by the Evil One, and, as Watchman Nee explains, one can thus be changed into a medium.

Such instructions unfortunately are found more and more in Christian books, and recommended as great 'experiences in prayer', especially in the line of literature from New-Pentecostalism. These statements will be illustrated by some examples. Larry Christenson writes in his widely-read book, *The Christian Family*:

> The prayer for guidance begins with a period of waiting. You come before the Lord, and you just get quiet. There is no activity, but rather a passivity. You are trying to hear.... You even quit breathing so you can hear better.[5]

Here we open ourselves to the spiritistic phenomenon of the hearing of voices. Almost the same advice can be found in the previously-quoted book by Greber.

Watchman Nee also believes:

> At this point Satan begins to feed them many exceedingly pleasant sensations and numerous visions, dreams and

supernatural experiences too. They receive them all as from the Holy Spirit, not realising that their inert spirit like a magnet draws in these counterfeit experiences. Had they known how to distinguish the sensational and the supernatural from the spiritual, these believers would have examined those experiences. Now however because of a lack of discernment combined with a passive spirit, they settle deeper and deeper into the enemy's deception. As the believer's spirit grows increasingly quiescent his conscience of course follows suit. Once his conscience is rendered passive, he next expects to be led directly by the Holy Spirit, either by voice or by Scripture verse...Satan alone will seize the occasion to replace the guidance of the believer's conscience and intuition with supernatural voices and other devices.[6]

Let us compare this with Larry Christenson's suggestions on prayers of meditation in the above-quoted book:

You may take a simple word or phrase, perhaps, the name of Jesus. You focus upon it and, maybe, see it in your mind in block letters, or you just say it, over and over again. (But it is precisely such practices of the passive emptying of our mind that our Lord forbids in Matthew 6:7—author's note) This ('Jesus-prayer') is a highly cultivated form of prayer in the Eastern Orthodox Church. In the prayer of meditation, spontaneous symbols and pictures will rise up out of the depths and you will just be in God's presence—for no other purpose than just to be there. You realise that you were in a state of prayer before you woke. That has been taking place in the depths of your mind, as you slept.[7]

Perhaps now we can understand better why the Scriptures exhort us to watch in prayer (Colossians 4:2). As much as some of Larry Christenson's comments about educational principles are good in his book, we also find those somewhat dubious and potentially dangerous instructions.

Thus God has given us a mind, and it is not His will that we should eliminate it, that is, become passive. I have in mind the book by John Stott, *Your Mind Matters*.* Also, many authors point out that we ought to understand, search and retain the Word of God. As a last resort we are not to rely on our mind, but we may and ought to consciously use it. The Holy Spirit illuminates our mind but does not eliminate it. Watchman Nee writes:

> A lively head is therefore an obstacle to the work of malevolent spirits. One of their greatest aims is to lead a person's mind into a blank state.... Only as his mind is functioning normally is the Christian fit to *discern* senseless supernatural revelations and various implanted suggestions and recognise their alien sources. A vacuous mind provides a foothold for the evil foe. All revelations and notions received by an empty head emanate from enemy sources[8].

Thinking of these strong admonitions, such suggestions for prayer as we find them recommended by Wilhard Becker—a leading man of the Charismatic movement in Germany—sound rather strange:

> In order that the presence of God also penetrates into the subconscious, he first of all speaks softly, in a slow rhythm, 'Jesus Christ', to himself. In doing so he tries

---

* In quoting this author I do not wish to intimate that I necessarily agree with everything else this famous Anglican theologian has to say. This also applies to some of the other authors quoted.

again and again to speak the name of Jesus while exhaling and Christ inhaling. After a while, through relaxed breathing and speaking of the name 'Jesus', the person praying acquires the ability to formulate the name in his thoughts instead of having to pronounce it.

Thereby the inner self is gradually filled with the name of the Son of God. If we repeat this exercise several times during the day it will lead to an attitude of life where the conscious process of our mind becomes passive and receptive to a leading force of the soul. This kind of prayer is especially helpful when in an upset frame of mind, and even for melancholia, and depressions. With the constant and rhythmical repetition of the name of Jesus the subconscious takes over the rhythm and the name of Jesus Christ becomes a ringing sound in the soul.[9]

Here it would seem that the concept of the subconscious and passivity, partly anyway, are over-lapping. Personally, such suggestions remind me more of 'Hatha-Yoga', and one can clearly recognise the principle of passivity which is explained impressively in *The Spiritual Man*:

Not aware of the possibility of accepting the teaching of evil spirits in their minds, Christians assume that anything which has suddenly burst upon them while in meditation is their own new discovery of faith. They write and preach these ideas as the fruits of their research. Upon hearing or reading these teachings, people marvel at the cleverness of these Christians. But do they perceive that many of these doctrines in reality emanate from the bottomless pit?[10]

In this respect we find a highly peculiar instruction for prayer again in the book, *The Christian Family*:

When you have a need that you want to pray about—
somebody else's problem—visualise yourself taking that
person into yourself before you begin to pray. You get a
whole new feeling. You are no longer praying at that
person. You have taken the person into your heart, and
you are now *involved*. God is in you, and in your heart an
interaction between that person and God is taking place.
Instead of beaming a prayer out to them, you take them
into your heart and let God, who is in you, begin to
transform that situation.[11]

This reminds us more of magic or spiritualism than of
prayer. In his book, *The Latent Power of the Soul*, Watchman Nee writes:

The prayers in the Bible are intelligent and not silly.
When the Lord Jesus teaches us to pray, His first words
are: 'Our Father who art in Heaven.' He teaches us to
pray to our Father in Heaven, but we Christians often
pray to the God in our room...God wants us to send our
prayers to Heaven by faith, regardless of whether our
feelings are good or bad, or even if there are no feelings.
If you pray to, and expect to be heard by, the God in your
room, I am afraid you will receive many strange feelings
and miraculous experiences and visions from the God in
your room. These are given to you by Satan.[12]

People who spread such teachings or open themselves to
these suggestions through passivity or 'letting yourself go', as
it is sometimes called, often have the very best intentions.
Bearing in mind all the statements of *The Latent Power of
the Soul*, and the statements made about the passive 'opening of self', I would like to quote a man whose sincerity and
dedication I do not doubt, but who gives rather questionable

suggestions for prayer. In his book 'Beten lernen' (*Learn to pray*, translated) Roland Brown writes:

> I let all my thoughts drop... After some time the physical relaxation itself leads into mental relaxation. Now you actually ought to feel the chair you are sitting on. You can really feel your weight. The chair is strong; it carries you; you completely trust it, and then you give yourself fully to it. Now you can imagine this chair becoming the arm of God. Allow yourself to fall into His arms, into the eternal arms of God. Allow God to hold you; trust Him. You are not giving yourself to Him—on the contrary you are abandoning yourself to Him, without any kind of effort at all. Let Him simply do with you whatever He desires. Then you also experience how the Holy Spirit comes into your soul.[13]

Apparently the warning of Watchman Nee is not unjustified:

> We know that in these latter times evil spirits especially engage in much teaching (1 Timothy 4:1). The Lord's people should guard against such teachings imparted to passive minds.[14]

This is the reason why the risk is taken here to call the people and things directly by name. Yet, in so doing, one usually meets with a lot of opposition. Who is it really who would like to prevent God's people from being warned explicitly?

Now perhaps it becomes more obvious why the Bible declares repeatedly, as we have shown to some extent already: 'Resist, test'; why the Lord Jesus warns us, especially in the hour of growing darkness (John 9:4) to watch and to pray (Matthew 26:41). To be awake is, in a spiritual sense, the opposite to a sleepy and passive condition. In Gethsemane the disciples literally went to sleep (Matthew 26:40) in this great hour of temptation (Luke 22:31). Perhaps we already find a similar situation among us. If we do not heed the warning in Peter's letter (1 Peter 5:8) and instead of being 'sober and vigilant', become passive and intemperate (how often do we find just that in the Charismatic movement), then the Devil will devour us, as the Word of God unmistakably declares and as Watchman Nee warns. Many a person can even report on how he started to speak in tongues in his sleep. What a widespread deception we already have today! (This is practically a literal fulfilment of Isaiah 29:9–10: 'This blinding spirit of deep sleep causing drunkenness.' In the 4th verse of the same chapter, we can read which spirit is speaking through such a one!)

It is clear that these principles of passivity are especially strongly marked in Yoga, hypnosis, auto-suggestion, group dynamics, the autogene training and above all in the Eastern religions. People, having such a past or even Hinduistic backgrounds, who find their way to Jesus Christ, must be especially watchful that they are not, in their 'devotional, meditative quiet time—that is, prayers', in reality practising a kind of transcendental meditation.

Watchman Nee writes:

Today many of God's children have fallen unknowingly into passivity.[15]

Compulsion by the Powers of Darkness

Let us go back to 1 Corinthians 12:2. The King James Version says:

Ye know that ye were Gentiles, carried away unto these dumb idols, even as ye were led.

The Menge (German) Bible renders it, 'being snatched away'. If someone is led away or even carried away against his will, then this is done through a false spirit, because 'the spirits of the prophets are subject to the prophets' (1 Corinthians 14:32). Yet today we hear and read more frequently of people being 'carried away', slain in the spirit, 'pulled away' and in some severe cases they even become unconscious. This clearly reveals compulsion controlled by an alien will.

So we distinctively read in a passage of Greber's spiritistic book:

> I cannot do otherwise...I am being forced...I must write...I do not know, but an irresistible power forces me to...[15]

Here the principle of compulsion very clearly stands out. As these truths became clear to me, many a report of 'great spiritual experiences' seemed rather questionable to me. For instance, we read in the main German Pentecostal magazine:

> Once when Bishop Burnett of Grahamstown meditated in his study he was thrown to the floor by a mighty wind. His body prickled and he made strange noises, and he later realised that he had spoken in an unknown language.[17]

Here, obviously, a wrong spirit is operating. In certain meetings the people are actually 'pulled away' or fall backwards on to the floor unconscious, even against their will (Isaiah 28:13). In the presence of God, if one falls, one always falls on his face (Matthew 17:6). Apparently it is not by chance that we read in 1 Corinthians 14:25: that the convicted sinner would 'fall down on his face'. Nowhere in the Book of Acts do we read of the apostles needing helpers to catch the people who had fallen backwards. Today, this is happening more and more in certain assemblies and is very clearly a sign of strong influences on the part of the powers of darkness causing the phenomenon known as 'slain in the spirit'.

A typical example may illustrate these statements. Barratt, who brought the 'Pentecostal Revival' from Los Angeles to Europe, in his own words describes his experience of the Baptism with the Spirit on November 5, 1906 as follows:

> The power came so suddenly and powerfully that I lay on the floor speaking in tongues incessantly for some time.... It seemed as if an iron hand laid over my jaws. Both jaws and tongue were worked by this unseen power.[18]

However, God never forces His creatures. His love leads and guides (Romans 8:14) but does not force. Let us also compare Romans 8:15a with 2 Corinthians 3:17—here slavery, there liberty. It is from such constraint as this that the Lord Jesus has set us free (Galatians 5:1). He has broken the merciless yoke of the enemy (Isaiah 9:4; Acts 26:18).

The Apostle Paul really says to the Corinthians: 'Well, you know; while you were still Gentiles, it just drew you to these dumb idols. Like robots you were pulled away.' If things like these are happening again today, it is hard to understand why it should suddenly be produced by the Holy Spirit. (Please see also 2 Timothy 2:26.) As already said, the Spirit of God never forces. Where through a growing influence obsession, compulsion, hallucinations, forced thoughts and pictures, even forced actions occur we find the influences of the powers of darkness.

> The satanic spirit however so puts the person under the oppression of an external power that it appears to him to represent God's will and compels him to act like a

machine devoid of thought or decision[19], writes Watchman Nee.

In this context the following report from the books of Kathryn Kuhlman is highly informative and instructive:

> And then I fell to the floor. Later Donna told me that while I had been lying on the floor I had banged my left leg up and down with such force that she had been afraid it would break. After a while some ushers helped me on to my feet again and escorted me to the platform.[20]

Let us imagine this for a moment: a person is lying helplessly on the floor with a quivering leg, furiously kicking it up and down. This reminds us, objectively speaking, rather of plain possession, a temporary seizure by an alien force, than of the work of God. The Bible explains that self-control, among others, is one of the fruits of the Spirit (Galatians 5:25). The Greek word 'enkrateia' ('temperance' as the King James Version says) also means self-control. We do not need a lot of imagination to recognise that something like this has nothing to do with self-control at all. If we just think of Watchman Nee's explanation of the subject of passivity, it actually describes exactly the opposite. Now out of concern and love for the churches we must plainly say that the power which so obviously acts unlike the Holy Spirit, is not of God.

At this point I do not wish to attack any person, but I would like to warn against the powers which hide themselves behind such manifestations. With Brandenburg, I would like to say:

> One will have to acknowledge objectively that these physical effects of power (trembling, shouting, falling over, etc) could not very well be attributed to the Holy Spirit.

From the same author we read in a different passage:

But it was wrong to understand the action of the spirit as magically powerful—with suppression of the human character. Here we come to a very important characteristic. Where, as we find in spiritism, the spirit of the person is paralysed or put to sleep to make room for another spirit, we can be certain that it is not the work of the Holy Spirit. The Holy Spirit does not kill or destroy, rather He renews, revives and quickens. He always gives us our own responsibilities. 'The spirits of the prophets are subject to the prophets,' Paul writes in 1 Corinthians 14:32. Where spirits are forcing a person against his will, there the Holy Spirit has certainly no part in it.[21]

In a book from Kathryn Kuhlman, in this same connection, still stranger things are taking place. It concerns the healing of a married couple. Here we only give the account of the husband who was healed soon after his wife had been healed.

At that time Bill had come to an all-time low. God had healed his wife and she had not even asked Him for it. Now Bill wanted to be healed too. She had never seen him in such a state during that night. He almost challenged God to do something. She did not understand anything about prayer yet she was scared when it was his turn to pray. He did not thank God, as they all did, but almost screamed at Him, and asked God how it was that they all knew Him and he didn't? He had healed Freda: why does He not heal him? God must prove to him that He existed. (If we think of the warnings in 1 Corinthians 10:9–10, we can understand how such behaviour can open the doors for the adversary of God. Author's note.) Suddenly Bill sailed past the people, as if an invisible hand had grabbed

him and thrown him across the room. He landed at the
door. Bill weighed almost 200 lbs, at the time, but this
power blew him over there as if he was just a feather.
There he collapsed. His head was leaning against the
doorpost.... With his eyes wide open he started to scream
again, that he was desperate and God should do something for him. And again he was thrown to the floor by
this invisible power as if he had been struck by lightning.
...Three of the people tried to bring him back on to his
feet but he was too heavy; they couldn't carry him. His
body was stiff and lifeless. They got frightened and he was
asked to get up. His lips moved and he whispered that he
could not move at all; he had no power over his body.
(Again the exact opposite to self-control. Author.)
...Suddenly Bill got up as if the same hand had hit him on
the back and he slid back over the floor into the kitchen
where he hit the refrigerator with great force. They were
all amazed and heard how Bill started to praise the Lord.
He prayed to Him and thanked Him for His mercy. He
asked Him for forgiveness just as a child would ask his
father.[22]

Here, hardly any comment is necessary. When people
regard such spiritism as the work of the Holy Spirit, it will
really not take long until they accept the antichrist in place of
the true Redeemer. Can we guess how far this undermining
has taken place already?

I would like to bring another example from counselling
which again ought to illustrate the above-mentioned principle of force. A young man from Holland was asked to fight
along in prayer (with others) for the deliverance of a
demonically-subjected sister. Several believers gathered
together in a remote room for intercession. This sister had
received seducing spirits of tongues through unbiblical laying
on of hands. It turned out that this young Dutchman also had

the gift of tongues. But as they spoke to him about this
subject and he saw his oppressed sister, he was willing to
renounce his gift of tongues. As he renounced himself from
it, the sister was bent down at the side by an unseen power,
while especially her hands, cramped like claws, were shaking
vigorously. One could really see the fury of the demonic
world as someone was ready, here, to abandon a gift from
'below'. After the young man had renounced himself by
prayer, the satanic spirit of tongues was commanded several
times to leave in the name of Lord Jesus Christ. Each time,
he confessed later, he had to press his mouth together as his
tongue vibrated against his will. Therefore it became very
clear that this was a forcing seductive spirit. As this happened, the fury of the invisible world was obviously
increased. The sister, for whose deliverance they had
gathered together in prayer, could not from that time on for
about half an hour, either talk or even utter one word. An
invisible power was holding her vocal chords. This was just
the more surprising as this sister had never had any problems
in this area before. These were obviously the same spirits
who wanted to demonstrate their control over the vocal
organs. There are several witnesses to this occurrence.

In addition I could quote more than a dozen such illustra-
tions of confrontations, yet I would like to leave it at that. I
am conscious of the fact this might seem unbelievable for
some. Indeed, I must confess that we were quite surprised
ourselves, as we really had not expected it, and such experience of the unseen world was rather strange to us. Had I not
seen this with my own eyes and heard it with my own ears,
and had not taken part in the active fight, I too would
probably have difficulty in believing it. However, these
occurrences demonstrate to us very effectively what kind of
deliverance we have in the Lord Jesus Christ and how far the
forces of the powers of darkness can go.

It could be helpful in this connection to include a passage

from the book, *The Psychology of Speaking in Tongues* by
John Kildahl:

> In our study persons with a low level of emotional stability
> tended to be extreme in their affirmation of the benefits of
> glossolalia. A well-integrated tongue-speaker generally
> made no wildly exaggerated claims for its powers, used it
> in a way that was not sensational, and did not allow it to
> dominate his life or use it as an instrument by which to
> manipulate others. In marked contrast, glossolalists who
> reported speaking in tongues at every moment they were
> not speaking English were psychologically in a similar
> condition to those who have an obsessive fantasy regard-
> ing numbers, or a hand-washing compulsion.[23]

Here too we have the same association. Where there is
compulsion and consequently the influence of the powers of
darkness, we find the strongest support and seeking after the
gift of speaking in tongues, and there we also observe the
strongest practising of it. One can therefore say that where
there is darkness, it leads to an over emphasis of this gift: it is
taken out of its biblical context and put into the foreground.
However, as we shall see, the Apostle Paul puts it last.

Counterfeit Tongues?

The 3rd verse of Chapter 12:

> Wherefore I give you to understand, that no man speak-
> ing by the Spirit of God calleth Jesus accursed; and that
> no man can say that Jesus is the Lord, but by the Holy
> Ghost

refers to the discernment between the genuine and the counterfeit speaking of tongues. The following is being expressed
here: If someone curses the Lord Jesus Christ with this gift of

tongues, then this kind of speech is being inspired by a false spirit. If Jesus Christ is called Lord during the speaking in a strange tongue, then the Spirit of God is speaking through this person.

Thus Michael Griffiths writes concerning the first verses of Chapter 12:

> The point made by Paul is that people speaking under inspiration may be divided into those who are speaking by the Spirit of God and those who, while certainly inspired, are *not* speaking by the Spirit of God.... Now previously the Corinthians had already been familiar as idol-worshippers with inspired persons, with oracles, speaking under the influence of false gods and moved by demonic influences (v 2). But even now, converted and in the church, there is still a danger that a spirit other than the Spirit of God speaks through someone in the congregation. This aspect of the subject is, oddly enough, sometimes not discussed at all in 'Pentecostal' literature. No reflection is implied on a genuine gift by asserting with Scripture that there are also spurious gifts. This is what Paul asserts at the very beginning of his discussion of the subject, and the order of the gifts explains why he does so... 'Glossolalia' is a widespread phenomenon also found in Islam, Hinduism, Mormonism, Spiritism, Voodoo and witch-craft. Clearly there is not only a genuine but also a spurious speaking in tongues. We may expect to find alongside the genuine, the Devil's counterfeit. We are used to counterfeit and true Christians. There is every reason also from Scripture to expect counterfeit tongues and counterfeit miracles.[24]

Lang similarly confirms:

> Another feature was an unwillingness by some to face the

danger of Satanic attack. This exposed souls to inroads of evil spirits.[25]

Love covers indeed, but real love will also seek to warn believers concerning such dangers of possible inroads of deceiving powers. This requires charity and proper judgement, as John MacArthur Jr in his series of messages 'What's Wrong in the Charismatic Movement?' once put it:

> I would say initially that we are thankful to God for the much good that is done as our brothers and sisters in Christ are sharing the gospel and winning others and so forth and we are not disparaging that for a moment, but only trying in the light of the Word of God to evaluate the movement so that we can get a clear understanding of what is good and what is not so good; to be able to make a proper judgement.[26]

Back to 1 Corinthians 12:3. This verse we often find wrongly interpreted, as it is assumed that someone who maintains that Jesus is his Lord, must therefore also have the Holy Spirit. This is contrary to Matthew 7:21–22 and other passages. The interpretation, given to me by Evangelist Ralph Shallis of the 2nd and 3rd verses, explains as follows: First of all, the speaking in tongues must always be in a language, otherwise the interpreter would not know what was being said. Where we find a phenomenon in the Bible for the first time, we usually also find the key to it. In Acts 2 it is clearly a question of languages as a miraculous sign. One is almost able to bring proof from the point of view of cybernetics that language means *order*—logos; babbling means *disorder*—confusion; alogos—darkness. The Holy Spirit is a Spirit of order (peace) (1 Corinthians 14:33), and the Lord Jesus Christ is called Logos (John 1:1). Secondly, another statement is made here—something that many believers do not recognise or believe to be possible: namely that a child of God is able to curse the Lord Jesus Christ with this 'gift'. This again is strong meat. Yet numerous cases in counselling have proved these biblical words to be true, and have brought this terrible truth into the light (Isaiah 29:3–4).

Here is one further example. A young man from charismatic circles visited a training camp for young Christians. There the lectures started to make him doubt his convictions held up till then, especially when it was biblically proved to him that the baptism of the Spirit and regeneration fall together. He fell into such doubts and crises that eventually he cried to God with all his heart to show him what was now right and if his gift was genuine or not. Afterwards he wanted to pray to God and he was horrified when he discovered that he was praying to the devil instead. After that he knew who had 'given this gift' to him. Similar frightening things are reported by missionaries and other counsellors. As we see and read how many an unsuspecting child of God has fallen victim to the deceitful attacks of the enemy (Ephesians 6:11), this ought to fill us with great sorrow.

> The enemy is very real. How can we afford then to be less watchful?[27]

says Watchman Nee. Yet, I would like to emphasise, the people concerned do not have any idea and are certain that they are serving God and worshipping Him. Their intentions are usually more than sincere. Sometimes they are like Peter who, in his zeal, wanted to keep Jesus from going to the Cross and thought to serve God at the same time (Matthew 16:22). However, in reality Satan was behind it (verse 23), and this in spite of the fact that just before (verses 16–17) the Spirit of God had clearly spoken through him. Although this happened before Pentecost it still ought to make us think. The enemy knows how to manipulate fleshly zeal.

About Spiritual Gifts

In 1 Corinthians 12:7 before the gifts are mentioned the statement is made that all the gifts are given 'to profit withal' and not for any self-interest. Indeed we read in the original Greek only 'for profit', but the translators have correctly, and in my opinion, not without good reason, given this translation. 1 Peter 4:10, where we are given to understand that every Christian is in possession of at least one gift, also discloses the basic reason for these gifts: we ought to 'minister the same one to another as every man hath received the gift'. The same principle is indicated in Romans 12:5, where in the following verses several gifts are named.

Paul also points out in this Letter to the Corinthians that the only reason for our having gifts and seeking after them, is the edification of the church (14:5,6,12,26). In Chapter 14:17 he rather warns: '...but the other is not edified'. He also gives us his own life as an example and he points out how he lives not for his own profit, but for the well-being of others (10:24,33). A gift given for selfish purposes contradicts the whole picture of the body of Christ, given by Paul in Chapter 12, as well as in Romans 12:4–5, in connection with gifts. Ephesians 4:11–13 shows the same basic principle. It even literally says: '...for the edifying of the body of Christ' (verse 12).

An independent member in the body is a contradiction in itself and an unnatural condition. It causes, in any case, only divisions (1 Corinthians 12:25), a phenomenon which today lays hold of more Christian communities. This also very often results from a certain gift which is simply being used for self-edification and thus must divide the body (see also 1 Corinthians 1:10,13). This connection would not seem to be perchance. William MacDonald commenting on 1 Corinthians 12:7, writes:

Each believer has at least one gift. In this way the Holy

Spirit can reveal Himself in the life of the believer. But these gifts were not given for self-edification, but for the blessing of the whole local body of Christ.[28]

Altogether we find the word 'charisma' seventeen times in the New Testament, seven times in 1 Corinthians. The word means 'completely undeserved gift of grace from God'. The list of the gifts in Romans 12 with 1 Corinthians 12 gives us about fifteen, and if we want to include Ephesians 4:11, eighteen 'charismata'. In 1 Corinthians 12:8–10 we are told of nine gifts. Here, as well as in the other enumeration of the gifts of the Spirit (28–30) the gift of tongues takes the last place, which is surely not a coincidence. In view of 1 Corinthians 14:33 this order is certainly not optional.

In Chapter 12:11 we are told that the gifts are 'divided to every man severally as God willed'—not as we will. In this connection it is interesting to see that it does not generally say that we ought to pray for these gifts. To my knowledge, we read that we ought to pray only for the gift of interpretation in Corinthians (14:13), and of wisdom, according to James 1:5. Otherwise the word of God says: 'Desire or covet' (12:31; 14:39 etc).

This should not be deemed 'hairsplitting'. There are definitely different concepts in the Greek. When we strive after, and are also, in my opinion, living in an active submission to God, then the Lord will bring the one or the other gift in us to fruition—according to His sovereign will. Nowhere are we instructed to wrestle for hours in fervent prayer for some gifts which would suit our flesh and ego best (Psalm 78:18). It would contradict the exposition of the first letter to the Corinthians.

If the sovereign God divides the 'charisms' (12:18) and they are freely given, without merit, then they could not be, strictly speaking, subject to human effort. Why then does it say in 1 Corinthians 12:31 that we are to 'covet earnestly' the gift? A mission leader believes it is because the Corinthians had turned around the divine order, as well as many other things, in regard to the gifts. They exalted smaller, inferior gifts to the disadvantage of the greater ones (see also Chapter 4:7).

William MacDonald expresses himself in a similar way:

It is interesting and perhaps significant that the list of the gifts start with those which are mainly concerned with feelings and emotions. The Corinthians had reversed the order in their thinking. They exalted the gift of tongues above the other gifts. They thought that the more someone possessed the Holy Spirit so much the more this must show itself in supernatural actions. 'They confused power with spirituality' (William Kelly). The order which Paul gives is the opposite to the way the Corinthians evaluated it. They believed that the less intellect and awareness were connected with it, the more they were under the power of the Spirit. Paul on the other hand shows that the highest spiritual gifts are exercised in connection with intellect.[29]

Also, Hans Brandenburg writes:

It is only in our deep repentance and genuine humility that God will answer with life from above. Beware, lest we seek gifts in order for us to be admired...or because we are looking for the unusual in order to have greater influence. If so, it will eventuate in a movement from below. It is dangerous wanting to be more than God desires to make of us.

Furthermore he comments on the same page:

As the body can develop power and energy, so also can the soul. Therefore we are able to 'intensify our emotions'. We can arouse and nurse our feelings. One thing the soul cannot do: it cannot give orders to the Holy Spirit. Whoever wants to obtain the Holy Spirit and His gifts by emotional means or even physical exercises (as we find them in India), becomes a religious dreamer.[30]

These explanations are of great importance in connection with prayer. Here especially we find too many false ideas.

Is there judgement as answer to prayer?

One can observe again and again, how especially followers of the Charismatic movement reject this idea and often are by no means ready to acknowledge the fact. Their main verse to refute such a possibility is Luke 11:13, a key verse of the whole Pentecostal movement. 'If you then, who are evil, know how to give good gifts to your children; how much more shall your heavenly Father give the Holy Spirit to them that ask him?' But in the original text we do not read here that we should ask for the Holy Spirit, since the word 'for' (ask *for* the Holy Spirit) does not occur. But the practical experience rather confirms that the Holy Spirit has a much better hold on those people who spend much time in prayer and intercession.

Believers should not ask for the Holy Spirit since they already *have* the Spirit as children of God (Romans 8:9). Also, Christians should not pray to the Holy Spirit. There is not one single example in the entire New Testament of this practice and therefore caution ought certainly to be taken here, because prolonged supplications in a misguided way can, as shown above, open the gates for the enemy.

In the same way, Barratt, whom we have quoted earlier and who is also called the father of the European Pentecostal movement, had also fasted and prayed for days in a completely unbiblical manner for the 'experience' of the baptism of the Spirit, until he finally received what he had asked for. Interesting in this context are the statements of A. E. Ruark:

> They seek to speak in tongues with the expectation that it is by the 'baptism of the Holy Spirit'. They thereby put themselves at the disposal of a demon spirit which may give the gift of tongues as a manifestation of the false doctrine ('Falsities of Modern Tongues', Prairie Bible Institute, p 1).

To assume that everything that concerns prayer must be coming from God is rather naïve. We are standing on the battlefield of an invisible war and not only good and positive forces are engaged in it. Not without reason does the Scripture warn us that we are to watch in prayer (Ephesians 6:18; Colossians 4:2). We are not only to turn to the true God in prayer but also we ought to be in agreement with His will. Believers who are praying but not in the centre of God's will are especially endangered.

We read in the Scriptures that sometimes God had answered prayers in such a way that He had to send judgement. We see this in Numbers 11:4–6 where the children of Israel were not content with the manna God had been giving to them. It is interesting to read in verse 4 that 'the mixed multitude that was among them, fell a lusting'. In any case, from the point of 'mixing' this is worth mentioning. They wanted more, they demanded meat. In a spiritual sense, our manna, our spiritual food, the Word of God alone, is not enough. We want sensations, experiences, visions, variety for the flesh.... The Lord's answer to the crying of Israel was:

> Therefore the Lord will give you flesh.... Ye shall not eat one day, nor two days, nor five days, neither ten days, nor twenty days; but even a whole month, until it come out at

your nostrils and it be loathsome unto you; because that ye have despised the Lord... (Numbers 11:18-20).

Psalm 78 says in connection with Numbers 11:

So they did eat, and were well filled: for he gave them their own desire: They were not estranged from their lusts. But while their meat was yet in their mouth, the wrath of God came upon them... (verses 29-31).

Thus the Lord gave them what they had cried for: yet the wrath of the Lord and judgement was connected with it (Hosea 13:11).

This again is strong meat, but it is very clear in the Bible and it is written for our admonition (1 Corinthians 10:6,11). Many a believer asks amiss 'that he may consume it upon his own lust' (James 4:3). In a similar way we read how the children of Israel asked for a king—again it was their own wish. They wanted to have the same things as the others around them. The story of Balaam and other examples make it clear that we are first of all to ask for the will of the Lord before we start to cry out for certain things or experiences. Nowhere in Scripture do we read that we are to pray for the baptism of the Spirit, or the gift of tongues or even for the outpouring of the Holy Spirit.

Baptism of the Spirit

Now we are going further along to verse 12 of Chapter 12, where we see the fellowship of believers described as a body, an organism of which the single believer is a member. The necessary requirement for it is regeneration, that is, the baptism of the Spirit.

In verse 13 there is the expression 'being baptized with the Holy Spirit', the only time in the Epistles. This term actually occurs seven times in the Bible, four times in the Gospels

(Matthew 3:11; Mark 1:8; Luke 3:16 and John 1:33) and twice in the Book of Acts (1:51; 11:16). For instance, the verses 14–16 of Acts 11 tell us that the baptism of the Spirit and the salvation of Cornelius were identical.

Passages in the Book of Acts have especially been the cause of considerable confusion and controversy about this subject. Concerning this whole critical area, Alfred Kuen makes an important point in his lecture entitled 'Werdet voll Geistes' (translated 'Be Filled with the Spirit'):

> If we believe that the Holy Spirit teaches the Truth in the Word of God then we must obtain our doctrines purely and simply from the Word of God and must make our expressions conform to those used by the inspired authors of the Bible. Therefore when we speak of 'receiving of the Spirit', of 'baptism of the Spirit' and of 'filling of the Spirit' we must use the same expressions and use them in the same sense as the Bible does. This is not merely a matter of strife over words. Words are bearers of spiritual realities and events and the history of recent decades provides abundant proof that blithely changing one word for another leads to spiritual confusion.

The well-known revivalist Charles Finney, for instance, described one special experience of his Christian life as 'Baptism of Power'. His friend and colleague in the school of Oberlin, Asa Mahan, named this experience: 'Baptism of the Spirit'. The evangelist Reuben Torrey took up this concept and systematically dealt with it in his book, *Baptism of the Spirit*. Torrey suggests that this is a special experience which the believer can have after conversion and that it equips him with special power from on high and gifts of the Spirit for our service for the Lord Jesus.

The founders of the Pentecostal movement took up this interpretation of Torrey's and added one further point: The sign of having received the baptism of the Spirit, they claimed, was speaking in tongues. Thus we have here the emergence of a doctrine which has been accepted by millions of Christians throughout the world today.

Before one accepts any doctrine, how necessary it is to examine that doctrine in order to determine whether it originates in the Word of God or in some historical development of dogmatism!

In asking oneself 'What does the Bible teach?' one must be willing to abandon the kind of methods unfortunately found in so many Christian circles where personal assumptions are allowed to override the Word of God. Any statement one makes concerning doctrine must have its basis in the Word of God.

It is commonly claimed today that one must first be converted, then later through a second experience one receives the Holy Spirit or the baptism of the Spirit. As proof of this the Apostles who received the Holy Spirit at Pentecost are cited, along with the Samaritans, the disciples at Ephesus and eventually also the Apostle Paul. Thousands of conversions referred to in the Book of Acts are neglected in the process. Instances where believers immediately received the Holy Spirit—without the laying on of hands and without the speaking in tongues—are not mentioned at all. Attention is never drawn to the fact that the Apostles never encouraged in any of the Epistles anyone to seek or to wait for such a second experience or baptism of the Spirit.

If one really wants to know what the Bible teaches then one must be willing to use the same inductive method employed by scientists in their research of the laws of nature. One must proceed from what the Bible says and from there draw one's conclusions only after one has honestly examined everything Scripture teaches on the subject.

If one wants to know what the Apostles taught one must first attempt to fathom their thoughts in the Epistles. This means one must start reading the Epistles and thoroughly examine the conclusions drawn from these letters, and then line them up with the Gospels and the Book of Acts—not the other way round. The Gospels and the Book of Acts inform us of a solitary, never-to-be-repeated series of acts in history. These include how the Word became Flesh, how the Lord Jesus suffered for us, His Resurrection on the third day, how He ascended into Heaven and ten days later poured out the Holy Spirit on His disciples. Like Good Friday and Easter Sunday, Pentecost cannot be repeated. To pray for a new Pentecost makes just as little sense as asking for a new Incarnation of the Lord Jesus Christ. Those who now enjoy God's unique salvation live in a new dispensation and not in a transitional time. We now find that no one ever has to move through such a transitional period as did the Apostles who moved from the Old Covenant to the New. In the Epistles we discover the truth of the New Covenant— baptism of the Holy Spirit is therefore the first step in the believer's life. We are buried with Christ by baptism into His death and with Him are raised up into newness of life in order to become members of Christ's body. Baptism of the Spirit is symbolically portrayed in baptism by water—a burial and resurrection with Christ. So far Alfred Kuen ('Bible and Church', translated, Oct.–Dec. 1975, pp 353–354 and 357). Those who hold to the unbiblical teaching of the baptism of the Holy Spirit as a second or special experience connected with holiness often cite the passage describing the baptism of Jesus in the Jordan River in support of their position. They claim that here Christ is supposed to have received the Holy Spirit or been baptised with the Holy Spirit. The Gospel of John, however, reveals to us that this visible descending of the Spirit was a sign for John the Baptist. Having thus seen it, John the Baptist was therefore able to bear record that Jesus was in fact the Messiah (John 1:32–34). However, to interpret this 'distinguishing sign' as if the Lord had only just received the Holy Spirit is not only risky but perilously close to heresy.

The Scripture is abundantly clear on the fact that Jesus Christ was naturally one with the Father from the beginning (Psalm 22:10) and full of the Holy Spirit. There is no other way to explain His absolute sinlessness and the fact that He never made a mistake. Concerning John the Baptist we read that 'he was filled with the Holy Ghost even from his mother's womb' (Luke 1:15). If this were true of John the Baptist, how much more would it need to be true of our Lord Jesus Christ. The Lord Jesus Christ was begotten of the Holy Spirit Himself, the fruit thereof being called 'that holy thing' (Luke 1:35).

Verse 13 of 1 Corinthians 12 tells us explicitly 'that we are *all* baptized into one Spirit'. The exact grammatical form is: indicative, aorist, passive—once and for all it was accomplished at regeneration. The word 'all' includes not only carnal but also spiritual Christians. They have ALL been made to drink into one Spirit. This ALL stands in contrast to verse 30, where the Apostle asks: '...Do all speak with tongues? Do all interpret?' To each of these questions a clear NO is expected. These passages express clearly that baptism of the Spirit and the speaking of tongues are two different things.

Perhaps it should be mentioned briefly that before the outpouring of the Holy Spirit these acts of God were described in Scripture through the use of the future tense (Acts 1:5,8 etc), while after Pentecost they were described in the past tense (1 Corinthians 12:13; 2 Corinthians 1:21–22 etc). Except for the 'filling of the Spirit of God' one finds reports of completed events.

It is something different, however, when the Bible speaks about being filled with the Holy Spirit. The expressions 'full of the Holy Spirit' or 'filled with the Holy Spirit' occur fourteen times in the Gospels and the book of Acts, and interestingly only once in the Epistles (Ephesians 5:18). This filling does not take place once and for all, but is a matter of daily surrender and dying to self as one accepts the Cross. Holiness and the Cross are inseparable. This is why we read again and again of this process of filling (Acts 2:4; 4:8, 4:31 and so on).

In Ephesians 5:18 we are commanded to be filled with the Spirit. It follows, consequently, after repentance and daily surrender. However, in contrast to this, baptism with the Spirit is not commanded. It should be noted that some authors speak about a 'baptism with the Holy Spirit', but really mean a 'filling of the Holy Spirit'. It should also be noted that there is no case of anyone's receiving the 'baptism of the Holy Spirit' after having received the Holy Spirit.

The meaning of the Body of Christ

On the illustration of the body, the Apostle now explains, in verse 26, why not every member can have every gift. This explanation is so simple that one can only wonder why so many people insist that practically everybody must have a certain gift. What sort of a body is this which consists only of one arm, one eye, or even one tongue?

As already mentioned and explained, the Corinthians are exhorted (verse 31) now 'to covet earnestly the best gifts'. Because we find a certain shifting of values here, we also find the clear invitation to strive for the greatest of all gifts, namely love (Chapter 14:1). This ought to be the main desire of a spiritual Christian, as everyone will admit. Unfortunately the believers had to be corrected here too. Not satisfaction of human pride and passionate desire, but the edification of the body of Christ to the glory of God and the salvation of many people, must be the governing motive. However, love is the better way than admiration of ourselves.

The Greatest of All

In Chapter 13 we have the incomparable and wonderful passage about love, which ought to be the central feature of our fellowship with believers. When we think of the references in 1 Corinthians 1:11,33 and especially the statement in Chapter 6:1–8, we see a predominant need here. It is surely not a coincidence that, in this main text about spiritual gifts—Chapter 12, the charismata in general and Chapter 14, the comparison of prophecy and tongues—love stands in the middle of these two. It should be the true centre, for we find the even argument about this subject of spiritual gifts has often severely quenched this love. This chapter unmistakably says that 'the tongues of men and of angels' without love are as empty chatter before God; that all prophecy, all knowledge and all faith without love are completely meaningless. May we draw from these statements (13:1–3) a sober conclusion, a conclusion which concerns myself and must be applied to my own heart: Without the fundamental surrender, holiness and love, the use of spiritual gifts becomes senseless, useless and means absolutely nothing at all.

This sounds awfully negative, yet at this time may we put the Word of God above all our own likings, opinions and feelings for, according to Chapter 14:37, this is the mark of true spirituality. This is what the Bible states very clearly. Measured by this criterion one must put a big question-mark behind some of these spectacular gifts of the Corinthians. These believers were divided, yet at the same time enjoyed sensational manifestations of charisma. Was it actually the work of God? Perhaps it was exciting for the flesh, yet from God's perspective apparently worth nothing at all. Yes, when we think of the admonitions of Chapter 11 then it was even worse than nothing at all. Looking at it from this viewpoint—and again my appeal is to obey the Scriptures rather than one's own preconceived ideas—the conclusion of 2 Corinthians 11:4 must almost force itself upon us. And it raises the alarming question: What kind of spirit is it which today puts similar emphasis on things which bring about spectacular gifts and yet divide the body of believers, just as in the days of the carnal Corinthians? Perhaps just the subject of tongues alone has already caused the most divisions and separations, and has possibly been the cause for the greatest unkindness among believers. Thus we find that one of the most blessed and strongest missionary societies, the Missionary Alliance, has split up over this regrettable issue. As a truly dedicated servant of the Lord wrote: 'This movement has never recovered from it completely.'

When we compare this with the statements of 1 Corinthians 13:1–3, I believe that the call for the hour for each one of us is not so much to look for the miraculous gifts, but rather to repent and deeply humble ourselves before our God.

For the time is come that judgment must begin at the house of God (1 Peter 4:17).

However:

When we would judge ourselves, we should not be judged (1 Corinthians 11:31).

Today when we observe the increasing secularisation of the believers we can also apply such passages of the Bible to ourselves (see also Luke 18:13–14).

What is Prophecy in General?

Now, love ought to be the one thing that we should really strive for most of all. In Chapter 14 of the Letter the Apostle now challenges the Corinthians especially to devote themselves to prophecy. According to 14:3 it serves for edification, for exhortation and for comfort; also according to verse 31 of the same chapter 'that all may learn'.

Perhaps we could also mention, without wanting to create a dogma, that today this function of prophecy (verses 3 and 31) has actually been transferred to the Word of God—that is, the proclamation of the Word of God. For example Hans Brandenburg writes:

> We should in no way think that the apostolic conditions could be repeated in our time. At the time of Paul, no written, fixed New Testament existed. None of the four Gospels had yet been written. The apostolic letters were not known until the next generation, within the churches here and there. Hence, the gift of prophecy was more important than today.[31]

However, we are exhorted to heed the prophetic word (2 Peter 1:19) and to desire the sincere milk (1 Peter 2:2) which is the Word of God. We are promised that we may become perfect through the intimate acquaintance with the Word of God and the obedience connected with it (2 Timothy 3:16). Significantly it does not say anywhere that we may become perfect through gifts or their use.

According to Numbers 11:29 prophets were people upon whom the Lord put His spirit, and it was through the prophet that the will of God was revealed. Now it is clearly visible that the Spirit of God identifies Himself with His Word (John 6:63; Ephesians 6:17). Michael Griffiths writes:

> According to 1 Corinthians 14:5, prophecy refers to the commonest and most edifying type of speaking in the assembly. This indeed has been the traditional evangelical understanding. The New Testament usage conforms far more to the Old Testament usage of a fearless proclama-

tion of the Word of God expounded in the light of the contemporary situation.[32]

Since the time of the New Testament the Holy Spirit has been living in each born-again believer (Romans 8:9; Ephesians 2:22), has anointed the believer and has been teaching him (1 John 2:20–27). We have the completed counsel of God in the Bible and according to my understanding, prophecy especially in connection with the Scriptures has ceased (Revelation 22:18–19). We find the fullness of the counsel of God in the Lord Jesus Christ. In this connection the statement in Revelation 19:10b is worth mentioning: '... for the testimony of Jesus is the spirit of prophecy.'

Paul uses the term in its widest sense as the speaking forth of the Word of God and in the narrower sense of revealing the future. Who are prophets in this sense? Not only those especially designated as such in the Old Testament, not only ordained ministers, but all believers. All true Christians are to be prophets of God, for the edification, exhortation of other believers and of unbelievers.[33]

Prophecy and Tongues

The Christians at Corinth are encouraged in this 14th Chapter to seek after prophecy and not after an unknown tongue. Beginning at verse 2, Paul gives the reasons, why prophecy is the greater of these two gifts. 'I would rather that ye prophesy, for...' (14:1–2). Then brings forward arguments against the overemphasised use of tongues, as was obviously the case in Corinth, and at the same time reasons for the use of prophecy. Principally he is saying: 'When you speak in tongues no one can understand you except God. But when you prophesy you edify and exhort others. When you speak in tongues you only edify yourselves; when you prophesy, you edify the church.' These are convincing reasons why prophecy presents the more desirable gift. The emphasis lies in verse 4 as well as verse 5 on the word *but*.

Those that push tongues, in order to biblically justify their emphasis, if they refer to the Letter to the Corinthians only and not to the Book of Acts, they usually quote four verses of 1 Corinthians 14, namely: 4,5,18 and 39. Of these four verses three of them have a following *but* or *yet* (verse 19 in connection with verse 18).

The remarkable thing now is that these points which Paul really directs *against* emphasis on the use of 'glossolalia', are accepted *for* a proof by these people today. 'I just speak mysteries in the Spirit, I only edify myself and this is commendable...'—we hear something like this again and again. One puts the emphasis exactly on the opposite side of the little word *but*. Yet this obviously contradicts the Spirit and the basic principle of the writings in Chapter 14. It will not do, to declare the counter-arguments of the Apostle as positive points or even to recommend them. With only just a little intellectual sincerity one ought to be able to recognise, or let ourselves be told, that here the facts are really twisted. The author of such an interpretation could not be the Holy Spirit, who will not as we all well know contradict His own Word. This frequently quoted verse 4: 'He that speaketh in an unknown tongue edifieth himself', giving this as a reason we should speak and pray in tongues, is to my understanding completely reversing the intended meaning of the statement. Strictly speaking the Apostle presents to the Corinthians almost an accusation or as already stated, a counter-argument. Gifts which are used for selfish purposes are highly questionable as already pointed out. Because the believers were puffed up (Chapters 4 and 5) it may not have been hard for them to live for their own edification and satisfaction, instead of the spiritual well-being of others.

John Stott states:

...while the tongue-speaker 'edifies himself' and therefore (Paul) is actively encouraging the practice of private tongue-speaking, I confess that I question whether this is the right deduction to draw. Two reasons make me hesitate. First, 'edification' in the New Testament is invariably a ministry which builds up others. In addition, Christians have a ministry of 'mutual upbuilding' (Romans 14:19) in which they are to 'build one another up' (1 Thessalonians 5:11; Romans 15:2; Ephesians 4:29; Jude 20).... Secondly we have to read the expression in the light of the teaching we have already considered that *all* spiritual gifts are service-gifts, bestowed 'for the common good', for ministry to others.... So for these two reasons it seems to me that there must be a note of irony, if not sarcasm, in Paul's voice as he writes of the tongue-speaker edifying himself. He takes it for granted that the Corinthians, to whom he has clearly explained the purpose of spiritual gifts in Chapter 12, will get his meaning and not need him to spell it out any further.[34]

Alfred Kuen considers this:

One can even ask if the apostle Paul, by the exceptional use of the verb (edifieth) in the reflexive form, does not want to draw the attention of the Corinthians, with a dash of irony, to a form of self-gratification. 'He loves himself and only serves himself,' to distinguish between love and zealous service ('Die charismatische Bewegung' ['The Charismatic Movement', translated], Brockhaus Verlag Wuppertal, p 55).

Hans Brandenburg believes:

The speaker of strange tongues is occupied with himself, the others disappear from his vision. They do not interest him. He desires after the supernatural. This apparently was the situation in Corinth.[35]

Many a believer becomes intoxicated with a feeling of power which seems to be brought about by the possession of the Holy Spirit. Pastor Grant Swank makes a similar observation in *Christianity Today* about speakers in tongues who came into his church:

> They were possessed with a counterfeit, a fake. They were living on an ego trip, a manufactured religious 'high' (February 28, 1975, p 13).

William MacDonald writes in a similar way about 1 Corinthians 14:4:

> This verse is usually given to justify the private use of tongues for self-edification. But the fact that we find the word 'church' eight times in the same chapter (verses 4,5,12,19,23,28,34,35) surely gives us the convicting proof that here Paul was not talking of an individual personal fellowship with God praying in our quiet little closet but the use of tongues in the local church. From this context one can see that here Paul does not recommend the speaking in tongues for self-edification at all but he condemns the use of this gift in the church as it does not help others.[36]

In any case a spiritual person will seek the edification of the church and of others and not his own ecstasy (Romans 14:19). Let us again compare this with 1 Corinthians 10:24,33. The carnal behaviour of the Corinthians has, as we have seen, resulted in the alteration in the meaning of many things. Michael Griffiths, also, does not seem to be very convinced of the private practice of this gift:

What is implied by the words, 'Let each of them keep silence in the church and speak to himself and to God' (14:28)? Does it mean that the use of tongues is a form of prayer which may equally be silent or spoken out loud? Or does it mean that the use of tongues should be confined to private devotions? It is this private use of tongues which is currently stressed in the Charismatic movement. This is an argument from experience rather than Scripture. The actual Scriptural warrant for 'solitary' speaking in tongues is not extensive. There is no example of it at all in the Acts narrative passages, and it is only understood by inference from the Corinthian passages. It could be urged, however, that in these chapters Paul is dealing largely with the public use and not with the private exercise of this gift of tongues. Private use raises the additional problem that it is not susceptible to the biblical test of genuineness in the way that public exercise may be. The individual is not able to apply these tests to himself when he is 'inspired'.[37]

A Bible teacher raised the question whether tongue-speaking is at all intended for worship. Many Charismatics claim to have a greater worship experience since they received the Spirit baptism. Now there are various gifts, talents and ministries. But concerning worship and approaching God all men are equal whether it is a simple cleaning woman or a gifted preacher, because God looks at the heart and He is not a respecter of persons.

Paul obviously expects an unequivocal 'no' to the questions asked in 1 Corinthians 12:29–30 (Are all apostles? are all prophets?...Do all speak with tongues?). Thus, as already mentioned, God has not given this charisma to each believer.

If a special form of worship were connected with this gift then God would be the author of favoritism, in that He permits some of His children to worship Him better and thus have a deeper relationship than other believers. This would not be on the basis of the attitude of the Christian's heart, but rather because of an external gift.

But this is in conflict with the entire teaching of the Scriptures, as this Bible teacher pointed out. This results in the divisions and party spirit, only too often seen in connection with the Charismatic renewal. Carriers of the gift of tongues often consider themselves to already being a little bit more sanctified, to have received a little bit more of the Spirit, whilst others are sometimes despised as 'outer-court-Christians'. It fosters their pride.

These expositions let the so-called practising of tongues for worship appear in a rather dubious light.

Altogether in Chapter 14 beginning from verse 12 to 23 the Apostle gives us about twelve reasons why speaking in tongues makes little or no sense in the way practised by the Corinthians. In the passage mentioned, verses 12 and 13 are sometimes produced as an argument for the use of Glossolalia. But again both verses emphasise the 'edifying of the church'.

More frequently indeed, verses 5 and 18 are mentioned in favour of tongues. But we have already shown that this is quite ineligible because of the following 'but'. Michael Griffiths also writes concerning 1 Corinthians 14:5:

> This verse has often been used to prove that all Christians ought to speak in tongues. Certainly taken at its face value it seems quite clear that Paul is expressing a desire that tongue-speaking should be universal among the Corinthian Christians. But to take just part of a verse in this way leaves one open at least to a sneaking suspicion that one is not really doing justice to Paul's argument in the passage as a whole. It is therefore unwise to quote only part of this verse without giving full weight to this particular Pauline mode of expression.[38]

The remaining passage in 1 Corinthians 14 is a pretty obvious correction for the Corinthians for their practical use and over-emphasis on tongues. Such an over-emphasis had to be rejected. Verse 6 says: '...what shall I profit you?'; verse 7: '...how shall it be known what is piped and harped?'; verse 8: '...who shall prepare himself to the battle?'; verse 9: '...for ye shall speak into the air'; verse 11: '...therefore if I know not the meaning of the voice.' Verse 12 again points to the gifts which edify the church and are much more desirable. Therefore the speaking in tongues, if at all practised, has to be interpreted, as we read in the next verse (13).

One can clearly see also in verse 26 and especially verse 28 how tongues alone, without interpretation, are worthless for the church and with interpretation have only limited use (verse 27b). Verse 14: '...my spirit prayeth, but my understanding is unfruitful.'

Concerning verses 14 and 15, I would like to quote from John Stott's book, *Your Mind Matters*:

Whatever Glossolalia may have been in New Testament days, whether a gift of foreign languages or of ecstatic utterance, the speech was certainly unintelligible to the speaker. And this is why Paul forbade its exercise in public if there was no-one to translate or interpret, and discouraged its exercise in private, if the speaker continued not to understand what he was saying. He wrote: 'Therefore he who speaks in a tongue should pray for the power to interpret. For if I pray in a tongue, my spirit prays but my mind is unfruitful. What am I to do? I will pray with the spirit and I will pray with the mind also... 1 Corinthians 14:13–15. In other words, Paul could not contemplate any prayer or worship in which the mind was barren or inactive. He insisted that in all true worship the mind must be fully and fruitfully engaged. The Corinthians' cult of unintelligibility was a childish thing. They should indeed be as childish and innocent as possible in evil, but, he added, 'in thinking be mature' (1 Corinthians 14:20).[39]

Verse 16 says: 'seeing he understandeth not what thou sayest?'; verse 17: '...for thou verily givest thanks well, but the other is not edified.' Verse 18 is often emphasised, while verse 19 is generally overlooked—yet it is connected with verse 18. Again the emphasis is on the 'Yet' and therefore on verse 19 and not on the oft-quoted verse 18. 'Yet...I had rather speak five words with my understanding that I might teach others also, than ten thousand words in an unknown tongue.' The ratio was 1:2000 and not vice versa. Now the question arises: May this ratio be taken so literally? 10,000 was the largest number in the Greek language, so that today the contrast between these figures could also be rendered by 1:1 million.

This tendency to obscurity is apparently not only childish but rather serious. John Stott writes in another passage of the above-mentioned book:

Leaving aside questions regarding the validity of what they seek and claim, one of the most serious features at least of some Neo-Pentecostalism is its avowed anti-intellectualism.[40]

Up until verse 19, the Apostle brings very simple and obvious examples to the carnal Corinthians to explain to them with rather plain and impressive concepts why their use of tongues is rather childish. We only have to think of verses 7 and 8 with the examples of musical instruments. Of course a small child is delighted to hear the different and peculiar sounds as well as being able to produce such incoherent noises himself, yet it is all pretty senseless (verse 9).

Starting with verse 20 Paul introduces the Corinthians to a deeper level of understanding and says: 'Brethren, be not children in understanding, but in understanding be men.' Therewith the Apostle brings them to a deeper basis of understanding, and in verse 31 allows Scripture, that is the Old Testament, to speak. Here completely new circumstances are revealed. First that the Apostle had suggested how senseless their behaviour had been with simple and clear arguments. Now he shows them through Scripture how they almost misappropriated this gift when used in such a way, that is, tongues without interpretation. 'It is for a sign to them that believe not and not to them that believe' (verse 22).

Tongues with regard to Unbelievers

Because we find many controversial points on this subject, first of all I would like to stress that the following ought not to be seen as a dogmatic absolutum, rather as a possible interpretation, or better, as a possible aspect of tongues. It is a partial aspect that we find especially in the Book of Acts. In the 2nd Chapter of the Book we find how tongues were given as a sign for unbelievers, for those who paid attention (verse 6) and God was able to convict many through the message of Peter. In one way it was the reversal of the consequence of the Tower of Babel. In Genesis 11 God confused the languages, turned away from the nations and called an individual, namely, Abraham (Genesis 12). From then on the revelations of God were only given to the Israelites in their language. At Pentecost God untangles the languages and this miracle indicates that now the counsel of God, the Gospel, becomes available to all people, 'languages' and nations. Therewith the character of the new dispensation was revealed right at the beginning. Just a note: the tongues of today often show this same disorderly Babylonian character. People who get along really well suddenly separate themselves. This rather indicates that the Lord as in Genesis 11 again is turning away from the nations.

The time of the Gentiles is indeed coming to a close (Luke 21:24). The time is at hand when God will literally revive Israel out of its graves (Ezekiel 37).

In Acts 10:45 we learn that tongues were given to the Jews as a sign because they, although born-again, would not believe that the Gentiles had received the Holy Spirit too, and in this respect they were still 'unbelieving'. Also in Acts 19:1–6 surely this was a sign for the Jewish people, who had not yet accomplished a clear separation from the Old Covenant. Owing to the sign of tongues they finally believed in the whole Gospel of our Lord Jesus Christ. In a similar way Michael Griffiths comments on this event when he writes:

> . . . This instance was a sign to the disciples of John: a sign that they had done the proper thing in moving on from John's teaching to believing in Christ.[41]

In this same sense, in my opinion, we have to understand the speaking of tongues as mentioned by the Apostle Paul in 1 Corinthians 14:18. On the missionfield the gift of tongues is of greater importance in order to reach the unbelievers who speak a foreign language.

William MacDonald writes:

> . . . Paul apparently could speak in more foreign languages than all the others. We do not know if he had received this ability by supernatural means or if he had learned these languages.[42]

Obviously MacDonald sees these facts in a similar way for he generally writes concerning the gift of tongues:

The gift of tongues was the ability to speak foreign languages without ever having learnt them. We are not of the opinion that babbling or ecstatic utterances are meant by this, but real foreign languages which existed in those days. To interpret tongues was the miraculous power of being able to translate something which was spoken in a foreign language without ever having learnt this language.[43]

This explanation of tongue-speaking as a real language and not just babbling, as already shown by 1 Corinthians 12:3, probably illuminates still another fact. Perhaps this is the reason why we never find the gift of tongues in the Old Testament, where otherwise all other gifts are mentioned (wisdom, healing, working of miracles, prophecy, etc). It was apparently not necessary as they all spoke the same language; it was just *one* nation. Also, the Lord Jesus Christ, who first of all came for Israel (Matthew 15:24) and lived during the time of the Old Covenant, never spoke in tongues (languages). He also never mentions this gift, as He is sending His disciples out to the lost sheep of Israel (Matthew 10:5–8) and this in spite of the fact that 'the Jews required a sign' (1 Corinthians 1:22). Nevertheless we read of this gift as He orders the same disciples to preach the Gospel to every creature in all the world, as He sends them out to other nations (languages) (Mark 16:15–16).

God had primarily meant this gift of tongues or languages for the communication of the Gospel to the unbelievers in their own language. No interpretation was necessary. Yet today the speaking of tongues without interpretation is being extolled more and more in the churches of today as the *great* experience just as it was at the time of the Corinthians with more or less the same results, namely confusion, disorder, divisions and disagreements (1 Corinthians 11:18). I am afraid that actually the real reason for the increasing popularity of tongues today and the growing sympathy for the situation in

Corinth is not to be found in the fact that we are so spiritual and balanced, but rather that we have become so very carnal.

Tongues with regard to Believers

Chapter 14:23 shows how the believers were probably used to practising their gifts:

> If therefore the whole church be come together into one place, and all speak with tongues, and there come in those that are unlearned, or unbelievers, will they not say that ye are mad?

In other words, they were in real danger, or may be this was partly the case already, of practising these gifts in a completely wrong way, as with many other things. After all we have heard so far this should not surprise us at all.

Verses 24–25 show, as a mission leader explained, that even in regard to the unbelievers, at least within the church, prophecy is the greater gift which also leads to repentance and worship. Now verse 26 shows the practice of the gifts within the church at that time, the spectrum of the gifts for the edification of the believers by which God intended to speak to the church. Here again speaking in tongues is connected with interpretation, since it would otherwise be meaningless for the church.

In verses 27–35 we find the biblical principles set down on how the gifts mentioned in verse 20 ought to be practised within the church at Corinth. But the instructions concerning the gift of tongues are not seen so much as a recommendation, De Haan believes, but are to be taken rather as a guide as to how to lead this 'awakening' into sober and orderly channels. Verse 27 stresses that only two, at the most three, should speak in tongues and only one after another and not simultaneously, and this only if there is an interpreter (verse 28). 'Otherwise let him keep silence in the church.'

Strictly speaking, verse 27 indicates once more that the Apostle is rather rejecting this gift, and I would again like to appeal to our intellectual sincerity. The definition 'at the most by three' really reveals that he would rather prefer less (two) than more people to speak in tongues. Verse 31 shows in comparison how 'all may prophesy' and how inspired prophecy is superior to even glossolalia with interpretation.

We can see in this whole essay on the 14th Chapter how the Apostle repeatedly shows the advantages of prophecy not only in the theoretical argument (verses 2–25) but also in the sphere of the practical application (verses 26–40), while he puts glossolalia back point by point. He rejects it in such a way that he even declares at the end 'and forbid not to speak with tongues' (verse 39). Naturally such an instruction would be unnecessary if he were to put such a gift into the foreground. Then we would have expressions like those he uses for the emphasis on prophecy, or he would declare it to be one of the great gifts. Strictly speaking we can say: In conclusion, Paul again summarises the basic outline of the two contrasting subjects, prophecy and tongues—here: 'covet', there: 'forbid not'.

The fact that we find this last inferior gift being exalted more and more today shows us very clearly that something must be definitely wrong. Some churches even put their main emphasis on this gift. Here obviously the divine esteem and order has been replaced by another. As is well known, God is not a God of confusion (verse 33). Indeed, verse 39 says, as previously explained, that we are not to forbid to speak with tongues, but it really says nowhere that we are to strive for this gift, that we are to covet it.

Where do certain circles and individuals, as well as preachers, get the right to urge other people to first of all strive for this inferior gift? What sort of a spirit is behind this? I am afraid that the statement—the false spirit urges the believers to pray first of all for this gift of tongues—may show the true situation pretty well.

Again and again we hear that we are not to quench the Holy Spirit. Yet to wilfully change God's order and to turn it upside down, in my opinion, would quench the Holy Spirit much more. According to verse 37 the mark of a Spirit-filled life is not so much the emphasis of a gift but rather the readiness to acknowledge the authority of the Word of God. Why do more and more people believe that the gift of tongues also belongs to true spirituality and the fullness of the Spirit? Why do we meet more and more people today who cry to God for days and sometimes weeks, animated by only one wish, to receive this 'beautiful' experience or charisma at last? What has really happened to us?

One young man lay on the ground for hours earnestly pleading for tongues. In another instance the subject had been urged by charismatic tutors to keep repeating the word 'Hallelujah' until he could break out in tongues. In both cases the subjects did acquire the coveted ability. Later testing, however, revealed that in each case a demon had entered the victim and had imparted the glossolalia (Gerald McGraw, *Tongues should be tested*, 'The Alliance Witness', June 5, 1974, p 4).

Today if we lift our voices in warning we are rather accused of a lack of love. But do we not render ourselves guilty if we keep quiet in the face of this distortion of divine standards with such consequences?

Of course, silence is a virtue, and in verse 34, women are even commanded to keep silence. Because many do not want to acknowledge this—we find in some circles that more and more women are leading—we ought to quote several more reasons.

We find that the word 'laleo' in the Greek in verse 34 and in 1 Corinthians 14, is usually mentioned in connection with 'glossolalia', tongue-speaking. To my understanding this does not refer to prayer or prophecy (11:5). While the Bible informs us that women have prophesied we do not find a definite case of them having spoken in tongues also. But because the possibility of deception in the spiritual— demonic area is much greater for a woman than a man (1 Timothy 2:14) they are usually the first ones to slide into such a movement. Women who play a leading role in a church, who preach and teach in a church, which happens in certain circles more and more today, are plainly acting against the Word of God (1 Timothy 2:11–12). Michael Griffiths believes in connection with verse 34:

Nevertheless, this consideration may well give us reason to pause in view of the very considerable involvement of women in the 'Glossolalia' movement.[44]

At this time I would also like to point to a comment on these verses in the Scofield Bible, where these principles are clearly summarised, and I would like to bring forward just one point: 'Those who speak must be able to control their gift because God is not the author of confusion' (verses 32–33).

Finally we can say: The initial use of tongues by the believers in Corinth was not an edifying gift. Speaking in tongues and other gifts are not necessarily a sign of spirituality and maturity. This letter proves that one can lead a carnal life marked by gross sins such as fornication, divisions, quarrels, etc and would still be able to practise many gifts. Gifts are not necessarily the criterion of spirituality but the fruit. Many Corinthians were almost 'specialists' in tongues yet this gift presented more of a problem to the church. The believers are frankly labelled as carnal. There is no shortcut to the fullness of the Spirit. Holiness is not a sudden acquisition of spiritual maturity through an exciting experience, a way which our flesh rather prefers, but on the contrary: a process of growing, through which we become more like our Lord Jesus, through the power of the Holy Spirit living in us—who gains room in our hearts on the basis of our obedience (Acts 5:32).

Basic Fundamentals in Danger

We learn in Chapter 15 that some (verse 12) did not even believe in the resurrection. This is very serious when we consider that the resurrection presents the centre of the Gospel and the hope of the church. Therewith the unique-ness of the message of salvation is in danger. Paul clearly indicates this possibility (15:2) and to meet with this trouble he again clearly lays down the foundations of the Gospel. Not by chance do we have the 'standard-definitions' of the 'Good News' in 1 Corinthians 15:1–5 and after that the wonderful testimony of the Resurrection. Already we can recognise the very doubtful fact of a changed Gospel in Corinth. Bible scholars who called this church one of the most unattractive have obviously not made this assertion without good reasons.

Now these are not insignificant matters which we can simply overlook. Let us only think of Galatians 1:8. Here it is a question of fundamentals and the Corinthians were in danger even here. Today in the same sense we find that the Gospel of the baptism with the Spirit is not the Gospel of the Bible any more. By this I mean the teaching that the baptism with the Spirit follows conversion as a separate work of the Holy Spirit and is connected with special holiness. Often it is also called 'the second blessing'.

The enemy, through the development of this teaching of the baptism with the Spirit into a false doctrine, takes advan-tage, of the sincere desires of many believers. They want to be set free from all bondages and chains and all conscious and known sins. How deceiving must be the message for many to believe that a single experience would set them free and acquit them of all battles. Instead of growing in simple faith and obedience in the grace and knowledge of our Lord Jesus Christ, one wants to 'leap into a higher life and another dimension'. With urging impatience and great wrestling one entreats God for this much-desired gift.

Has it finally happened, one is almost drunk with a feeling of happiness at first; then believes that he has finally received the baptism with the Spirit. The acquired condition is valued as a higher form of Christianity, in contrast to a mere conversion to the Lord Jesus and the acquired justification.

With this kind of doctrine and the 'experiences' connected with it (these can really be very 'blessed' as I know from my own experience) we are actually tearing apart the work of the Lord Jesus Christ and the work of the Holy Spirit, we are separating the work of the Cross and the Spirit of God. We have another Gospel: a 'Cross-plus-experience' message and we are eager to pass it on in the churches, usually through laying on of hands. Not by coincidence does Paul mention to the Corinthians in 2 Corinthians 11:4 that they might well bear with another Gospel. What a serious statement is made in such a verse!

In any case, the Apostle did not preach the baptism of the Spirit but the Cross. Let us compare Matthew 3:11 with Acts 13:25–30. Instead of speaking about the baptism with the Spirit, as John the Baptist mentioned, Paul speaks of the crucifixion of Christ and our guilt. *This* is the way, as an unbeliever, to experience the baptism of the Spirit, namely conversion or regeneration, as already stressed many times—when we accept the message of the Cross, of salvation, for ourselves, when we say 'Yes' to the Cross, when we make our decision for the Lord Jesus Christ.

For example, 2 Corinthians 12 reveals to us that Paul had a

spiritual experience once. Yet verse 2 of the same chapter tells us that he kept it a secret for over fourteen years. In other words he had never mentioned it in his preaching. He did not travel around and tell the congregations of his wonderful spiritual experiences, visions and so forth, as we find this happening more and more today. In the case of the clairvoyant Mrs White it led to the founding of the Seventh Day Adventists. Such practice will cause the increase of sectarian divisions.

In Colossians 2:18 Paul warns of people who 'intrude into those things which they have not seen, vainly puffed up by their fleshly minds', yet who are able to behave very meekly and humbly. It is worth mentioning that 2 Corinthians 12:7 indicates the danger of 'being exalted above measure through the abundance of the revelations'. This other gospel can cause a believer to slip into an emotional and increased religious performance, apart from the basis of trust and obedience. The beginning was spiritual and we finish up in the flesh, in self-righteousness. Hence the result is very often an increased emotional godliness, where one calls Jesus the bride-groom of the soul with an infatuated, activated religiosity. As shown in Colossians, all this can hide itself under the pretence of what seems to be humility.

In such a condition of religious deception one sometimes even believes in having to suffer with Jesus; one bewails the Cross and the scars of the Lamb. It all seems very humble and godly, yet this really is, to answer with the Word of God:

After the commandments and doctrines of men, which things have indeed a show of wisdom in self-made religion and humility, and neglecting of the body; not in any honour to the satisfying of the flesh (Colossians 2:22–23).

The Lord Jesus said: 'Daughters of Jerusalem, weep not for me, but weep for yourselves, and for your children'

(Luke 23:28). Interestingly, it was the women who bewailed and lamented Him (verse 27). Jesus addressed them as they were apparently especially inclined to do so. It is not by coincidence that we find such behaviour pre-eminently in the circles of women and sisters more and more. For instance the famous Catholic saint Therese Neumann, called Therese of Konnersreuth, started to bleed from her eyes as she deeply translated herself into the passion of Christ.

Signs, wonders, visions, dreams and trances are reported more frequently today—instead of leaving the proclamation of the Word of God in the centre. We are moving away from the true basis of the Gospel more and more and are opening ourselves to the workings and insinuations of seducing spirits, of which the Bible speaks so clearly (1 Timothy 4:1). For example, Schlatter writes:

> ...a trap, through which a deceiving spirit can sneak with the help of the art of deception: The godliness, which resembles the Holy Spirit, is intensified in an infatuated way, equipped with extraordinary power and passion, perhaps even with the ability to work wonders, to see visions. Salvation is felt in a wonderful, emotional way, perfectly presented to the soul, so that the desire for daily cleansing of sins through the blood of our Lord Jesus Christ is lost and the faith connected with Him becomes irrelevant. This is the main purpose of the satanic seduction: to separate from Christ, to lure them out of Him and to stimulate such a fullness of indwelling power of the Spirit that it seems unnecessary to further seek our redemption in the Cross...[45]

But a passion for wonders and miracles is against the theology of the Cross. Our Lord Jesus remarked several times, with disapproval: 'an evil and adulterous generation seeketh after a sign' (Matthew 12:39; 16:4). We honour God through faith and without faith it is impossible to please Him (Hebrews 11:6). The search for wonders and signs will slowly but surely lead to another basis, to the shaky foundation of feelings and experiences. Gradually we are drawn away from the basis of faith into a false doctrine (heresy). However, God would like to take us into His school of faith (2 Corinthians 1:9).

As we know, faith is the opposite to sight (2 Corinthians 5:7) and a non-doubting of the things not seen (Hebrews 11:1). This is a very hard and unpleasant way for our old nature. Instead of believing, the natural man and emotional Christian would rather see, hear, feel, taste, experience the supernatural, etc. But this means a falling away from our faith about which the Bible speaks explicitly (2 Thessalonians 2:3).

Contrary to the plain teaching of the Epistles, Yonggi Cho, pastor of the Full Gospel Church in Seoul, South Korea, emphasises the importance of visions. Speaking at the International Conference of Itinerant Evangelists in Amsterdam in 1983, he declared:

Vision and faith are essential to a successful life. A vision produces faith. To have great faith you must have a vision.... Our forefather Abraham did not just say that he believed. First, he received a vision from God, then he believed.... Without dreams and visions your faith cannot be produced.... Without a vision there is nothing in your heart and mind to believe for, so nothing can be created.[46]

This is more or less the opposite of what was stated before:

Now faith is the substance of things hoped for, the evidence of things not seen (Hebrews 11:1).

One begins in the Spirit and ends up in the sentimental flesh (Galatians 3:3). Naturally we find that another spirit is behind all this, which then must be called upon with much prayer, fasting and entreaty. When we see how many a child of God is led to cry for the receiving of the Holy Spirit, whom he already possesses, then we must remember the question of the Apostle Paul, which he surely did not ask the Corinthians without good reason: 'Know ye not, that ye are the temple of God, and that the Spirit of God dwelleth in you?' (1 Corinthians 3:16).

As already stated, this letter, for the main part, contains corrections, explanations and reproofs. The church was in a highly deplorable condition and here we possibly find the explanation of another fact. This again should not be connected with any critical assertion or dogmatic statement. But it might be worth mentioning that in his letter the Apostle Paul does not ask the Corinthians for their intercession. Otherwise we find this in all the other letters to the churches (Romans 15:30; Ephesians 6:18; Philippians 1:19; Colossians 4:3; 1 Thessalonians 5:25 and 2 Thessalonians 3:1), except also in the letter to the Galatians, where we find, among other things, a bewitching (Galatians 3:1) and the practical acceptance of another gospel (Galatians 1:8; 5:2–4). The church at Corinth was obviously in a pretty unspiritual state. The believers, through their conceit and pride, 'super-spirituality' and sins, caused the Apostle much grief, sorrow, headache and heartache (2 Corinthians 2:4)—a rather sad if not discouraging fact; then as well as today.

For I fear, lest when I come, I shall not find you such as I would, and that I shall be found unto you such as ye would not: lest there be debates, envyings, wraths, strifes, backbitings, whisperings, swellings, tumults; and lest, when I come again, my God will humble me among you, and that I shall bewail many which have sinned already, and have not repented of the uncleanness and fornication and lasciviousness which they have committed (2 Corinthians 12:20–21).

Test the Spirits

The above-mentioned misinterpretation of the gift of tongues may be the reason why investigations of people on this subject, either in the counselling of the occult or in the purely psychological area, have come up with such negative results. While counsellors are reporting on terrible deceptions and great errors, we also find that linguists are making shocking statements. Dr William Welmers, Professor of African languages at the University of California, Los Angeles, writes:

> I am told that Dr E. A. Nida of the American Bible Society has reported similar impressions of glossolalia recordings. Our evidence is still admittedly limited, but from the view-point of a Christian linguist the modern phenomenon of glossolalia would appear to be a linguistic fraud and monstrosity, given even the most generous interpretation of 1 Corinthians 12—14.[47]

In another instance, John Kildahl writes in a similar way in the book quoted earlier:

> Linguistic scholars work with precise definitions of what constitutes a natural human language. Glossolalia fails to meet the criteria of these definitions.[48]

Therefore it falls below the biblical standard. When we consider that this doctor has investigated this phenomenon in America for ten years, then we have very serious facts in front of us. Further on in the same book:

In order to investigate the accuracy of these interpretations, we undertook to play a taped example of tongue-
speech privately for several different interpreters of
tongues. In no instance was there any similarity in the
several interpretations.

and

The belief that tongue-speaking is caused by direct mechanical movement of the vocal chords by the Holy Spirit
made group members accept almost anything that was
uttered as glossolalia.[49]

In fact it is precisely this 'mechanical movement' which
again reminds us of the forcible-demonic influence. It is
obvious that a lot of counterfeit can creep in through such an
attitude, as the investigations of John Kildahl suggest. Not
without reason does the Apostle Paul explain in 1 Corinthians 14:29 that we ought to judge any speech. We are to
exclude an unconditional approval of just anything that is
prophesied or spoken in tongues; the church ought to 'prove
all things' as we are literally told in 1 Thessalonians 5:20–21.
This exhortation stands in direct connection with the
prophetic speech which is mentioned just before this. Verse
22 reads: 'Abstain from every form of evil.' This was surely
not written in such an order by mere coincidence, but one is
obviously connected with the other and in direct relation to
the previous statement; namely, through prophecy the devil
can creep in, this time as an 'angel of light'. When we do not
test such prophecy, we will naturally not be discerning, but
will accept it as the real thing. Thus it comes to adulteration,
to an infiltration and deception.
As we have seen, prophecy is a greater gift than speaking
in tongues. However, we find false prophets, that is, false
prophecy, in the Old Testament as well as in the New Testa-

ment. It is evident that when the enemy is able to imitate the greater gift—and we are explicitly told to prove prophecies—it would be much easier for him to imitate an inferior gift. Therefore, tongues-speaking wherever it may appear ought to be tested, whether it has a spiritual, emotional or even spiritistic-demonic source (Zechariah 13:2).

Michael Griffiths writes concerning the testing of tongues:

Because the gift is not self-authenticating, in 1 Corinthians 12:3 we are clearly warned to apply certain tests; it is therefore in accord with Scripture and not in any sense quenching the Spirit or tempting the Spirit to put the test of asking whether the spirit will confess that 'Jesus is Lord'.[50]

There is the further test given to us by the Apostle John (1 John 4:1). But very often we find a real reluctance, a strong antipathy towards allowing the gift or the speech to be tested, which usually hides itself behind a biblical vocabulary. Many speak of an unloving attitude. Love covers or tolerates, so it is claimed, these Charismatic manifestations. Whereas it will accept the believer in Christ, yet real love will not contradict the Bible but rejoices in the truth (1 Corinthians 13:6). Only a soulish love will compromise with and tolerate error and unscriptural phenomena and gifts. Real love will also try to warn us, as Merrill F. Unger did in his book, 'What Demons Can Do To Saints':

Prominent healers and charismatic leaders make a fatal blunder in mistaking these abilities for the genuine gifts of the Spirit. They should renounce them.... The ever-expanding charismatic confusion in the Church today represents a clever halo-crowned strategem of Satan to divide God's people and to bring them under a very subtle yet real type of occult bondage.[51]

It shall be emphasised here that I do not want to write off tongues as being always demonic. God may give them on special occasions. But here this particular movement shall be referred to as having a false source. There is also enough potential in our flesh and emotions for such phenomena. Kildahl came to the conclusion that it was nothing more than learned behaviour. Yet, such warnings show the importance of the issue. Perhaps we understand, why the test itself is not some possibility or suggestion by the Word of God, but a commandment. We have a duty to test the source of visions, uncovering of sins, healing, peace, joy, etc.

Watchman Nee believes:

Doubting is the prelude to truth. By this is not meant to doubt the Holy Spirit or God or His Word but to doubt one's own past experience. Such doubt is both necessary and scriptural because God commands us to 'test the spirits' (1 John 4:1). Believers often embrace a wrong idea: they are afraid to examine the spirits lest they sin against the Holy Spirit. But it is He Himself who desires us to make the test.[52]

And today this power appears to be craftier than ever. It is driven by a spirit of imitation, often copying the Holy Spirit exactly; it is a spirit of sublime counterfeit, which disguises itself with increasing craftiness as the endtime draws near. At this point, not to test is spiritual suicide. To say it in someone else's words: 'With the false Pentecostal spirit it is a question of mixing truth with error.' Consequently his spirit is much more dangerous for the church than open attacks and open enmity. Do not let anyone keep us from our right and our duty to test, to unmask, to warn. Gerald McGraw writes:

The deceptiveness of false tongues spirits is seen in the

ways they take advantage of the victim, diverting from him serious spiritual exercises and centering his life around tongues, as well as in their misleading names and their tactics to fool the person who seeks to expose and dislodge them. Satan's whole kingdom is skilled in deceit, but probably no evil spirits are more sly than tongues spirits who simulate God's Holy Spirit. The fourth lesson I have learned in tongues testing is the seemingly slight ground that can admit a tongues demon, particularly where an unscriptural view is entertained. An Alliance pastor became invaded when, while visiting a Pentecostal home, he simply gave credence to the view that it would be desirable to have a tongues gift. He had neither prayed for tongues nor seriously pursued them, but a gift suddenly came upon him.[53]

This is also my observation.

Brethren who are under the influence of the false Pentecostal spirit are wrongly accusing those discerning believers that they are against 'gifts of the Spirit' and 'tongues', and that they have no idea of the Holy Spirit. Those brethren, in so doing, are really drawing a wrong battle-line. The fight is not directed against the gifts of the Spirit; also not against mistakes and abuse of the gifts, but the fight is against the false spirit, who imitates the divine gifts of grace, and hides himself behind them, cunningly disguised. He would like to creep into the churches through these imitations and split them bringing another gospel and at the same time a spell over the believers.

Yet this same false spirit will not come into the light, but will stay hidden and often confuse sincere brethren with many innocently disguised lies as: 'You are of little faith, you are grieving the Holy Spirit, you are doubting God Himself, etc.' We find very often that the testing or questioning of the genuineness of the gifts is equalised to the quenching of the

Holy Spirit. Hypocritically disguised, one emphasises that we ought not to 'judge'. Some seem to be extremely perplexed about it and over-spiritual people even claim that one is blaspheming the Holy Spirit. However, He does not contradict His Word (Revelation 2:2) and He commands us to prove everything—even the spirits (1 John 4:1–3).

Sometimes we find certain people and preachers who are really very nice and spiritual, yet this must never be a final criterion. It is a big mistake to judge a movement by some nice person I know. We are not to believe and obey our feelings and opinions, but the Scriptures, which tell us: 'Test the spirits.' It does not say: 'Test one person in this or that movement, his sincerity, discipline, love, his zeal and dedication, and so on.' All these are superficial criteria which could still cover up a bad root; yes, especially through these. Let us think, for instance, of the discipline, joy, zeal and the real dedication of the Mormons.

The church of Thyatira had love, faith, works, service and patience and the saints were models in many respects. However all of these positive characteristics and fruits did not protect the church from deceit. There was a toleration of false doctrine. Therefore the Lord warned this church of impending judgement (Revelation 2:18–20).

Especially today we repeatedly hear these final comments about spirit-testing: The brother is so spiritual, so quiet, so disciplined, he practices the gift only for himself, he has been walking with the Lord for so many years, he radiates such joy, he does not belong to any extreme movement, he has spiritual authority, he lives a dedicated life, and so on. Initially, all these qualities must be taken into account, but in spite of everything, such tests finally remain on the surface. And again, as so often happens, we have tried the person and not the spirit.

A very impressive example, that even the most outstanding life in dedication towards Christ need not necessarily be a protection against false inspirations and visions, is perhaps Sadhu Sundar Singh. The self-sacrificing character of this man and his outstanding discipleship have deeply impressed me. One can only talk about these qualities with great respect. On account of his exemplary courage in witnessing most of the believers accept that his experiences and visions concerning the 'spiritual world' must be without question truly from God.

Nevertheless we read about these visions in the following way:

Swedenborg was a great man, philosopher, scientist and above all a seer of clear visions. I speak often with him in my visions. He has a high position in the 'spiritual world'. He is a marvellous man, but humble and always ready to serve. I also see wonderful things in the 'spiritual world', but cannot describe them with the same accuracy and skill as Swedenborg. He is a highly gifted and well educated soul. After having read his books and having contacted him personally in the 'spiritual world', I can unhesitatingly recommend him as a great seer.

In a personal letter from May 30, 1928 Sundar Singh wrote:

Yes, I have seen the honourable Swedenborg many times in my visions. He is an amiable personality and he assumes a high position in heaven... (A. J. Appasamy, 'Sundar Singh' Verlag Friedrich Reinhardt AG., Basel, pp 271 and 273, translated).

Swedenborg, about whom Sundar Singh talks so enthusiastically, ranks as perhaps the greatest spiritist of the 18th century. For him there is neither devil nor hell. He allegedly conversed with beings from the moon, Mars and Jupiter in the course of his talking and communication with the 'spirit world'. He despised the teaching of justification of sinners through faith in Jesus Christ and emphasised that Jesus' spiritual return is fulfilled in him.

When Swedenborg assumes a high position in heaven, as Sundar Singh emphatically declares, then we read the Bible to little purpose. Then the Gospel is wrong to say the least.

We should be honest enough to admit, if even someone like Sundar Singh, whose being a child of God should by no means be called in question, has been deceived with his visions, then each one of us can become a victim of delusion if we rely on our own experiences and not on Scripture.

Here I also want to emphasise, by mentioning these names, one should not get the impression that I, as author of this book, am therefore better or more spiritual than the people whose supernatural experiences are refuted. Often it is the most dedicated and burning Christian who opens himself to these trends. However, these souls are worth telling them the truth, even if the messenger is just an unprofitable servant and a sinner saved by grace and by no means any better.

On a similar level is McGraw's conclusion when he observes:

A second lesson I have learned is that strong Christians can be invaded by a tongues demon. In the course of a year's Sunday school lessons on the deeper life I spent several weeks exploring the gifts of the Spirit with my adult class...I closed my treatment of tongues with a simple statement that anyone with a gift of tongues should make certain the gift was not a satanic counterfeit, since missionaries have reported hearing tongues speakers blaspheming in the language they had used on the mission field. Tongues should be tested.... The only person from the class who approached me was an outstanding Christian lady—capable, talented, balanced, dependable, a soul winner. She said she never used her tongue except in private... I just could not imagine that this fine believer could have a tongues demon. I told her so.... Yet it was undeniable that a demonic tongues spirit inhabited her.... Others who have had tongues tests are utterly sincere and deeply spiritual people. The lives of several show marked evidence of conversion, spiritual hunger and growth. I do not believe that a tongues demon can sever a person from Christ's love. I have no doubt that many in the charismatic movement are earnest Christians, with more zeal and love than their anticharismatic critics. Yet my experience of testing makes me suspect that multitudes of tongues enthusiasts are deluded.[54]

I wonder whether such warnings are still heard, or are they rejected as too extreme?

Too often one only tests if the person concerned is a child of God. If the test turns out positive then one opens himself to this brother rather quickly and completely without reservation, for example through laying on of hands. However, this is already sin and disobedience. I myself committed this error, or rather, disobedience. Some years ago I met such a lovely, harmonious and obviously blessed brother who had the gift of tongues that I allowed him to lay hands on me. In those days I longed for the experience of the baptism of the Spirit. The reason why I quote 2 Corinthians 11:4 so very often lies perhaps in the fact that I have personally experienced the truth of these words. It was really a 'beautiful' and intoxicating spirit, which brought the much-desired feeling of 'power' in me, only, unfortunately, it was not of God. I had only superficially tested. It does not say: 'Try the people, if they are of God (that is, born-again)' but: 'Try the spirits, whether they are of God' (1 John 4:1).

Especially the believer who knows of the reality of the unseen world ought not to confine his evaluation to the visible criteria only, but should also question authenticity, through testing. Of course, if the test is done, then we find, as a rule, an enormous deception revealed. In the case of my own confrontation the total result of the testing done according to the Bible is alarmingly negative (1 Peter 4:17–18); so negative, that arguments of the above-mentioned nature— 'he is so dedicated, and so on'—hardly impress me any more. Sometimes our heart is much more deceitful than we could ever imagine (Jeremiah 17:9).

However, along with these experiences I started to understand a little bit better the meaning of Jesus' warnings in Luke 11:35: 'Take heed therefore, that the light which is in thee be not darkness.'

Watchman Nee again writes:

The Lord's saints should not receive everything supernatural without question, for Satan too can perform supernatural deeds. No matter how the feeling is during the moment of experience nor how the phenomenon appears or declares itself to be, believers should investigate its source. The charge of 1 John 4:1 must be strictly observed.... The counterfeits of the adversary often exceed the believer's expectation. If the Lord's people will humble themselves by admitting that deception is quite possible to them, they will be the less deceived.[55]

May the Lord grant us mercy for such a humbling of ourselves (1 Corinthians 11:31).

Further Observations

The previously quoted John P. Kildahl informs us of a real dependency syndrome in his book:

Without complete submission to the leader, speaking in tongues was not initiated.[56]

This dependency is visibly demonstrated through the laying on of hands. It means, as we shall see later, identification, surrender to someone else.

For instance, we also find this dependency syndrome typically amongst the believers in the Corinthian church, and we are naturally not referring to the apostolic glossolalia. 'For while one saith, I am of Paul; and another I am of Apollos; are ye not carnal?' (1 Corinthians 3:4; 1:12–13). How far this dependency goes is clearly explained in the work of Kildahl. There we read that tongue-speakers are influencing whole groups with their manner and style of glossolalia. Had the leader used more Hebraic sounds, then this affected the whole congregation. Had he used rather Spanish diction or mannerisms then the followers also developed that style. This dependency leads so far that linguists could even tell which prominent glossolalist had introduced a congregation to tongue-speaking. Finally we read the sobering remark on page 53:

> The glossolalic styles of Bennett, Bredesen, Christenson, du Plessis, Mjorud and Stone are distinctive enough to be identifiable by observant linguists.

We could hardly imagine a more impressive indication that in these cases it is not a question of a gift of God, but rather one of human manipulation on a suggestive, group dynamic, as well as, psychological level. Believers who are still on the lookout for the 'strong delusions' of last days (2 Thessalonians 2:11) ought to realise that the church is already in this situation. The command of the hour is indeed: 'Watch!' (1 Corinthians 16:13; Mark 13:33).

I would like to relate something out of my own personal

counselling experience. While testing these gifts, and the spirits, I repeatedly made this observation: First of all I found an unbelievable mixture of light and darkness. In my opinion it is not a coincidence that the first letter to the Corinthians shows this mixture of light and darkness as well. John Kildahl again writes (on page 54 of his book) that hypnotisability is a presupposition for tongue-speaking. Hypnosis actually functions on the basis of a stronger influence of the powers of darkness. This power of darkness sometimes finds its entrance through heavy sins, especially in the sexual realm. Once when I read the passage in 1 Corinthians 6:9–10, where Paul quotes great transgressions, I noticed some parallels. We learn in verse 11 that several of the Corinthians had practised these things before their conversion. I personally believe that the Holy Spirit is not throwing light on the background of the Corinthians by accident. The sins quoted there, according to my knowledge, cause strong bondage to Satan, even as far as indwelling of demons. When these things are not brought into light after conversion then we find this mixture.

Again, this is not referring to the guilt (burden) of sin, which has been forgiven once and for all and cancelled through the blood of Christ ('ye are washed, ye are sanctified, ye are justified...' 1 Corinthians 6:11), but to the power of sin. There, where the Cross, which has overcome all these sins, abominations and powers, has not yet been able to perform a deeper work in the heart of a believer, then these strong bindings signify the real danger of mixing—especially when one lives more a life of disobedience than holiness which is usually the case in a superficial conversion and repentance; sometimes also because we do not take our discipleship seriously enough and we fail to find a really deep understanding of sin. Just as there are carnal Christians it is likely that there are a lot of 'carnal conversions' as well (1 Corinthians 10:5).

Thus A. Schuetz writes under the title, *Repentance still is and will always remain a principal part of our faith*:

In 2 Corinthians 7:1 Paul speaks of the 'defilement of the spirit'. Here we find the reason why so many men have not pleasure in the Word of God, why so many women fail to live a life of victory and so many young people do not pray. Repentance remains superficial, it does not reach into the depth of our heart. We forget the cleansing of our hearts by the blood of Christ. Of course we have the forgiveness of our sins but we were not saved from the power of sin.[57]

But holiness and the Cross are inseparable, as well as the Holy Spirit and the Cross. Watchman Nee even believes:

Many, if not most, believers were not filled with the Holy Spirit at the moment they believed the Lord. What is even worse, after many years of believing they continue to be entangled by sin and remain carnal Christians.

Perhaps for the following reasons:

Many Christians are unaware how drastically the Cross must work so that ultimately their natural power for living may be denied.[58]

This increased mixing deprives us of the blessing, and brings judgement upon us (Revelation 2:14–16). Extensive counselling experience reveals that people with such a background are especially susceptible to soulish as well as demonic tongue-speaking. These gifts are sometimes very strongly defended by such believers, in whom the darkness has found entry and whose temple has partly become or still is the dwelling place of demons, even if they are not practising these charisms themselves. Unfortunately, Watchman Nee may be right in saying:

> It is to be sorely lamented that so many Christians, unaware of the basic difference between the activity of evil spirits and that of the Holy Spirit, have unconsciously permitted the enemy to enter and occupy their minds.[59]

In my opinion, it is because these grave sins, as well as other snares of demonism (drugs, demonic music, yoga, hypnosis, meditation, Asiatic religions, autogenic training, growing heresies, and so on) are so strongly on the increase today, that we find such an enormous increase in tongue-speaking lately. Missionaries and counsellors have explained to me that where we find occult bondages and oppressions, these gifts are not genuine. Thus we can observe that in countries where the practice of witchcraft, especially spiritism, is widespread, the Pentecostal movements are also growing and gaining influence very rapidly. Obviously McGraw's warning is not unjustified:

> Tongues are no plaything.... But it appears much of the current wave of tongues-speaking is satanic delusion.[60]

These are strong statements, yet, after many years of counselling experience and observation, I have come to the same conclusion. Similarly, as in Corinth, the mixed or occult background has the effect of an over-emphasis of these gifts, especially the sign-gifts.

> No spiritual speaking gift today enjoys more popularity than tongues and none harbors such inherent possibilities of deception.[61]

stated McGraw.

When we also consider that the marks of the occult are especially 'gifts' and powers (clairvoyance, telepathy, visions, and so on) then we have to look at many a 'spiritual' movement with a new perspective. Especially a person entangled in grave sinning, as well as a demonically-subjected person, desires after gifts, power and experiences, just as the story of the sorcerer Simon shows us (Acts 8:9– 19). Even the daily newspapers are reporting today that we are living in a time of 'occult revival'.

If we also consider that Jesus' first answer to the question of His second coming was a warning against deception (Matthew 24:4; 2 Thessalonians 2:3a) then we would think that the current emphasis on revival and charismatic over-spirituality is rather strange (Matthew 7:22). Again the Epistles speak of a falling away of the church towards the end of the age of grace (2 Thessalonians 2:3b), 'giving heed to seducing spirits and doctrines of devils' (1 Timothy 4:1), and prophesy the coming of 'perilous times' (2 Timothy 3:1), 'false teachers and damnable heresies' (2 Peter 2:1), error (2 Peter 3:17) and teachers of fables (2 Timothy 4:3–4). The Gospels predict an increase of unbelief and false prophets (Matthew 24:11–12), even a real decline of faith for the last days (Luke 18:8). In the light of all this the constant emphasis on world-wide revival and on charismatic super-spirituality is more than strange.

When the Lord Jesus speaks of the end-times He emphasises again and again that we ought to watch and pray (Mark 13:33–37; Luke 21:36 etc). In some circles invitations are given to foster and regard dreams. This is rather peculiar as it principally means to sleep and dream, whereas the Lord Jesus urges us to watch and pray.

The Ecumenical Alignment

Today we are living in the middle of the preparatory age of the appearance of the Antichrist. The Bible reveals to us that the Antichrist will receive world-wide worship when he will appear in his deceptively religious garment. This deception is made possible through signs and wonders (Revelation 13:13–14; 16:14). The coming of the false messiah will presumably be initiated by a world-wide 'revival' (Revelation 13:8), brought about by signs and wonders (2 Thessalonians 2:9), gifts, visions and prophecies (1 Kings 22:22–23; Jeremiah 23:15b). When we observe how an increasing number of Roman Catholics are receiving the 'baptism of the spirit' and how many a Protestant movement feels itself drawn towards the Catholic direction because of tongue-speaking, and when right in front of our eyes we can see big 'fraternisation scenes' between Protestants and Catholics on the basis of 'gifts of grace', then we can also realise that the possibility of a charismatic 'superchurch' is not such a strange thought any more.

Here I would like to let the Charismatic advocates speak and quote from their magazine 'Wort + Geist' ('Word + Spirit'', translated):

10,000 spirit-baptised Catholics, from 60 countries, came together for a charismatic conference during the Pentecostal holiday weekend in Rome. Laymen, bishops and cardinals united themselves in songs of praise and tongues in St Peters Cathedral. Before 60,000 members attending mass this modern miracle of Pentecost took place: After Cardinal Suenens had read mass they all proceeded to the papal (pontifical) altar, with raised arms and jubilant songs and choruses, with clapping hands and speaking in tongues. There, several prophetic messages were delivered.... And something else also happened: A Catholic priest fell down on his knees and asked the one standing next to him: Pray for me, that I may be baptized in the Holy Spirit. Several formed a ring of prayer around him and prayerfully laid their hands on him. After a few minutes he got up: His eyes were shining with joy, he had experienced his pentecost.... There are distinct parallels between the Charismatic movements of the Protestant and Catholic churches and the classical Pentecost revival. The leading men of the Catholic Pentecostals regard these three currents of the Pentecostal movement as the result of the outpouring of the spirit, which has the same origin (source).[62]

What source is this really? Let us examine this source more closely. We generally agree that the Pentecostal movement of our time had its beginning in Los Angeles at the start of this century. Concerning this 'revival' we can read the following in the report of a very objective writer, H. Lang:

One further matter deserves special mention, because it provides a test in some other vital questions. From the very first, and throughout all the early years, there was persistent assertion that the second advent of Christ was just at hand.... Many of the utterances were quite precise, as that the Lord will come 'this year', or within two years, or that this may be the last winter before He comes. Few speaking from their own mind would be thus daring, it suggests an outside foreign source or impulse, but this source could not have been the Spirit of Truth. This false prediction was so constant, so emphatic, so universal as to constitute a major feature of the whole Movement from its start, which forces serious doubt as to the energy animating it.[63]

Now, according to Deuteronomy 18:21–22, this is just the test for false prophets. Because the source is obviously false, one has to ask, how can the movements coming from such a source be any better? This mixed trend is growing in alarming proportions today and is penetrating the Catholic church more and more.

How strongly this ecumenical and mixed spirit is already working is shown in an alarming way in the book, *Glossolalia*, by Arnold Bittlinger. Here, for instance, we read 'as positive proof for genuine tongue-speaking in the church history' the following:

> The Jesuit-priest Joh. Bapt. Scaronelli (died 1752) describes the experience of the mystics with the following words: 'Just as such who are drunken with wine are not able to lead an orderly conversation...so here too the soul breaks out...in completely unrhymed praises to God, because the love filling the soul hinders it from putting words in order.'[64]

But in his letters to the Corinthians Paul is fighting this exact emotional confusion. Again we read on page 22 of Bittlinger's book:

> The Franciscan mystic Harphius (died 1477) describes his mystic experience: 'The amorous rapture itself...with some in jubilation and song, with others in crying out and sighing, again with others in unusual words and disconnected sentences....' Probably, the mystic Jacob Boehme also had the gift of tongues (1575–1624).[65]

In this book we find a colourful mixture of Catholic saints, mystics and founders of monastries and orders (page 54) and so on. But it gets worse. On page 23, on the list of 'blessed' charismatics, even Ignatius of Loyola is mentioned. Now this is really going too far. Anyone who regards the founder of the Order of the Jesuits as possibly inspired by the Holy Spirit really confuses light with darkness and Christ with Antichrist. No Order has taken the Holy Scriptures away from so many Christians, has consequently persecuted the 'heretics' (non-Catholics) and destroyed the biblical faith, as the Order of the Jesuits. And to describe the founder of it as inspired by the Holy Spirit, moreover to quote this as proof of the genuineness of biblical tongue-speaking, is really the height of delusion, a complete lack of spiritual discernment. Here we do not find orientation according to the Word of God any more, but mystic experiences and occurrences are taken as guidelines. This is in principle the deception spoken of in Revelation 13:14.

In other passages Bittlinger is quoting (on pages 35–39) the highly spiritualistic medium Therese of Konnersreuth. He presents her inner voices and visions as gifts of the Holy Spirit and describes in detail this great 'work of God', this miracle of tongues. This book, *Glossolalia*, in its enumeration of 'blessed' Charismatics is an unbelievable mixture of mysticism, spiritism, Catholicism and also the genuine work of God—it could hardly be worse. What immeasurable deception! Anyone in such ecumenical confusion is able to explain just about everything as the work of God. What makes it worse still is the sad fact that this book is recommended in groups which claim to be Bible-believing, so that even a conservative Charismatic writes about Bittlinger:

> It is primarily due to Bittlinger that the Charismatic revival in the German-speaking churches is running without the help of the American Pentecostals, with such a big success.[66]

It ought to be very clear what sort of spirit is creeping in here. In a recent article published by the World Council of Churches Arnold Bittlinger's promotion of syncretism has become even more obvious. Under the title *Integrating Other Religious Traditions into Western Christianity* he states:

When I discovered that many charismatic elements in those churches had also roots in the African pre-Christian traditions I began to look for charismatic elements also in other religions. I discovered that especially the charismata of 'healing' and of 'prophecy' were sometimes more convincing in those religions than in the charismatic renewal—at least as far as it is influenced by the North American type of Christianity. In Shamanism I found fascinating parallels to the ministry of Jesus, whom I began to understand as an archetype of Shaman. Concerning 'healing' I was especially impressed by the holistic approach to healing, which I found among American Indians.... Concerning 'prophecies' I am impressed by experiences in Hinduism. Some of our European 'prophets' discovered and developed their prophetic gifts under the influence of Hindu gurus. Also other charismatic experiences have some very impressive equivalents in other religious traditions (eg 'praying in the spirit' in Japa yoga). I am convinced that the charismatic renewal will become more significant—especially for the mission of the church—if it also takes seriously the charismata of other religions.... We also had conferences on the Chinese I Ching and on the Tibetan Bardo Gödol. But our main concern is to go back to our own Celtic and Allemandic traditions and to revitalize them in order to integrate them into our Christian belief (ed. by Tosh Arai and Wesley Ariarajah, Spirituality in Interfaith Dialogue, Geneva: World Council of Churches, 1989, p 96–97).

It has already been mentioned how people who are spiritually defiled with occult oppressions (2 Corinthians 7:1) are more inclined towards this mixture and confusion of the Corinthian situation. Due to the occult revival of today, their number is considerably increasing. One has 'defiled' his garments (Revelation 3:4) and opened himself to many trends.

Here also we find the reason for the large numbers of 'charismatic' and ecumenical enthusiasts, as these two movements are a literal realisation of 2 Corinthians 6:14–16. One actually mixes believers with unbelievers, light with darkness, Christ with Belial (Antichrist).

Something that unfortunately only few people know ought to be stated here: The Epistles to the Corinthians are the 'standard' letters for the subject of intermixture and pluralism. Like no other letter, the first letter to the Corinthians shows the nature of the infiltration of the believers. We only have to think of the permeating action of the 'leavened lump' (1 Corinthians 5:6–7). God's children who are harbouring ungodly connections (darkness) in their temples (1 Corinthians 6:19) for some reason or another, and who are therefore mixed or leavened through to various degrees, are especially open to this letter and defend the Corinthian conditions. This Epistle is the real 'indicator' for this mixture. Movements which are strongly grounded or leaning on the Corinthian Epistle are mixed movements.

Carriers of such 'mixed spirits', as Peter Mayer writes, do respond strongly to this Corinthian situation and very often don't accept any warning and sometimes are especially opposed to any suggestions of the possibility of deception, intermixture or occult bondages. Instead of taking God's warnings seriously to separate ourselves, come out from among them, touch not the unclean thing, (2 Corinthians 6:17), we are invited more and more frequently today, or directly or indirectly to 'let us gladly take part in it, be progressive, join in it, open ourselves to all kinds of movements, and so on'.

If one has not died to his emotional life but earnestly seeks sensational events, he will be easily duped... it can be stated that present day Christians are particularly susceptible to trickery in supernatural matters,[67] Watchman Nee states again.

We agree with Arnold Bittlinger when he writes:

We are not to underestimate the ecumenical effect of tongue-speaking. The charismatic prayer-services of today have ecumenical character as well. The speaking in tongues creates a mutuality which is stronger than all the barriers of confessions and denominations.[68]

We can see much more clearly how this very blinding and syncretic spirit works, from the book by John Sherill 'They speak with other tongues' (Hodder & Stoughton, p 84). He tries to prove that speaking in tongues has existed throughout the centuries of Church history. When he deals with the 19th Century, the founders of the New Apostolic Church (Mary Campbell and Edward Irving) are mentioned first. Then, one will be surprised to hear, the Mormons are named in a positive sense for their 'charismatic' experience. Sherill writes:

USA, 1855: The Mormons speak in tongues in their colony in Nauvoo, Illinois. The 7th Article of Faith of these Latter Day Saints states that they believe in the gift of tongues, prophecy, revelation, visions, healing and interpretation of tongues.

The creed of the Pentecostal and Charismatic movement sounds similar. There upon Sherill writes the following, again in a positive sense:

Deep in Czarist Russia there are reports of Pentecostal manifestations in the Greek-Orthodox Church.

We can see clearly owing to the phenomena of speaking in tongues, that all movements, no matter how unbiblical, can be united.

Today, with the increasing appearance of such 'gifts of grace', we are not experiencing a new awakening, but an invasion of the old serpent, disguised as an angel of light, coming into the ranks of our churches, usually starting with mixed and carnal believers. The frightening credulity of many children of God shows the superficiality of our acquaintance with the Word of God. Let us think for instance about the letters to the seven churches in Revelation. Just these are also showing us (Revelation 2:14–15; 2:20, etc) how the enemy had already partly undermined, infiltrated and leavened the churches. There is hardly a better illustration of slow infiltration than the one of the leaven. Imperceptibly, everything under the surface is undermined and infiltrated, until we find something completely different.

According to biblical prophecy there will be in the last days a great world-wide church which the Word of God calls 'Babylon the Great' (Revelation 17:5). Many Bible scholars see in the Roman Catholic Church a system which has definite parallels to the Babylonian Cult. It seems the most obvious interpretation is, that this 'Super-Church', a fusion of the ecumenical movements and Rome, will be made up of all the apostatised Christians (not only from the Catholic Church) throughout the world.

It is important with such statements to differentiate between the doctrine and the person. There are Catholics who fear God. The above statement does not mean that there are no re-born Catholics. The Roman Church however as a system is definitely unbiblical.

It can be clearly observed how the Charismatic movement is moving more and more towards Rome. In doing so it is providing a bridgehead from Protestantism to Catholicism.

Philip Potter, general secretary of the ecumenical World Council of Churches in Geneva, said:

The Charismatic renewal is the bond between the churches of the Reformation, the Roman Catholic Church, the conservative Evangelicals and the Orthodox Church ('Erneuerung in Kirche und Gesellschaft', 'Renewal in Church and Society' translated, No. 7, 1980, p 26).

In an 'idea' (Information Service of the Evangelical Alliance) Publication from October 28, 1981 (page 2) appeared the following statement under the headline 'Charismatic Movement records world-wide break-through':

From the beginning of the sixties the Charismatic movement has reached almost all the churches world-wide. This revival-movement is being especially promoted by the Roman Catholic Church, but the leadership of the Protestant State-Church is in favour of it as well.... Prof. Dr Lorenz Hein...said further that the Charismatics are more open for cooperation with Catholics and the World Council of Churches and that they are not so hostile in their theology as 'pietism'.

This becomes even clearer through the following statement:

Coming directly from a visit to the Pope at the Vatican, du Plessis told about his impressions: 'You would think the Pope is a Pentecostal. He talked so much about Pentecost and why one should be baptized and filled' (CZB, 'Impuls,' translated, No. 5/81).

In the book 'Angels on Assignment' Charles and Francis Hunter write:

> God told me that the Pope has neither greater influence than the least Christian, nor greater privileges. However because of the great influence he has on the people his election becomes a matter for God. He has chosen a man named Karol Wojtyla from Poland to become Pope.[69]

Every Bible-believing Christian should be able to recognise which 'God' is talking here. The present Pope has never made a secret of the fact that he receives his special power from the Black Madonna, the national religious symbol of Poland. On his last visit to Nigeria he told the people that Muslims and Christians may call themselves brothers in one God.

Such a man has been chosen by God to be Pope according to 'Angels on Assignment'. A Pope who is very much involved in Mariolatry and shows clear counter-reformatory tendencies. Protestant missionaries in Catholic countries tell how their work has become increasingly difficult since John Paul II came into office.

The Bible states that the worship of Mary is idolatry and the Word of God admonishes us not to have fellowship with idolaters.

T. W. Cooke writes in a little leaflet entitled 'The Gift of Tongues' the following:

> We are living in the latter days, when much of the Spirit's work is counterfeited. Consider the following for instance. In his book 'Catholic Pentecostals' Kevin Ranaghan says: 'The baptism of the Spirit leads to a greater love for Mary, greater veneration for the Pope, greater devotion to the Catholic Church, increased regularity at the Mass, and more power in witnessing to these

things.' This alone should convince Evangelicals that there is more than one source of spiritual influence, as Rome's ecclesiastical system cannot be of the Lord. Any manifestation which supports it should be avoided.

The above emphasises why the Roman Catholic Church so strongly promotes the Charismatic movement. Even the traditional Pentecostal circles do not reject the worship of Mary any more. In an article in 'idea' of November 25, 1981 (translated) under the headline 'Mary does not question Jesus—Pentecostals open themselves to the veneration of Mary', the following statement is found:

The agreement between Catholics and Pentecostals is deeper than any differences which still exist. (Excerpt from the ninth communique between leading representatives of the Vatican and the Pentecostal Churches...). The Catholics realized how Mary had found a place in the preaching and worship of the Pentecostal Church.

The whole development reminds one of a statement Leonard Ravenhill made about ten years ago:

Moreover, the devil has substituted...familiar spirits for the Holy Spirit, Christian Science for divine healing, the Antichrist for the true Christ, and the Church of Rome for the true Church. ('Why Revival Tarries', Send the Light Trust, p 3).

As already noted, the great problem is that more and more churches which several years ago clearly rejected on biblical grounds any relationship with Rome are now enthusiastic about this type of ecumenical fellowship. One is no longer a 'brother' on the basis of the Bible, repentance and the acceptance of God's Word, but on the basis of a Charismatic experience. I would like to quote John Stott again:

> My third example is Pentecostal Christians, many of whom make experience the major criterion of truth.... One of the movement's leaders said recently, apropos of the Catholic Pentecostals, that what matters in the end is 'not doctrine but experience above the revealed truth of God'.[70]

Do we realise the power of this deception which is already taking place? There, where a person imagines himself wiser than God's Word, may it be through intellect or 'blessed' experiences, the road to destruction begins; judgement is imminent.

If we are mindful of the fact that the Lord Jesus warned of signs and wonders (Matthew 24:11,24), then the increasing passion for charismatic experiences and signs (Matthew 16:4) and wonders as well as the growing manifestations of such, really ought to open our eyes completely. (Divine miracles of today should not be denied here.) What sort of basis do we still have here if we depart from the Holy Scripture? As we can see, only our intellect and beautiful experiences as well as emotions. Thus a pretty shaky foundation, as we have shown before. We read in *The Spiritual Man*:

> Overstepping the bounds of the Word of God ushers in countless perils.[71]

Has Joel not Prophesied a Great Revival?

In order to be able to maintain the unbiblical doctrine of the world-wide revival of the end-times, Acts 2:17–18 is quoted again and again in connection with the prophecy of the prophet Joel. Now the first part-fulfilment of this prophecy actually took place at Pentecost, with the beginning of the

Church. First of all now, it should be mentioned, as explained before, that the secret of the Church revealed in the Book of Acts but in the Epistles (Eph 3:1–5). And here we not only fail to find expectation ui a revival at the end of the Church-age, but we come across the exact opposite. It would be possible to quote approximately seven Bible passages, as worked out above, which are showing the whole spectrum, starting with the deception to the falling-away in the latter times.

To try to neutralise these clear statements with falsely interpreted passages from the Book of Acts is exegetically untenable and is intellectually dishonest. As we all know, we ought to interpret the Bible with the Bible. Thus the Lord Jesus does not say one word about revival in these passages about His second coming (Matthew 24) but He speaks of persecution, deception and in verse 12 of the exact opposite, namely the prevalence of unbelief, not faith. Only a quick look at the world today is sufficient to thoroughly confirm these statements.

Secondly, when the Apostle Peter mentions these verses of the Old Testament, he is standing in Jerusalem. In this connection let us think of Zechariah 12:10 where it is emphasised that 'the Lord will pour upon the *inhabitants of Jerusalem* the spirit of grace....' The Apostle initiated the Church first of all in Israel for the Jews. He does not quote this passage from Joel when he is speaking to the Gentiles. He primarily prophesies for his people (Acts 3:26) in that he bridges over the millenniums and combines these two events of the first and second outpouring of the Spirit.

Zechariah 12:10 shows just how often prophecy has a twofold fulfilment. We generally understand this verse to be the conversion of the people of Israel, which still lies ahead of us. But the evangelist John also quotes this verse concerning the crucifixion of Jesus (John 19:37), that is, Jesus' first coming.

Now the question is, when does this second outpouring of the Spirit take place? Here again one must interpret the Bible with the Bible. When we look at the other verses (Isaiah 32:14-18; Ezekiel 11:17-19; 36:24-29 etc), which speak of this event, then we can understand that the second prophetic outpouring of the Spirit stands in connection with the gathering of the people of Israel, and probably coincides with the beginning of the millennium. For instance, Ezekiel 39:28-29:

Then they shall know that I am the Lord their God, which caused them to be led into captivity among the heathen: but I have gathered them unto their own land and have left none of them any more there. Neither will I hide my face any more from them: for I have poured out my spirit upon the house of Israel, saith the Lord God.

Characteristically the famous passage in Joel is found between promises (Joel 2:27) and events centred around Israel (Joel 2:32; 3:1-3).

Thirdly: according to Ephesians 3:1-5 and Colossians 1:26, to none of the prophets of the Old Covenant the future dispensation of grace (Matthew 11:13; Luke 16:16) was revealed. They prophesied of the future blessings of Israel.

The following verses in Acts 2 in connection with Revelation 6:12, indicate the approximate time of these events. This will not take place in the dispensation of grace, but in the Tribulation period. It is also obvious (Acts 2:19-20) how Israel stands primarily under the disposition of signs but the Church first of all under the Word of God.

A second outpouring of the Spirit of God will take place over the remnant of Israel (Isaiah 10:21-22), probably the frequently mentioned 144,000, the inhabitants of Jerusalem (Zechariah 12:10). (Please see also the Scofield Bible.) The immediate verses before that passage show the judgement situation of the nations and the events around Israel, that is, Jerusalem.

Fourthly: according to Romans 11:25 the nation of Israel will not be converted during this dispensation of grace. Yet God has promised the salvation of all Israel (Romans 11:26). Therefore it is obvious that the Lord will again intervene in a special way, though not during the time of the nations any more, but in relation to His people of the Old Testament Covenant.

In any case these events are still before us, in the future. The Holy Spirit has long since been poured out abundantly for today's dispensation of grace (Titus 3:5–6), and the Church has not to wait to a second Pentecost but for the return of our Lord Jesus Christ. But in applying Israel's promises to the Church (as for instance also the 'latter rain' which according to Hosea 6:1–3 stands in connection with Israel) one only encourages the existing false doctrines and errors. Very often the Bible knowledge of many is so superficial that it is not through the Word of God but through personalities and experiences that believers are controlled, if not manipulated.

In order to prevent any misunderstandings, I would like to say that the impression should not arise that I am against revivals. On the contrary, we hope, pray and believe that the Lord will still be working locally, in a mighty way. However, to expect a global, world-wide revival is unbiblical.

The thing that makes the Charismatic movements so doubtful and suspect to me is the observation that almost all Pentecostal circles usually quote this passage in Joel or the verses in Acts 2 connected with it as biblical evidence for their emphasis on and unfolding of just such a remarkable gift. This is, so to speak, the written proof. Here and there wherever one goes, people are referring to this passage in Joel. It is considered to be the basis for the manifestation of such peculiar events today. This is how it is taught, sung, printed, disseminated and repeated. But we can show just how these passages, at least in the second or complete fulfilment of them, have really nothing to do with the Church age at all. And it is also a fact that the Holy Spirit does not make any false promises. What sort of a spirit is it then who twists God's promises in such a way? Here I would like to appeal to intellectual sincerity. Surely the following question is justified: When the headline of a subject is already incorrect, then how can that which follows be much better or more accurate? Do we find a reason here too, perhaps, why missionaries and counsellors are making such shocking discoveries when testing the spirits, and are anxiously warning against deception? Visions which are based on the passage in Acts 2 are therefore to be 'considered' with the greatest precaution, as well as people who are referring to these verses for their prophecies (Zechariah 13:2).

A missionary wrote to me that he can see the judgement of God over the churches in the 'Charismatic renewal' (Judges 9:23; Isaiah 28:11–13), because they would rather seek more frequently after sensations and religious bliss and less and less after the Cross of Christ. In fact he came to this conclusion after studying this subject in Isaiah, especially in Chapter 33:1; 33:19. When I think of some statements in 1 Corinthians, especially of the 11th Chapter, then I am inclined to agree with him more and more.

God allows it that spiritual darkness is sent out in judgement (Isaiah 29:9–10). Today we observe, in a certain sense, as predecessor to the outpouring of God's wrath in the Tribulation (Revelation 16), a 'pouring out' of deceitful spirits. When we think that in regard to the end-times the Bible even speaks of strong delusions (2 Thessalonians 2:11) which God will send, and Scripture admonishes us repeatedly to be sober, then a Bible-true Christian really ought to recognise what is going on. As a whole, we are not facing 'revival' but the infiltration of the Church in the end-times.

Summary

To summarise, I would like to name the three main criteria by which we can soon recognise the false gift of tongues. Bearers of such counterfeit gifts are usually very quick to lay hands on someone else, which the Word of God explicitly forbids (1 Timothy 5:22). Where this attitude comes from, as we will later show in detail, we can discover from Acts 8:19. Sometimes it is even done without asking the person concerned. Any comment is unnecessary here. Sometimes we also find a spirit of pride, a disinclination to be instructed (compare James 2:15 with 2:17) and sometimes a certain super-spirituality is displayed.

Secondly, the gift is strongly emphasised, put into the foreground and mostly presented in such a way, as if the life of a Christian would not have fulfilment without it. Yes, sometimes it is almost forced upon us. In the case of Charismatics who are more deeply rooted in the Word, it is put very cunningly into the centre. After all that has been said, we do not have to mention that this clearly contradicts Scripture. Would this gift, recommended in such a way, really be from God, it would never find such an emphasis. Believers who are stressing or defending this gift (the spiritual Apostle Paul plays it down very definitely) could without their knowledge become the source of mixture and spiritual infection, manipulated by the enemy. They are very often motivated by the noblest and most 'biblical' intentions, and to emphasise it again, usually true believers.

Thirdly, with this shifting of the crucial point, the Holy Spirit usually receives a strong and frequent mention too, as well as special interest. Also the concept of 'baptism with the Spirit' is used very often. One frequently has the impression that it is not the Lord Jesus any more but the Holy Spirit who has become the central figure. Even if we are only just a little acquainted with Scripture, we realise that the Holy Spirit does not want to be in the centre (John 15:26) nor does He want to speak of Himself (John 16:13). He wants to make the Lord Jesus the central point, wants to glorify Him (John 16:14). Also, according to John 16:8–11 the Spirit of God works in such a way that He primarily leads people into repentance. But many have become proud of their gifts.

I would also like to summarise the crucial statements which we want to draw from the letter to the Corinthians in this book, namely the parallels between now and then.

The Corinthians had a strong pagan or occult background. Today we have 'apostasy' and growing occultism. Through sexual sins (Chapters 5 and 6), partly remaining from their past, they were a 'leavened' people. Today we have the pornographic wave and an unbelievable moral decline. Through worshipping idols (Chapter 10) spiritual fornication took place in Corinth which amounted to the defilement of the spirit, and therefore again to the mixing with darkness. Especially today we have many movements which lead to the same result without the visible identification (fornication). These are practices in which we open ourselves to demonic powers, becoming one with them, with forces which strongly defile the spirit. Among other things there are drugs (especially LSD), Yoga, Transcendental Meditation, passivity, hypnosis, parapsychology, and autogenic training.

This intermixture and syncretism because of lack of holiness and sanctification caused the believers in Corinth to over-emphasise certain gifts (Chapter 12–14), especially such with sign characteristics. We see the same today. Chapters 4 and 9 reveal pride and partly that they refused to take advice, and some Corinthians even rose up against the spiritually mature Apostle Paul. Chapter 15 shows that some did not take the Gospel, that is, the Scriptures, very seriously at all. In this respect we can find Bible criticism there. Especially today we see the rapid decline of reverence for the Word of God. Francis Schaeffer interestingly states:

One can also see a parallel between the new Pentecostals and the liberals.[72]

The fact that Bible criticism and liberal theology are breaking into the assemblies and churches like wildfire may be common knowledge by now.

The Corinthians were also inclined to unite with unbelievers because they themselves were mixed, that is, they could not discern between Christians and pseudo-Christians any more, as we see in 2 Corinthians 6. They were, so to speak, ecumenically orientated. We also find this only too evident today, as we have mentioned briefly before. Believers who are mixed are stained—have 'defiled' their garments (Revelation 3:4) and are more or less inclined towards such mixed movements and trends.

I believe that these relationships ought to be brought to light, even if many will not be happy about this book. Yet I also know that believers who really give the Lord Jesus Christ and His Word the first place, that is, with their heart and not with their lips only, are thankful for the presentation of these observations. This book was written for just those people.

Final Words

After all the warnings and rather negative things we still want to put a positive ending here. Above all the terrible deception of the end-times stands the unsurmountable victory of our Lord Jesus Christ; a victory that is so mighty that even the weakest child of God is called a king and a priest, and still has authority in this invisible world in the beautiful name of our Lord Jesus Christ.

The more than deplorable condition of some believers in Corinth caused the Apostle Paul to write the unique treatise of the resurrection. Obviously no church, as already shown, had caused the Apostle more inner grief than the Corinthian. Nevertheless we do find just there the unprecedented cry: 'O death where is thy sting? O grave where is thy victory?' (1 Corinthians 15:55). The 'grave' is spreading today with giant leaps, yet the promise of the Lord Jesus in Matthew 16:18 remains firm as a rock. When we cling to the basis of this victory, our work is not in vain for the Lord; on this foundation of the eternal victory alone we can be firm and immovable (1 Corinthians 15:58), as the Word of God promises to us, even if the world seems to collapse.

Not in our experiences and feelings do we find comfort and anchor for our souls (Hebrews 6:18–19) but in the irrefutable promises of God and the total victory of our Lord Jesus Christ on the Cross. May the Lord grant us that we, like Abraham, do not look at our dead bodies (Romans 4:19), neither our emotional and religious experiences, but like him, the father of all believers (Romans 4:17), look only to the promises; cling to them (Romans 4:20) and thereby give glory to God, to whom alone all honour and glory is due.

In the resurrection of the Lord Jesus we possess the most immovable hope, we are immensely rich, and in trusting thereupon we have the victory (1 Corinthians 15:57). May the Lord grant that we are more concerned with our wonderful Lord Jesus and less with ourselves and our experiences. May the Giver direct our lives. In looking up to Jesus may we become free from ourselves and may we be filled with a burning love for the Lord Jesus and His wonderful Word. He is and always will be the mightiest Victor, the King of Kings, and Lord of Lords. He is our only hope, He alone is our wisdom, sanctification, righteousness and redemption (1 Corinthians 1:30). To Him alone be thanks, for He confirms and holds us, in spite of all our failures, right to the end (1 Corinthians 1:8). Is there a more wonderful God, a mightier Saviour? What immense riches we have in our Saviour Jesus Christ. To Him be the glory for all Eternity.

2

THE QUESTION OF SPIRITUAL DARKNESS IN RELATION TO GOD'S CHILDREN

Are there Bondages?

We have already shown in the treatise on the letter to the Corinthians how a mixture or syncretism of light and darkness is obviously possible. But because we find many, even fine and spiritual Christians, who have real problems and questions here—I personally was for some time also convinced that such a mixture is impossible—an attempt to present some kind of Bible study about this subject will be made.

Experience may be very nice and pleasant, but the Holy Scriptures must always speak the decisive and final words. Does the Bible give us reference points in this regard or not? It is not my desire to appear all-knowing and dogmatic, but that this synopsis should mainly stimulate us to meditation and thinking.

To put a definition first:

'Pneumatic' = 'Spiritual'—according to Scripture is that which the Holy Spirit alone creates, who puts Jesus Christ as our Saviour and Lord into our hearts. 'Psychic' = 'Soulish'—according to Scripture is that which comes from natural impulses, powers and tendencies of the human soul. It is this area in which the life of the Christian is lived. Depending upon which one of the two areas he gives way to, he is either called a carnal or a spiritual Christian.

Hebrews 12:1 tells us that sin 'easily besets us'. Sin can therefore become a trap. It is quite clear that the more deadly the sin the stronger the bonds are tightened (Isaiah 28:22). 'The wicked himself shall be holden with the cords of his sins' (Proverbs 5:22b). Now the Bible mentions that believers can be literally bound. First of all we read of David in the Old Testament, that 'the sorrows of hell compassed me about: the snares of death prevented me' (Psalm 18:5). He expresses the same in Psalm 116:3. In Matthew 22:15 we read that the Pharisees wanted to 'entangle' Jesus in His talk. Still today the adversary is constantly out to ensnare believers. In 1 Timothy 3:6 it is stated that a Christian can 'fall into the condemnation of the devil'. This probably is in connection with Revelation 12:10. The absolutely holy God is also perfectly just towards His worst enemy. Verse 7 of this passage in 1 Timothy speaks very clearly of the snare of Satan into which a believer can fall. This undoubtedly means: subjection to the powers of darkness. 1 Timothy 6:9 similarly states that one can 'fall into temptation and a snare'. However, we ought to 'depart from the snares of death' (Proverbs 13:14).

1 Timothy 5:15 speaks of the fact that obviously a child of God can turn aside and follow after Satan. It is clear that such a 'following' is only possible when the believer has been caught in the snares of the enemy and is obviously bound, and thus pulled in the satanic direction. Such bondages are usually grave sins or on the other hand strong 'religious' deceptions. 2 Timothy 2:26 states clearly that one who is imprisoned in the snares of the devil is doing the will of Satan. Believers who are doing the will of Satan are often, without their knowledge, in the power of the enemy. Here already we are faced with the question to what extent the ones concerned are controlled. Thus Psalm 106:36 shows us how far fellowship with demons can become a snare for us.

Such bondages can be broken in the name and power of

our Lord Jesus Christ, that is, through prayer and sometimes prolonged intercession. Matthew 12:29 reveals that the Son of God has bound the strong man; it is thanks to the victory of the Lord Jesus that such freedom from bondage is possible at all. Luke 13:16 indicates that bondages of Satan can be loosened. Mark 7:35 may point in that same direction. Perhaps it might be worth mentioning here that in 1 John 3:8 it literally says: 'For this purpose the Son of God was manifested that He might "loosen" the works of the devil.' In principle it is finally always the Lord Himself who breaks these bonds, that is, snares (Psalm 107:14; 116:16; 124:7 etc), who even promises to deliver us from the snare of the fowler (Psalm 91:3). Indeed, the Lord Jesus came to open the prison to them that are bound (Isaiah 61:1) and to preach (bring) deliverance to the captives (Luke 4:18).

At this point I would also like to mention the story of Lazarus, the brother of Martha and Mary, although not everyone has to agree with this interpretation. In some respects Lazarus is a picture of regeneration, spiritually interpreted. Through the calling of the Lord Jesus, a dead person awakens to new life. Also John 5:24 expresses this in a similar way. Although it was clearly a miracle and a complete transformation took place—we read that he was bound on hands and feet and his face was hidden (John 11:44). He was, so to speak, marked by death, the world. The hands were, as I have read in an English commentary once, not yet ready for service, the feet were not able to move and his eyes were not yet able to perceive clearly. He could not see very clearly; he did not have real discernment.

The Lord Jesus commanded His disciples to loosen him from those bands and grave clothes. We do not want to create a doctrine here, and coming back to what was said already, we are not even allowed to do so, yet it is not a coincidence, perhaps, that God's Word records it in such a way (John 11:44b).

Another thought, also taken from an English commentary, may be fitting perhaps. We are informed in John 12:11 that because of Lazarus many Jews 'believed on Jesus'. It was important that he was freed from all grave clothes, otherwise the testimony of his resurrection would never have had, we can assume, the same impact. Afterwards everyone could see it clearly. Believers who have laid aside all connections with the world, which is, as we know, marked by death and who follow Jesus whole-heartedly, cause many people to believe in Christ. For this reason Lazarus should have been killed by the Pharisees (John 12:10). Where such grave clothes still exist, we usually find little or no fruit for Jesus, therefore God is not glorified (John 15:8). Thus the adversary has sufficient interest in the fact that those bonds are not brought into the 'light'. However, as stated before, this is an allegorical interpretation one may accept or reject.

Francis Schaeffer asserts on the basis of Romans 6:13a that the devil can use believers as a weapon in his fight against God. This is my own conviction as well. In my opinion God's children are found to be destructive on all fronts today (Romans 14:20; 2 Timothy 2:18). The adversary cares very little about the theological doctrines of the one in question. Thus Watchman Nee writes:

> The consequences of a misconception of truth such as this are: (1) the believer himself ceases to be active; (2) God cannot use him because he has violated His operating principle; therefore (3) the evil spirits seize the opportunity to invade him since he unwittingly has fulfilled the prerequisites for their working. Due to this misinterpretation of the truth, and his practising of death, he becomes a tool of the enemy who has disguised himself as God.[1]

There are Christians who will not acknowledge that God's

children can be bound. But I fear that Watchman Nee is right when he writes:

> Many who are deceived and bound by the enemy need to be released. Not only is there need for release from sin and self-righteousness; many who are bound as well by supernatural experience need release also.[2]

Watchman Nee writes further:

> He should ever and anon declare: I choose freedom...I refuse to be passive...I insist on knowing the wiles of the evil spirits...I will sever every relationship with the powers of darkness. I oppose all their lies and excuses.... Just as in the beginning the believer permitted the evil spirits to enter, so now he chooses the very opposite, the undercutting of any footing of the enemy.... The greatest hindrance to complete liberty is the believer's unwillingness to recover all territory carefully.... But if he genuinely wills to be released and prays for God's light, the Holy Spirit gradually will reveal the past to him.... By patiently pressing forward he will experience deliverance in one area after another. He is on his way to freedom.... The child of God must reclaim all foothold until he arrives at the freedom he first enjoyed.[3]

Here we conclude our consideration of bondage which is clearly shown in the Bible.

Can a Child of God Be Possessed?

A much more difficult question is the controversial subject of whether a born-again Christian can be 'possessed'. May I bring a definition here first. 'Possessed' means: to be in the compulsive power of a supernatural being. With reference to Christians, this is usually not the case. Perhaps only in situations where God's children, in extreme charismatic directions, are giving themselves over completely to another spirit, and are also showing symptoms which occur in cases of direct possession, such as distortions of the face, wild twitchings, groanings, rolling from side to side, and such like. I myself use the concept of 'indwelling' in regard to satanic spirits in believers. That means: the powers of Satan are present, but cannot or can only partly affect the spiritual walk, because the believer is fighting spiritually. In some cases the discipleship can, nevertheless, be strongly hindered. Possession would mean that such believers would have to do the will of the enemy. This would again mean 'force' in its highest degree, if we think of the principle shown before. But a child of God can usually defend himself spiritually.

The concept of 'indwelling' is taken as a counterpart from the positive sphere. In 1 Corinthians 3:16 the Bible speaks of the indwelling of the Holy Spirit. Since there is a satanic counterpart to everything divine—doctrines of the Bible and doctrines of demons (1 Timothy 4:1), table of the Lord and table of devils, the cup of the Lord and cup of devils (1 Corinthians 10:21), Christ's apostles and satanic apostles (2 Corinthians 11:13; Revelation 2:2), fellowship with the Lord and fellowship with devils (1 Corinthians 10:20), Gospel of Christ and 'another' gospel (Galatians 1:8)—the expression 'indwelling' seems appropriate to me. The Lord Jesus says in Matthew 12:45 literally: '...and they (the unclean spirits) enter in and dwell there...'

It is certainly not my wish to create new theological concepts. It was shown previously in this book what sort of confusion this can create. It should rather serve as an aid in the understanding of this very complex subject. The translated word of 'possessed' in our Bibles really means 'demonised' or 'controlled by demons' in the original text. Here we obviously do not find fixed categories, but rather gradual nuances (bound, Luke 13:16; tormented, Acts 5:16; overpowered, ruled or possessed, Acts 10:38) from very light cases to that of the Gadarene, ie legions. However, these things must be understood spiritually; also the question, where these powers live, that is, dwell, as all this takes place in the invisible world.

The Bible calls 'flesh' those areas of the soul and the body which are not controlled by the Spirit, that which remains in the self-life. Here may be the point of application and basis of operation for the enemy.

As long as I regarded the whole person as a vessel, the question of 'indwelling' darkness in believers was a problem. But the human being consists of body, soul and spirit (Hebrews 4:12; 1 Thessalonians 5:23). Today the enemy invades a believer more and more as an 'angel of light' with regard to these emotional physical relations. The soul now, is closer to the body than to the spirit, and this may be the explanation for the fact that many a 'charismatic experience' can have such a clearly visible physical and emotional effect (eg shaking). Usually this emotional phenomenon is exceptionally religiously disguised. Many Christians know nothing of the possibility of such competitive influences. We read in *The Spiritual Man*:

> The emotional part of the soul also can be aroused easily by the adversary. Since many believers crave joyful feelings and the sensations of having the Holy Spirit, of the loveliness of the Lord Jesus and of the presence of God, evil spirits will supply their senses with many strange experiences.... The evil spirits can even impart visions of lofty thoughts to believers, lulling them into thinking that since these are supernatural they must be of God. And so the saint slips into deeper and deeper deception.[4]

I believe that there are several passages in the New Testament which show very clearly how believers can come into the area of influence of the adversary, that is, where 'indwelling' can result. First of all Ephesians 4:27 commands that we shall not 'give place to the devil.' In the Greek it says 'diabolos'. Since all sin is conformity to the will of the adversary (we know from the Bible that ultimately evil is personal), it is practically only a question of the gradual opening of oneself to the enemy to determine how much room he will win. However, we can imagine that in the case of too much opening, it can result in an 'indwelling' of the 'Diabolos', as it obviously happened to Ananias.

In Acts 5:3 it says that 'Satan had filled' the heart of Ananias. In the book, *Satan is Alive and Well on Planet Earth*, Lindsey and Carlson take up this subject on the basis of this passage and give an affirmative answer to the question of 'possession' of God's children.[5]

In the same way McGraw also writes:

I already knew that some contemporary theologians had reversed their position upon discovering strong evidence that Christians can be invaded by evil spirits.[6]

It is also shown in the book just mentioned how the expression 'filled' ('Why has Satan filled your heart?') is the same Greek word as in Ephesians 5:18: 'Be filled with the Holy Spirit.' It means here also: to place oneself unconditionally and voluntarily under another person. People who do not want to see these obvious relations to darkness state that Ananias and Saphira were not really saved. In my opinion this is not correct, as they could not otherwise have lied to the Holy Spirit (Acts 5:3)—as mentioned earlier.

The second crucial passage is 2 Corinthians 11:4. There it is written very clearly that believers can 'receive another spirit'. This formulation would make little sense if such a thing were not possible for a child of God. Let us also note the verse immediately preceding this. This passage alone should be sufficient to resolve the above question. Paul writes to the carnal Corinthians here. When we walk carnally, we can actually mistake the cunning work of Satan for the work of God. The Bible tells us in the same chapter that the enemy can appear as an 'angel of light' (verse 14). Verses 19–20 show how these powers of deception are operating. The Corinthians bore it well when entangled with the yoke of bondage (Galatians 5:1b). I am afraid that many have, instead of a baptism with the Spirit, received a 'baptism of spirit'.

These verses were sufficiently quoted in the exposition of the Letter to the Corinthians, so that I am really repeating myself here. The same goes for the following Bible passages; yet for the sake of a general thematic view, they shall be quoted again.

We find the third biblical statement in this connection in the church at Corinth. However, I would again like to just briefly take up verses 2–3a of 1 Corinthians 12. As we have seen they are dealing with the discernment of false gifts in general and the gift of tongues in particular. It is evident that a child of God will never consciously curse the Lord Jesus. This is therefore only possible, then, when a believer has, at least temporarily, opened himself completely to a deceiving spirit. This spirit may cause, especially through this identification, altogether beautiful, glorious feelings. In the joining of man to a harlot the Bible gives the best picture in the seen world for wrong spiritual identification (1 Corinthians 6:16).

If we call Jesus Christ the Lord with this gift of tongues, then it is a gift of God. 'In such cases one is—as also with prophecy—driven by the Holy Spirit or otherwise by an evil spirit' (comments on 1 Samuel 10:6; 18:10 by the German Elberfelder Bible).

A further passage that is reasonably clear is 1 Timothy 4:1.

Here the Bible speaks, beyond any doubt, of believers who are opening themselves to the insinuations of the enemy in such a way that they fall away. The Luther text speaks of 'hanging on to the deceiving spirits'. This could reveal an identification, especially when we think of the same word in connection with 1 Corinthians 6:16–17. Merril F. Unger states in *Unger's Bible Handbook* in regard to this passage:

> We do not have a neutral ground on which a person who knows Jesus Christ can move. 1 Timothy 4:1 points to this fact: 'Now the Spirit speaketh expressly, that in the latter times some shall depart from the faith, giving heed to seducing spirits and doctrines of devils.' 'Departing from the faith', which is clearly part of the doctrines of the apostles (Acts 2:42) means that even a born-again Christian can give heed to 'seducing spirits' and 'doctrines of devils'. From Paul's viewpoint the 'latter times' refer to the whole church-age. Only a short glance at the history of the church shows how far this prophecy has been fulfilled and still fulfils itself.[7]

Also 1 Peter 5:8 allows such a conclusion. To be devoured by the devil obviously means to fall into the power of the forces of darkness, to be conquered by evil spirits. In this connection let us also take notice of 1 Timothy 5:15.

In my opinion these are some of the direct references in the Word of God.

Allegorical or Other References

In the Old Testament we possibly find a pictorial description of these circumstances. Let us take the blessed land of Canaan as a parable for the life in which God wants to unfold His fulness, in which He wants to reign. Now as the people of Israel moved into the land, the enemy was not yet banished immediately therefrom. By faith, his strongholds and fortresses had to be captured systematically. Perhaps this is a picture of the repeated exhortation to the believers in the New Testament to 'put off' the old (Ephesians 4:22; Colossians 3:8). In the case of disobedience of His people, God proclaims that He would not 'drive out any of these nations from before them' (Joshua 23:13). In the Book of Judges, Chapter 2:21, the Bible tells us that unfortunately this actually happened. Because of the lack of surrender to God the enemy could not be 'driven out' any more. This is, in my opinion, a picture of how many believers are stalled in their life of holiness. After initial victories, compromise and lukewarmness set in and the enemy hits back. In the time of Manasseh we finally find the carved image of an idol standing in the house of the Lord (2 Chronicles 33:7).

We are told in 2 Thessalonians 2:4 that the adversary 'sitteth in the temple of God, showing himself that he is God'. Today, spiritually seen, the temple of God is the Church and the individual saint. This verse may, apart from the actual, visible fulfilment, also show the fact that the spirit of the adversary implants himself right into the centre of the Church, disguised as an 'angel of light' to pass as divine. Since the Greek word 'naos' is used here, which Paul in his Epistles always means to designate the Church or individual believer (1 Corinthians 3:16–17; 6:19; Ephesians 2:21), this interpretation may not be so farfetched. It is my personal opinion that this 'invasion' has already happened to a great extent. It leads to a mixture against which the apostles fought wholeheartedly (1 Corinthians 10:20–21; 2 Corinthians 6:14–16). Perhaps the cleansing of the temple, figuratively, teaches us something similar. Anything ungodly was vigorously cast out (Matthew 21:12a). There remains little doubt that in the case of many believers—in the present temple of God therefore (1 Corinthians 3:17)—many a thing would have to be abandoned if the Lord Jesus would really be the Lord of their temples. May we also remember

the letters to the seven churches in Revelation
and 3), for they also show how the enemy may br
Church and is able to adulterate it. At this poi
remember the working of the leaven. This ou
purged out (1 Corinthians 5:7). Peter exhorts: 'Pu ,y your
souls.' 'Keep yourself unspotted from the world,' writes
James (James 1:27b).

However, every time the children of Israel were ready to
repent and to obey God, they had victory, even when the
enemy was the more numerous in the land. It is my observation also that believers with strong bondages, and definite
'indwelling' of the powers of darkness, can have victory and
bring real fruit as well, if they are ready to obey. Therefore,
simply because the Spirit of God is infinitely stronger, the
Lord very often defeated gigantic armies with just a few
people as recorded in the Old Testament. But if such
believers are not obedient, then the enemy very often strikes
back, as was also the case with Israel time and again.

The two spheres of influences in a human being, the
soulish and the spiritual, could in extreme polarisations go
sometimes very far. This is a little strongly stated—that
believers could be under the blessing of God and Satan's
'blessing' simultaneously. On the one side they are fighting
spiritually and are obedient to the Word, but on the other
side they give much room to the soulish—emotional areas,
and rely on experiences and feelings as well. This mixture
and such bondages, as well as the defilement of the spirit and
the flesh connected with it, will only be separated or
dissolved through the Cross, will only be driven back or
removed (2 Corinthians 7:1b) through a life of holiness. Thus
James also invites the believers to submit themselves to God
and consciously draw nigh to Him (James 4:7–8). The
frontiers of these unseen realms are clear cut at the Cross.
This became alarmingly clear to me in the course of my
book[8] *The Theory of Relativity and the Bible*. Matthew

16:16–17 and verse 23 clearly show this. Through the same Peter, through whom the Spirit of God had just spoken (verse 17), Satan already works and the disciple wants to hold his Lord back from the Cross. Although his motives were more than innocent and were meant well (verse 22), the enemy was already standing behind this soulish—human behaviour.

Our theological convictions may be correct, but they do not disturb our adversary as long as the way we live contradicts biblical truths. He knows that he is defeated only at the Cross. There, where the Cross does not reign, he has already gained power. Where the flesh rules and not the spirit (Galatians 5:16–18), we may not be surprised if the enemy infiltrates and strongly uses us, even if we deny it and explain dogmatically that such a thing is impossible. Only where the Cross reigns this opponent is powerless. Where experiences and feelings rule, the soulish sphere in other words, the enemy can usually record a 'revival', which is promptly regarded as a real work of revival by many believers.

Watchman Nee writes:

Emotions may be denominated the most formidable enemy to the life of a spiritual believer.[9]

According to my knowledge, the Bible calls all areas of the human life which have not gone through the Cross, to be flesh or darkness. All too often many believers unfortunately do not really live surrendered or crucified lives. (Let us think of verses such as Philippians 1:21; 2 Timothy 1:15; Luke 18:8, or the words of the Lord Jesus in the open letters to the different churches in Revelation.) Only the Cross and repentance bring sins into the light and His blood cleanses us (Ephesians 5:8,13). The Bible teaches us that the powers of Satan are ruling in darkness (Ephesians 6:12). Now if we can show that children of God can contain areas of darkness, then it becomes rather clear to us that the devil and his angels can join in to rule even there. Apart from this indirect conclusion the Bible tells us undoubtedly that believers ought to put away or resist this darkness. Ephesians 5:11 exhorts us not to have any fellowship with the unfruitful works of darkness. If we are not obedient, or not discerning, then this is possible, as the previous verse states, with more or less intensity according to circumstances. We read of instances in the Bible where believers have given themselves to fornication or prostitution. If someone opens himself to the powers of darkness too much, it can finally come to the stage of 'indwelling'.

The Bible also says of believers that they can have darkness. Yes, even the Lord Jesus warns 'that the light which is in thee be not darkness' (Luke 11:35).

I know of two passages where the Bible mentions darkness in connection with the children of God, namely Romans 13:12 (indirectly) '...let us therefore cast off the works of darkness...' and 1 Corinthians 4:5 (very directly—again in Corinth). According to Ephesians 6:12, the enemy may consequently exercise a certain controlling influence over a believer as well.

Naturally the Lord Jesus Himself was without darkness (1 John 1:5; James 1:17). For that reason He could say: '...for the prince of this world cometh and hath nothing in me' (John 14:30). On the other hand we can see how the enemy can gain power over us through dark deeds, just as the formulation of the same verse suggests in the Luther text: 'He has no power over me' (translated).

In closing, another parable which the Lord Jesus gives to us and which, in my opinion, can be interpreted in a similar way is in Matthew 13:31–32 where the Lord tells us in the second parable of the kingdom how the birds of the air lodge in the tree grown from a mustard seed. The mustard tree sometimes grew up to three metres high. Here we see how

Christendom has grown beyond the standard. Now who are the birds? In the same chapter the Lord states that they are a picture of the devil (Matthew 13:4,19; Revelation 18:2). Obviously the Church, through secularisation, or alienation from the Cross, becomes so big that demons can comfortably live in it, or 'indwell'. (See also Scofield Bible.)

This is also the sad experience in practice as a lot of counselling cases prove.

The parallel parable in Mark shows us, moreover, where these birds dwell, namely in the shadow of great branches (4:32). In James 1:17 it says that God is light 'with whom is no variableness, neither shadow of turning'. One can see these shadows allegorically as darkness. The branches, the disobedience, the worldliness and the sins become so big that the birds live in this shadow, as we read there literally.

A question: When must the enemy come into sight? When we cut or saw off the branches and twigs. We have to 'circumcise' ourselves, the Word of God says, and the Bible also speaks of God purging the branches (John 15:2). This cleansing usually means real repentance and brokenness. Thus it happens again and again in cases where people bring their sins into the light during counselling sessions— 'through removal of these branches'—that 'birds', or powers of darkness are suddenly manifested and become apparent. It is wonderful to see how the Bible indirectly and directly declares these realities; realities which are confirmed in practice.

But I would also like to mention here, that not everyone agrees with this interpretation. They see this parable positively, as a picture of security and delightful growth. Nevertheless, I would still like to bring the following considerations. In regard to the mustard tree mentioned above, the normal proportion was exceeded by far. It became much bigger than it should have, according to the law of Creation. As we have seen, the believers at Corinth were also 'puffed up'. And this is a snare par excellence of the enemy, for pride was his pristine sin.

In this church, as we have seen, the power of darkness had actually settled in. Somehow it becomes obvious now how counselling and cleansing therefore reveals such realities again and again. Thus Petrus Oktavianus reports in *Call from Indonesia*:

> This took place as the Lord completely broke us teachers, because we saw what kind of seed was coming up in our pupils, and as the Spirit of God was working among us, something peculiar took place; the spirits were starting to become active. For a long time they had remained hidden and undetected, and now they were moving. People who seemed to be difficult before, students whom we also served frequently in counselling, suddenly turned out to have an evil spirit. Others were thrown all over the place in such a terrible manner that we had to speak of possession. Bible students and teachers—more than one teacher—observed: I am not only a subjected person but also a possessed one; I am not filled with the Holy Spirit but with the anti-(godly) spirit. Satan fears nothing as much as the Spirit of God and he continues to sleep, so long as the Spirit of God does not work.[10]

'Therefore let us cleanse ourselves from all filthiness of the flesh and spirit, perfecting holiness in the fear of God.' (2 Corinthians 7:1).

Looking unto the Lord Jesus

At this point I would especially like to mention that it is not so much a question of whether such 'bondages of darkness' are present in a child of God, but rather if the one in question is prepared to obey God, to fight spiritually and to lead a life of holiness.

This subject can lead to an unhealthy introspection in an inexperienced and immature believer. One searches oneself to see whether certain symptoms and signs of occult oppression or even 'indwelling' are evident. One becomes unnatural, inhibited, neurotic and possibly highly introspective. This introspection is always the beginning of spiritual defeat—just as Peter started to sink as soon as he looked away from the Lord (Matthew 14:30). However, this book wants to show how dangerous it is not to walk by faith (2 Corinthians 5:7), but to heed feelings, experience, signs and wonders and lastly to concentrate on one's self in a certain degree.

Should this book have such an effect on any one reader, then this negative result would have defeated its purpose. We are to become watchful and sober, but biblical faith does not look at oneself and the weaknesses of the flesh. A true Christian life neither consists of proud sinlessness nor of an unhealthy occupation with our own mistakes; it consists of a trusting obedience towards the known will of God and the loving service towards our fellowman.

Abraham, who did not work one sign, is called the father of all believers in Romans 4:12 and 16. It is said of him that he did not look at himself, his dead body (his feelings, possibilities, strength)—as already briefly mentioned earlier—but he only clung to the promises of God; he held fast the promise of the Lord and therefore only looked unto Him. He was his real consolation, the true anchor of his soul (Hebrews 6:19). Through this faith he became strong and honoured God. It was a faith which was established in the invisible world, and which expected everything from God and nothing from itself, a faith which counted on God. Abraham had no more hope in his own strength, nothing visible to which he could cling. But he did not let go of the promise of his Lord and in looking upon it he became the conqueror, the father of all.

'Abraham believed God, and it was reckoned to him as righteousness. Therefore, be sure that it is those who are of faith who are sons of Abraham. And if you belong to Christ, then you are Abraham's offspring, heirs according to promise.' (Galatians 3:6,7,29)

Thus we should not walk by sight or look at ourselves, but walk by faith and lay hold of the promises of God in His wonderful Word; hold fast, no matter how positive or negative our feelings or the opinion of the world may be. This kind of faith proves God right and therefore let us look unto the Lord Jesus, the author and finisher of our faith (Hebrews 12:2); and not unto Satan, author and finisher of unbelief, no matter how bad it may be with us. 'Mine eyes are ever toward the Lord; for he shall pluck my feet out of the net.' (Psalm 25:15). Such faith may claim:

We know that whosoever is born of God sinneth not; but he that is begotten of God keepeth himself, and that wicked one toucheth him not. (1 John 5:18)

and

The God of peace shall bruise Satan under your feet shortly. (Romans 16:20)

3

CONSIDERATIONS CONCERNING THE LAYING ON OF HANDS

Laying on of Hands in the Old Testament and the Gospels

According to Hebrews 6:2, the doctrine of laying on of hands belongs to the foundations of the New Testament. This subject shall primarily be contemplated here from the point of identification, 'becoming one' before God. This is best illustrated in the Old Testament by the laws that God gave in the Book of Leviticus. If any of the people or even a priest had sinned, then an offering was needed, which was shown at the door of the tabernacle (Leviticus 1:3). Then there followed the laying on of hands and I quote from a Bible dictionary:

> The person offering put his hand on the head of the innocent sacrifice and thereby transferred his sin unto the sacrifice.[1]

In Leviticus 4 this identification becomes very clear, where the laws concerning the sin offerings are recorded, and the laying on of hands is mentioned five times (verses 4,15,24,29 and 33). The principle of the transference of sin becomes very apparent in Leviticus 16:21. The high priest had to lay his hands upon the live goat and confess the iniquities of the children of Israel. Again, in a certain sense, transference took place. Such a victim could only be killed after the sinner had made himself one with it. We have the symbol of the scapegoat before us, a beautiful illustration of

142

the substitutionary sacrifice of Jesus Christ. The confession of sin and the identification with the Lord Jesus (Romans 6:6)—by acceptance of the Cross—are the two presuppositions for our justification. All this takes place at conversion.

When two creatures or two people declare themselves one before God, then this is a very serious matter in the eyes of God. The Lord sees them as one. Their identification with one another brings about certain results. For instance, God regards the sinner as holy and clean through the Lord Jesus (Colossians 1:22). Every blessing that God intends for a human being is derived from our oneness with the Lord Jesus, therefore we also read that we have died with the Lord Jesus and have been raised up together with Him to sit in heavenly places (Ephesians 2:6).

Someone who identifies himself with the Lord Jesus receives the Holy Spirit. Transference takes place.

Generally speaking, by means of identification of two or more persons, spiritual powers can be exchanged in the invisible dimensions. As someone once said, sin binds us together with the enemy. Various sins can open us to the devil so much that he finds entrance into our heart and soul, as mentioned earlier. Those transgressions which are an abomination unto God in the Old Testament cause an identification with Satan and lead to demonisation. A drastic example which the Bible cites to explain this principle is that if anyone makes himself one with a harlot, then transference can result and unclean spirits can enter the one concerned, as explained several times before. Anyone being aware of this fact will naturally consider carefully with whom he makes himself one (we could almost say: 'whom he marries').

The laying on of hands signifies in the spiritual realm an identification, presented in a visible way. It becomes conceivable from this perspective why Paul wrote to Timothy: 'Lay hands suddenly on no man...' The reason why follows: '...neither be partaker of other men's sins: keep thyself pure' (1 Timothy 5:22). Therefore we should not too hastily lay hands on anyone, since we may make ourselves one with a person of whose spiritual condition we may not really be aware. In that way, one can become part of other men's sins; yes, an invisible transference of darkness can occur, even spiritual defilement.

Many a person does not want to acknowledge this. But once we have perceived the basic spiritual outline, then it will not seem to be so incomprehensible any more.

It becomes clear from this viewpoint why the disciples never laid hands on anyone while casting out demons. Unfortunately this is practised more and more frequently today. In doing so, one identifies oneself with darkness, with the bondage. Thus Peter Mayer writes:

> In the counselling of people under the bondage of the occult, the question often arises, how far the laying on of hands is necessary or desirable. We hold the opinion that, referring to this fact, caution seems to be advisable; under no circumstances may hands be laid on anyone who is under strong demonic subjection or possession. The Lord Jesus never laid hands on while releasing a possessed person; counsellors who had done this came under the spell of the dark powers themselves, those which they had tried to cast out. In the New Testament we see that hands were laid mainly on the sick...[2]

In the case of healing the sick we do not necessarily have to speak of identification. This is actually differentiated in the Gospels again and again, for instance in Luke 4:40–41. These verses, in conjunction with their parallel Matthew 8:16, shows that the Lord Jesus cast out the evil spirits with His Word and laid hands on the sick (also Mark 6:5 and so on). This indicates a significance of laying on of hands, namely that of recovery and healing of the sick. We find this in the case of our Lord (Mark 8:23) and also of the apostles. Thus we read in Acts 28:8 that Paul laid his hands on the sick father of Publius and he recovered. This is in agreement with the statement in Mark 16:18b, where the character of the apostolic signs stands in the foreground. Where the Church of Jesus Christ has been formed, there the letter of James shows how this ought to be done. The sick person has to call for the elders of the Church (therefore not miracle workers, apostles, healers or 'itinerant evangelists'), that they may pray over him (James 5:14–15).

It is clear that the Lord Jesus identified Himself with sinners, for He was made 'sin for us' (2 Corinthians 5:21). Thus we read that He, the clean one, touched lepers and the unclean (Matthew 8:3, etc). The Lord Jesus Himself is only light; whoever came in contact with or was touched by Him, became clean accordingly, or blessed (Mark 10:16). To my knowledge we read of only one case where our Lord laid hands on a satanically-subjected person, namely the woman who had been crippled for eighteen years. This, essentially, was also a case of sickness as it speaks explicitly of a 'spirit of infirmity' (Luke 13:11). The Lord Jesus thus identified Himself with His people—as it surely says that He 'Himself took our infirmities and bare our sicknesses' (Matthew 8:17). It becomes clear that this is only and exclusively valid for our Lord and only to be used by Him and not by us.

With this we want to leave the Gospels behind and turn our eyes to the principle of identification in the Book of Acts. In this book the laying on of hands is reported six times. The sixth and last case (Chapter 28) has already been mentioned. Here, the remaining five cases will be examined more closely, some of which are very controversial.

...And in the Book of Acts

Jerusalem

In Acts 6:6 this action is first mentioned. It had come to disagreements within the first Church and seven deacons were appointed who had to look after the fair distribution of relief funds for the widows. They were set before the apostles, who in turn prayed for them and laid their hands on them. Why was this necessary? With this act it was shown to the whole church that the apostles identified themselves with their responsibility and were clearly standing behind them. This signified, in other words: 'Look, if you do not obey these deacons, then you really do not obey us (apostles) in this matter. Therefore accept their instructions.' Such an investiture is also paralleled to some degree in Numbers 27:18–23, on the principle of identification. We find this kind of equalisation in the Scriptures again and again. It is finally given also in the relationship of Jesus to His Father as well as to His disciples (Luke 10:16). Whoever thought that he had to obey the apostles only was therefore corrected.

There is no order without authority. Visible unity was demonstrated in Jerusalem, an apostolic authority was delegated to the trustees of alms. One knew therefore that behind the deacons stood the authority of the apostles. The unanimity and therefore the peace was restored by this act as well.

Samaria

The second event of this kind is recorded in Acts 8:17. This report has caused much confusion. Why did the apostles have to come and lay on hands? We learn that Philip, one of the deacons (according to verse 1 the apostles were in Jerusalem at that time), was preaching among the Samaritans with great power and authority. Although the Lord confirmed mightily the preaching of Philip (verses 6–8) and many were baptised (verse 12), they had not yet received the Holy Spirit (verse 16). How can this be explained? The Samaritans, although baptised in the name of the Lord Jesus, became believers only in the sense of the Old Testament dispensation of Law in which one had not yet received the gift of the Holy Spirit (Ephesians 1:14; 2 Corinthians 1:22; 5:5). First of all we notice that a new nation was reached with the Gospel here. The Samaritans were a very mixed nation, not only in religion (2 Kings 17:41) but also racially (2 Kings 17:24)—and this since the time when the Israelites had mixed themselves with all the different nations of the Assyrian Empire. The Apostle Peter received, symbolically speaking, the keys to the Kingdom of Heaven. He actually opened the door to the Christian Church for Israel and later on he will also open the door for the Gentiles in the house of Cornelius (Acts 10:34–38).

Each new beginning was connected with visible events, as this is quite evident for the beginning of a new dispensation—as for instance, the speaking in tongues (Acts 10:45). Therefore we find the reason for the laying on of hands in the fact that Peter (as the 'key apostle') had to come first of all, before a New Testament Church could be formed in a new nation. (Incidentally, the fact that Peter and John were sent out by the other apostles [verse 14], in connection with John 13:16, clearly disproves the papal primacy, as taught by the Roman Catholics.)

Yet another explanation for this behaviour is worth mentioning, and seems to me to be the most satisfactory. According to John 4:9 the Jews and Samaritans had no fellowship together. They were declared enemies, and in Flavius Josephus' *The Jewish War* we can read that a hatred of immense degree flared up between them. The smallest incident caused conditions almost like a civil war, with real massacres. One mutually considered the other as renegades and dogs. The one worshipped in Jerusalem, the other on

Mount Gerizim. The word 'Samaritan' was an insult to the ears of a Jew (John 8:48). Now into such a situation the apostles were sent.

It is conceivable that the believing Samaritans, in spite of everything, would take their racial prejudice into the Church. It is well known that many a thing is only yielded gradually, many a carnal idea withdrawn very slowly (Ephesians 4:22). One needs only to think of how even the believing Pharisees were still partly clinging to the old (Acts 15:5), and among other things wanted to introduce the circumcision into the New Covenant. Thus it is conceivable that the Samaritans, if the Holy Spirit would have at this stage come into their hearts by the preaching of Philip, would have rejected the authority of the apostles and renounced the Israelites (perhaps remarking that they possessed everything and did not need the 'Jewish guardianship'). The body of Christ would have been separated. Yet the Spirit of God knows no racial barrier (Colossians 3:11); after all we are built upon the foundation of the apostles and prophets (Ephesians 2:20), who were Israelites. It is easy to see—as hatred always causes separation—that this situation called for a special act, even that of identification.

Therefore the apostles had to come and had to visibly declare themselves one with the Samaritans through the laying on of hands. As Ralph Shallis once said, it was probably a very humbling experience for both parties. They who had once called each other dogs (Goyim) now declared themselves one in the Lord Jesus. Every unbelieving witness had to acknowledge that in Christ there is actually no more prejudice, no more separation. What seemed to be completely unimaginable and impossible, was now accomplished through the power of God and the finished work of the Cross. Jews and Samaritans became one heart and one soul. After their mutual humbling act of accepting the Crucified One, the Holy Spirit came at once (Acts 8:17). In Chapter 2 of Acts the Holy Spirit penetrates the language barriers; in Chapter 8 the racial barriers.

It is exegetically invalid to conclude from this report that laying on of hands—if possible by an apostle—would always be necessary for the receiving of the Holy Spirit. This, unfortunately takes place more and more in certain movements today. John Stott gives similar reasons when he writes:

> Instead, as has been urged above, the reason why the Spirit was not given seems to lie in the historical situation. And since this historical situation was unique and cannot be repeated (the Jewish-Samaritan schism having long since been swallowed up by the universal Christian mission), I cannot myself see how the abnormality in the Samaritan reception of the Spirit could be taken as a precedent for today.[3]

Damascus

The third case is reported in Acts 9. An event of enormous significance had occurred: the conversion of Saul of Tarsus. He had arrived in Damascus blind and broken inwardly. One can hardly imagine what sort of a shock the realisation must have been for him that the Lord Jesus is the true Messiah. The whole of his old life—everything he had done before— had been destroyed in that moment of encounter on the road to Damascus. Therewith he had lost all his old friends, namely the Pharisees, who were yet to become his worst enemies. He had persecuted the Christians with all intensity. Who would now stand with him? Actually he sat there completely alone and forsaken and prayed. Now God started to build this man up again and to prepare him for his service (9:15).

Initially, we are told expressively that hands were to be laid on him in order that he might receive his sight (verse 12). Indeed it is also clear that in this case a special act of identification was necessary, as Saul was really the worst persecutor of the pristine Church. Ananias calls him brother (verse 17) and Saul had to realise that this was not just lip-service. By means of laying on of hands (as a Pharisee he knew exactly what this meant) it became rather clear to him: 'Indeed, is this possible? Although I persecuted the Christians in such a way, they are not resentful to me, they even declare themselves one with me and I am really their brother.'

It seems to be almost a confirmation of Jesus' call: 'Why persecutest thou me?' (9:4). The Lord does not say: 'Why persecutest thou my disciples?' Interpreted in a figurative sense one can say that because Saul identifies himself with the Christians, he receives his sight again and therewith receives the true Light, namely the Lord Jesus. Previously he was spiritually blind, being completely deceived.

Here we find a special event as well which is accompanied by special circumstances and actions.

Antioch

We find the next case at the commencement of the 13th Chapter. The explanation is quickly found. It was the first time that a church was sending out missionaries. For people on the outside it might have looked as though Paul and Barnabas were leaving the disciples and separating themselves from them. Although in some respects a separation actually took place, the laying on of hands declared: We are one, we are behind you. Even if we are geographically going separate ways now, we are still completely united with one another in heart (1 Thessalonians 2:17). By this identification the church that was sending them was really declaring that they were, spiritually speaking, going with them (verse 3).

This report usually serves as proof for the idea that hands should still be laid on during mission services. I really do not want to say that this is not good, yet we ought to remember that we do not necessarily have an instruction for the Church here but a simple report. Here we have a book of history. Furthermore it is a matter of a first event and this is usually, as already stated, connected with special actions and conditions.

Ephesus and Malta

In Acts 19 we are informed of the fifth and most difficult case, difficult from the point of interpretation. This passage is a favourite one of many false teachers for instance the 'New Apostolics', a group which originated from the 'Pentecostal revival' of Edward Irving from Scotland in 1830. These verses are often used as a reason why the laying on of hands should be necessary.

Let us therefore approach the somewhat difficult task of interpreting this passage. Here also as in other cases, the evangelist Ralph Shallis has given me the basic explanation. First of all these disciples were in all probability followers or 'converts' of Apollos (18:24). We read of him that 'he spake and taught diligently the things of the Lord Jesus' but 'knowing only the baptism of John' (18:25). In other words, the transition from the Old to the New Covenant was not yet completely accomplished.

John the Baptist was the last and greatest representative of the Old Testament time (Matthew 11:11; Luke 16:16) and he had many followers. With the beginning of the age of Grace something completely new was brought about by God (2 Corinthians 5:17). But many a person found certain things of the Old Covenant so nice that they would rather have saved some of them for the new dispensation (Acts 15:1). Thus we read that it was especially the pristine Church that was threatened with intermixture in this area (Galatians 3:1; 5:4; 6:12). Because of this question of intermingling of the Old and New Testament, most heated discussions and quarrels developed (Acts 15:2,6,7; Galatians 2:5–6). When the Lord

Jesus spoke on this subject (His disciples were requested to fast by the followers of John, Matthew 9:14). He gave the famous answer that one does not put new cloth on an old garment, neither does one put new wine into old bottles: therefore, no mixing of old and new. In the beginning God had indeed still 'tolerated' a few transitions, yet in principle a clear separation and clear distinction is demanded.

Now the disciples at Ephesus were really confused in this regard. Almost literally they had the 'new wine in old bottles'. On the one hand they knew about Jesus; on the other hand they knew only the baptism of John, as Apollos did (verse 3), and they had not yet received the Holy Spirit (verse 2). Like the people in Samaria, they believed in the concepts of the Old Testament. Here the danger of intermixture was especially obvious and Paul knew that a clear decision and a definite action was necessary. When this Apostle—this distinct personality—laid hands on someone and therefore made himself one with him, he did not adapt himself to the opinion of the other person, but rather the other person had to follow his convictions. With the act of laying on of hands, the Scriptures indicate that Paul executed a clear separation from the Old Covenant, from John the Baptist (and John himself would certainly have agreed with this, John 3:30). Thus people who are turning to the Lord Jesus ought first of all to renounce the world and the old life. To many this might have appeared as being too radical, but the following sign of tongue-speaking confirmed the correctness of this act of the Apostle. One can have different opinions about this passage. However, one should not derive church doctrines or behaviour patterns from it, because we have a very unique case here. Thus Dr Wasserzug writes:

This same sign of tongue-speaking was given once more when twelve men were baptized by Paul in the name of the Lord Jesus Christ in Ephesus, after they had previously received only the baptism of repentance after the manner of John the Baptist. These twelve men had remained in the period of the Kingdom which John the Baptist had preached; owing to the preaching of Paul they were now introduced to the new Church period. It was a unique case and the admittance of these twelve men into the church was therefore accompanied by this sign of tongue-speaking.

With reference to the 'Pentecost of the Gentiles' in the house of Cornelius the same writer points out:

Peter emphasized that they 'had received the Holy Ghost as well as we'. The speaking in tongues, that is, in a foreign language, was a sign which was meant for the believing Jews who had come with Peter and were shocked to find that the Gentiles had received the Holy Spirit. Today the acceptance of Gentiles into the church does not cause any upheaval among the Jews any more. Therefore no more signs are required.... On the contrary, the sign of tongues is mentioned only three times as a peculiarity in the Book of Acts: on the day of Pentecost with the believers of Jews, in the house of Cornelius with the believers of the Gentiles and in Ephesus with twelve men in the Jewish 'Diaspora', who were still living in the time of the promised Kingdom.[4]

These passages are often read to biblically inexperienced believers since Charismatics want to show them how ubiquitous this gift ought to be. In the twenty-eight chapters of the book of Acts speaking in tongues seemingly consistently occurs, yet if we remember that this Book was written over a period of approximately thirty years and we only find three definite cases of tongues mentioned, it then appeared to be the exception rather than the rule. This sign accompanied only special events.

In Chapter 28 of Acts we have the sixth and last case (when Paul is on Malta). Here we read about the healing of a sick person as previously recorded. Here as well as in the following case of laying on of hands (verse 9) it is not primarily identification.

Laying on of Hands in the Epistles

The laying on of hands is mentioned three times in the Letters to Timothy. Both passages 1 Timothy 4:14 and 2 Timothy 1:6 really render the same event.

Thus the Bible dictionary states:

> The ministry of Timothy was that of an Evangelist (2 Timothy 4:5); he was therefore not restricted to one place. He was appointed to this ministry by means of prophecy (1 Timothy 1:18; 4:14), and had received special gifts for that purpose (2 Timothy 1:6), when he was appointed by the laying on of hands of Paul and the elders.[5]

The Bible text speaks of a gift—which one it was cannot be said with certainty—perhaps that of an Evangelist. The third passage was quoted earlier, namely 1 Timothy 5:22.

Finally the letter of James speaks of this in connection with the healing by the elders (James 5:14) although the laying on of hands is not specifically mentioned.

Otherwise this act is only mentioned once more in Hebrews 6:2 where it is shown to be one of the fundamentals of biblical doctrine.

Following the Gospels the laying on of hands is found eleven times in the New Testament. Therefore it must be explicitly stated that the laying on of hands itself is actually biblical. But there, where the church situation is introduced to us in the Epistles, we realise that the laying on of hands has to be done by the elders and within the church. Thus we read this in James and also in the first letter to Timothy.

This purely biblical fact is certainly no guard against any misuse as is too often the case with divine matters. One may only think of the Lord's Supper. After all Paul had certain apostolic powers of authority (for instance to complete the Word of God, Colossians 1:25), probably also in regard to the conveyance of gifts (2 Timothy 1:6). It is also worth mentioning that Paul and Timothy knew each other already for a long time and were practically colleagues. The Apostle writes: 'But thou hast fully known my doctrine, manner of life, purpose, faith, longsuffering, charity, patience...' (2 Timothy 3:10–11). A greater agreement between two people is hardly conceivable. Here the laying on of hands was only a visible demonstration of an already invisible reality. Paul himself considers therefore his admonition well when he says to 'lay hands suddenly on no man' (1 Timothy 5:22). A similar relationship existed also between Moses and Joshua.

Yet certain groups want to neutralise the statement in this verse and assert that this refers only to the ordaining of the elders. We actually do find that in Chapter 5:17 and 19 of First Timothy the elders are mentioned, and it is quite possible that this is meant also, but in 1 Timothy 5:22 we clearly read 'no man'. Not only the elders, therefore, are not to be treated suddenly in this way. We are also told in the only passage in Acts 14:23 where we find the ordaining of elders that they indeed prayed and fasted, but the laying on of hands is not mentioned. However, no doctrinal statement ought to be made here since the book of Acts is not a book of doctrinal teaching.

Misuse of the Scriptures

One of the main desires of Satan is to deceive us with false doctrines, if possible in regard to Bible passages

passages (Matthew 4:6), for example. Watchman Nee points out the following:

> The peril for the Christian is to have false teaching injected into his thought life so as to lead him astray from a sincere and pure devotion to Christ. These are the works the 'serpent' is perpetrating today. Satan has disguised himself as an angel of light to lead saints to worship with their intellect a Jesus other than the Lord, to receive a spirit other than the Holy Spirit, and by these to propagate a gospel other than the gospel of the grace of God. Paul pronounces these to be nothing else than the deeds of Satan in the Christian's mind. The adversary translates these 'doctrines' into thoughts and then imposes them upon the mind of the Christian. How tragic that few appreciate the reality of these activities.[6]

How true these words are!

The whole truth of Scripture as we find it finally in the Epistles is the armoured shield against false teachings. Therefore it should be emphasised once again that the Book of Acts is not a book of doctrine. Peter Mayer writes:

> The Book of Acts is not a book of doctrine about the life in the Christian community or about the Holy Spirit. The Book of Acts is a record of the events that took place during the transition from the Old Testament (Law) to the New Testament (Grace).[7]

We must distinguish between instruction and information. To raise information of special events in the Bible to doctrines leads to error and heresy. This is the history of the origin of almost all sects.

John Stott gives us the same advice when he says:

It would be easy to misunderstand the point I am trying to make. I am not saying that the descriptive passages of the Bible are valueless, for 'all Scripture is inspired by God and profitable' (2 Tim 3:16). What I am saying is that what is descriptive is valuable only in so far as it is interpreted by what is didactic.[8]

The laying on of hands in the Book of Acts represents special situations. To take from such information that one needs the laying on of hands for the 'baptism of the Spirit' or even for the receiving of the Holy Spirit for all future time is, as shown above, biblically unfounded. For instance, Acts 8:17 should serve as proof, yet we read in the previous chapters how thousands believed without mentioning any laying on of hands.

Thus Michael Griffiths writes:

There are many other places in the book of Acts where it is recorded that people came to genuine faith, but without any special manifestation of the Spirit apparently being bestowed. Hoekema lists them as follows (p 80): 'The lame man is healed in Acts 3. Those who subsequently believed (4:4). Those who believed after the death of Ananias (5:14). The great company of priests (6:7). The Ethiopian eunuch (8:36). The many who believed in Joppa (9:42). Those who turned to the Lord in Syrian Antioch (11:21). The proconsul at Cyprus (13:12). The believers in Pisidian Antioch (13:43). The believers in Iconium (14:1). The disciples at Derbe (14:21). Lydia (16:14). The Philippian jailer (16:34). The believers in Thessalonica (17:4). The Bereans (17:11–12). The Atheneans in 17:34. Those in Corinth (18:4). Crispus and other Corinthians (18:8). Some of the Jews at Rome (28:24).' It is thus impossible to set this isolated Samaritan event against all these other events and argue that what took place in Samaria was the normal thing and typical of what happened whenever anyone in the Acts period became a Christian.[9]

In similar way he comments on Acts 19 in regard to the disciples in Ephesus: 'Again it can be argued that at Ephesus there were special circumstances.'

To derive from these special cases that the laying on of hands is necessary for the receiving of the Holy Spirit contradicts very clearly the Letters of the New Testament also, where we find the situation for the local church explicitly set forth. Thus, characteristically, Paul writes especially to the Ephesians that they were sealed with the Holy Spirit when they had first believed (Ephesians 1:13). Moreover, he also asks these disciples at Ephesus whether they had received the Holy Spirit since they believed (Acts 19:2). In agreement with this we read in Galatians that we receive the promised Spirit through faith (Galatians 3:14), not by any law or works (Galatians 3:2). One may notice that one or two Bible verses out of context result in false teaching. 'Text out of context is pretext.' The whole Bible presents doctrine.

If we look at 1 Timothy 4:1 once more, we must assume that such activities of the adversary may increase very much in the last days. Is this perhaps the reason for distortion supposedly supported by Scripture (2 Peter 3:16)?

The misuse of Acts 19 which is used especially by New Apostolic groups, as well as some Pentecostal movements, is actually quite sobering. Many unsuspecting believers, who are very often sincere and serious, come into this 'undertow' of deception. The confusion is alarming. We have already briefly referred to the origin of the New Apostolic church. If we compare the events of that time with those things happening very frequently today, one gets the impression that the Church has learnt little, and furthermore has grasped little of the principles of Satan's deceptions. As to the history of this sect, I would like to quote Bautz:

His (Irvings) followers were certain: The end of all things had come near (1 Peter 4:11), yet they were equally convinced that a 'new Pentecost' would have to precede the end of the world and the second coming of Christ. They begged for it in fervent prayers and waited in feverish suspense for a new pouring out of the Spirit and the revival for the new apostolic gifts of the Spirit. One did not have to wait very long for the day of Pentecost. In Fernicarry in Scotland... on 21st March 1830 a needlewoman received the 'gift of tongue-speaking': she babbled unintelligible prayers. Shortly afterwards sensational cases of healing occurred in the family of a ship's carpenter in near-by Glasgow, on the other side of the River Clyde. One was beside oneself with joy and jubilation. Now the desired apostolic gifts of the Spirit were here. Only the apostles were still missing.... Therefore one impetuously prayed in the assemblies: Send us apostles.... The movement spread like a fire. Everywhere new assemblies gathered in houses. Tongue-speaking, healing and prophecy were its special characteristics. The movement increasingly assumed charismatic character. Irving could not prevent the speaking of tongues starting in his church as well, and it became increasingly more important in his services.[10]

One could almost say that he could not get rid of the spirits that he had called. If we read 'revival reports' of Pentecostal circles today, they practically sound the same. Are we ready to learn from history? What is really written? That revival will come—or that strong delusions will be sent? May the Lord give grace and open blinded eyes.

Signs and Wonders

We have to notice here, as briefly mentioned, that the apostles had certain special positions and authority, just as their letters have a special significance. Moreover, the apostles were serving under certain sign aspects, and were therefore endorsed with signs and wonders (2 Corinthians 12:12). Thus we are told of Paul that handkerchiefs and aprons from his body drove out demons and healed the sick (Acts 19:12) and that he raised Eutychus from the dead (Acts 20:9–10). Dr Wasserzug believes:

It is of utmost importance to us to clearly understand the Word of God, inspired by the Holy Spirit, that Paul was a true apostle, who was proved as such by the signs of the apostles. His letters belong to the most important writings of the New Testament.

If he is an apostle, then all his writings and each word have divine authority for us. If he was not an apostle then his letters have only the value of a subjective testimony which may be valuable, but not necessarily binding for us. The apostles have left us the written Word in the New Testament, which is under the testimony of the Holy Spirit: 'All Scripture is given by inspiration of God' (2 Timothy 3:16). This revelation of God in the New Testament was completed within the time of the apostles and nobody can add even one word. The New Testament is the Word of God and as such does not require any signs and wonders. Its authority is divine and does not need to be submitted to proof. Therefore the signs and wonders of the apostles disappeared also with the apostles. Today we not only have Moses and the prophets but also the Lord Jesus Christ and the apostles in order to examine every message for any falsehood.

Today it is potentially dangerous to ask for wonders and signs. The Lord Jesus Christ warns us of this and says:

'For there shall arise false Christs and false prophets, and shall shew great signs and wonders; insomuch that, if it were possible, they shall deceive the very elect.' (Matthew 24:24). It is just the sign of the last days, that so many even among the believers desire after something special, and are not willing to be satisfied with the plain, beautiful Word of God.[11]

This concern is justified. Some people are longing for the 'apostolic' times and experiences. That requires the regular occurrence of signs and wonders. We have already pointed out how the Lord Jesus has warned against the desire after signs. Yet the Bible itself does not include great miracles all the time. One can recognise that miracles are usually accompanied by new revelations in God's plan of redemption. Thus Paul emphasised that the signs of an apostle were wrought among the believers (2 Corinthians 12:12). In other words he considered these signs as 'apostolic'.

We can also recognise the special status of the apostles from the following event. In Acts 8 Philip evangelises among the Samaritans with obvious success, as already mentioned. Yet the apostles still had to come for the laying on of hands. The reason for this has already been given. Yet we are faced with the question: Why could Philip not lay hands on them? Because he was a deacon and not an apostle. It should make us think that practically the whole Pentecostal Movement refers to this passage, among others, in order to 'biblically' prove their arbitrary actions.

It is also worth mentioning that the words 'signs and wonders' no longer appear in the report of Paul's second missionary journey. Indeed, in his third journey, special miracles are mentioned only once (Acts 19:11) of the Apostle, and one can say generally that miracle signs decreased.

Signs usually accompany first events, they are at the

beginning of each new dispensation of God. Thus Alfred Kuen states:

> The three cases (of speaking in tongues, author's note) mentioned in Acts refer to 'historical breakthroughs' of the Gospel into new spheres: establishment of the first church (Acts 2), conversion of the first gentiles (Acts 10), disciples of John the Baptist (Acts 19), and if one wants to add Acts 8: the Samaritans.... Each one of these cases, one can safely say, is an exception.[12]

Does this mean the miracles of today are unnecessary or even impossible? I would like to answer together with Hans Brandenburg:

> We know that nothing is impossible with God and that He most certainly works extraordinary things upon the prayers of His children. Why then should we not also speak of miracles? But these are personal experiences of faith which do not belong to the general preaching or even publications in which one calls similar things a sign of elevated Christianity.[13]

Thus Hebrews 2:1–4 also brings out the conclusion that in principle God shifted His work from signs to the written Word. We have seen in the treatise on the Corinthian letter how the Lord still intervened in judgement and how He also judged the first sin in connection with the first Church in a visible way (Ananias and Saphira). It would be dangerous and misleading if one generalised the extra-ordinary to promote something as a doctrine which was at first more of a confirmation of the Word with signs by God (Mark 16:20b).

It should be illustrated by the following quotation just where this emphasis can lead and what religious disguise can be connected with it:

O then ye unbelieving, turn ye unto the Lord; cry mightily unto the Father in the name of Jesus, that perhaps ye may be found spotless, pure, fair and white, having been cleansed by the blood of the Lamb, at that great and last day, and again I speak unto you who deny the revelations of God, and say that they are done away, that there are no revelations, nor prophecies, nor gifts, nor healing, nor speaking with tongues, and the interpretation of tongues; Behold I say unto you, he that denieth these things knoweth not the gospel of Christ; yea he has not read the scriptures; if so, he does not understand them. For do we not read that God is the same yesterday, today and forever, and in Him there is no variableness neither shadow of changing?[14]

It sounds very pious and biblical, except it is found, strangely enough, in the *Book of Mormon*. It should make us think, when several circles of the Charismatic movements are arguing in a similar way, frequently in connection with Mark 16:17–18, the passage which interestingly enough is quoted in the same chapter of this passage in the *Book of Mormon*, namely verse 24.

It does not say, the Lord *does* the same, but that He *is* the same throughout all eternity, of which there is no doubt. But He does not always act or work in the same way, as Hebrews 1:1 clearly states. The foundation is laid only once, as we know (Ephesians 2:20). 2 Thessalonians 2:15 shows us, as well, how the Apostle Paul knowingly established the believers in the Scriptures, in contrast to the deceiving signs and wonders which he mentioned earlier in this chapter (2:9–11). Luke 16:29–31 informs us of the same.

Now whoever would ask the Lord to again intervene and act as He did during the time of the early Church would also have to ask the Lord to visibly judge sin as He did with Ananias and Saphira. Yet no fervent prayers are offered in this direction. One devotes one's supplications more to the pleasant and more comfortable manifestations of the presence of God.

One can essentially say for other areas also that anything which may be obtained by natural circumstances and means, a person should not seek to attain by supernatural, possibly sensational, methods from God. Thus the Lord gave manna to His people for as long as they remained in the desert. However, this stopped when Israel moved into the promised land, where food was available in abundance by natural means. In my opinion, miracles cannot reveal the true depth of the Godhead to the same extent as the Word. John 14:21–23 may point to that. The Lord really says that He wants to 'make His abode in us', wants to reveal Himself to us through His Word. Obviously the more we love His Word, the more He can reveal Himself to us and can gain room in us. Thus we learn in John 2:23 that many believed in the Lord Jesus when they saw His miracles. However it was obviously not through saving faith. After all, the next verse reveals to us that the Lord Jesus did not commit Himself unto them. The faith which justifies consists of a mutual giving of self. The following well-known story of Nicodemus illustrates well how one can be spiritually dead in spite of seeing signs and wonders. But the new birth (John 3:3) takes place through faith in the finished work of the Lord Jesus and the acceptance of the Lord as Saviour, not by events which impress our senses.

When a disappointed, wonder-seeking crowd (John 6:30) turns away from the Lord Jesus (6:66) then Scripture declares to us, practically in contrast to this hunger for signs, that the Lord Jesus has the Words of eternal life (John 6:63,68).

It may also be worth mentioning that signs are necessary for communication between two people who are out of hearing distance. But we know that we have direct communion with the Lord through the Spirit of God and His Word and do not have to consult a prophet for God's will as in the Old Testament, where the Spirit had not yet been poured out. We do not want to make dogmatic statements about this, yet John 20:30–31 also points to this conclusion, how obviously the written Word has taken over the function of the signs. Thus R. C. Trench writes the following in regard to the Greek word '*semeion*', meaning 'signs':

> It is contained and declared in the very Word itself that the prime object and end of the miracle is to lead us to something out of and beyond itself: that, so to speak, it is a kind of sign-post of God...[15]

We can follow this same kind of development in the Bible. The signs are never an end in themselves. Where they take on this function, they are a cause of distortion of the faith-life of the believer. Usually the carnal Christian regards signs and wonders as the more exciting and greater thing. But the spiritual Christian knows that the Word is to be regarded as the authentic standard. After all, the Apostle Paul has declared in great detail in 1 Corinthians 14 why the gift of proclaiming the Word is greater than the sign-gifts. Our Lord Jesus also contrasts these sign and miracle workers (Matthew 7:22) with those who are obeying His Word in simple faith (Matthew 7:24).

John 20:8–9 also tells us how, in certain respects, sight indicates lack of spiritual understanding. For: 'Blessed are they, that have not seen, and yet have believed.' (20:29). We are admonished to walk by faith and not by sight (2 Corinthians 5:7), to look at the invisible and not at the visible (4:18).

Misuse of the Laying on of Hands

I would like to say here directly—although I am aware that it may cause annoyance to some: the sudden laying on of hands is spiritual fornication (thinking of identification), a real epidemic and, in my opinion, one of the greatest dangers of the Church. It is connected with the occult and sorcery and, therefore, is increasing parallel to it.

We read in Acts 8 of the 'conversion' of a certain sorcerer named Simon (verse 13). Before Philip came the people had confused his satanic power with the power of God (verse 10). Today this also happens more and more among believers. Anyone who expresses doubts in the case of certain 'miracles' and 'experiences' is all too often silenced on the pretext of unloving judgement. As Simon now sees that the Lord works great wonders through His disciples, he offers them money in order to receive this power, to mediate the Holy Spirit through laying on of hands (verse 19). The sins of sorcery cause pride and a swollen head (verse 9). Simon wants the same powers as he had previously as a magician. He obviously takes his occult history along with him into his new faith, only now with different prefix. This story illustrates very impressively where the inspiration for a sudden laying on of hands may come from and the dangers of attempting to mediate the Holy Spirit through laying on of hands. Watchman Nee writes:

> The flesh continually furnishes bases for the enemy's operations. If man's mind is not renewed after his spirit is once regenerated, he exposes a great deal of territory to the machinations of the evil spirit. While many saints do have their mentality changed at the time of repentance, nonetheless the eyes of their heart once blinded by Satan have not yet been enlightened entirely and may still be veiled in many areas. These darkened corners are the old operation centers of the evil spirits.[16]

A past life involved with the occult or with drugs can also furnish very strong bases or darkened corners, especially in the case of a superficial conversion or unbiblical laying on of hands.

While Simon Peter perceived such actions, many believers of today read these reports in the Bible, and in many a heart these same thoughts and desires are stirred, and they refer to such Bible passages only to justify their own arbitrary actions. Behind all this and very 'biblically' disguised is, of course, the father of all pride, the old serpent. The Greek word for sorcery is *pharmakeia*. By this word alone one can clearly recognise how drugs are related to it. Since the consumption of drugs and occultism have become so very popular, we can also assume that such 'Simon-like' desires, doctrines, and actions will increase steadily. People with a drug history are especially in danger of falling into unbiblical movements. Anyone who does not believe this can read it in the books of David Wilkerson. There we find, among other things, those false teachings.

However, the Bible does not teach that one will be delivered from drugs or other subjections by means of speaking in tongues, but through repentance and through the victory of the Lord Jesus on the Cross of Calvary. In the Swiss newspaper *Die Tat* on 22nd August 1973, appeared an article called, 'Laying on of hands is trumps'. There we read how the miracle worker Hermano frees the people from alcohol, drugs and cigarettes with great success by means of the laying on of hands (for which one must pay 50 Swiss Francs each time)—in the case of cigarettes even with a positive 90 per cent deliverance. Deliverance alone need not in itself be the proof of divine working or activities of the Holy Spirit. For example, Guru Maharaj Ji has many followers who have come out of the drug scene and who have been 'freed' by him.

In Revelation 13:2 we are shown by the example of Antichrist how he receives his great power from Satan. There are many today who do not have their 'wonderful' and great power from God. Anyone who seeks after honour and power and not after the Cross of Christ, which breaks us, can receive a lot of 'gifts' from below (Matthew 4:9). If Satan did not even shrink back from Jesus with such propositions, then he will try it with us the more. Many a person started out in the Spirit, became puffed up and proud, and ended up in the flesh.

We read of Hermano in the above article that he made quite a name for himself as a hypnotist in show business during the war. If we remember that the medical practitioner, Dr Kildahl, literally reports in his book *The Psychology of Speaking in Tongues* that the basic predisposition for tongue-speaking is presented in the ability to be hypnotised, then we perhaps have an idea of what is really happening. To some extent one creates nearly the same 'showbusiness' today with 'conversions, miracles, healings and the healed'. The fact is that where sorcery or magic is practised, new 'apostles, great prophets, supercharismatics—even christs and messiahs' arise.

From these aspects the feeling, as well as the conviction of a 'special calling', emanate. Pride and spiritual arrogance frequently accompany such false gifts. In his above-mentioned book, Kildahl writes:

So do tongue-speakers. They join a group of their fellow practitioners and they support each other in multiple ways so that they feel themselves to be a company of special people.[17]

Here we find the great danger in striving after the sensational; Watchman Nee writes:

Due to curiosity and the prospect of pleasant sensations,

Christians gladly welcome these supernatural phenomena, not recognising that these merely puff up their pride without producing any real or lasting result in terms of a holy and righteous life or spiritual work. When the evil spirits succeed in their deceptions they gain a footing in the believer.[18]

Kildahl further noticed:

All tongue-speakers entertained a certain magical notion of what glossolalia meant. The term magical was defined by the belief that God or the Holy Spirit controlled and directed believers' lives in a mechanistic way. For instance, one person in the glossolalia group prayed: 'God, make me a puppet.' He believed almost literally that God would pull the strings and he as a puppet would respond. (In this connection, remember the previous study on passivity. Author's note.) Others declared: 'God now directs my life; that is, God directly controls the movement of my tongue; and He allows me to make these sounds.' Such believers usually developed tremendous feelings of worth and power. 'To think that God has singled me out to make that very sound' was a typical self-assessment.[19]

It should be evident, having in mind such an attitude, that one would not be especially pleased about the wish or command to test the gift or about the suspicion that a deceiving spirit could be involved in it. A marked refusal to accept advice is usually connected with it. Sometimes any objection of others will be ignored with a superior smile. We can frequently observe a distinct aversion to the advice of others. Such people have the inner conviction that they are especially blessed. They point to the things which the Lord has already worked through them, believe themselves wonderfully led and see this as a confirmation of their way and as a vested right not to have to be corrected. Very often one's wilfulness prevails and is connected with going one's own way, even at the expense of others. One demands unconditional obedience ('Children of God', Jim Jones) and anyone not submitting to it is taken as unspiritual. With biblical passages one 'proves' one's attitude; in extreme cases one even walks (in a figurative sense) over the dead.

The latter occurs, as we have already mentioned, sometimes as a consequence of the sins of sorcery and involvement with the occult, but can also be the result of unbiblical laying on of hands.

Sometimes gross sins of the flesh, similar to those in Corinth, are close companions of super-spirituality. We sometimes find in such circles real chaos and a deplorable situation concerning sexual matters. Charismatic movements are especially susceptible, as the false Pentecostal spirit runs parallel to the spirit of lying, fornication and pride. Such believers can soon be used and redirected by the enemy, at least some of the time, as pride is Satan's special talent. This spiritual arrogance is often imperious. And this pride gets especially hurt if one suggests deceit or fraud. Very often this is the reason for fiery resistance.

We observe such a reaction in 2 Chronicles 18, where 400 prophets prophesied unanimously that God would grant Ahab the victory (verse 5). This was overwhelming evidence. Then came one man, namely the prophet Micaiah, who was unpopular, as he usually did not have anything good to prophesy (verse 7). It was suggested to him that he should agree with the general opinion and understanding and to keep his far too negative view to himself. The other prophets had reached such a wonderful unanimous precognition and deep understanding (verse 12). One could almost say, in the concepts of today, that an intensive group-dynamic pressure was exerted on him to make [ ] with the opinion of the majority.

Now Micaiah states, not very flatteringly, that th[ ] derful unity among them was the result of a lying spirit [ ] God had sent to entice Ahab, king of Israel, to dea[..] in battle and that a false spirit was speaking out of the prophets (verses 21–22). The prophet Zedekiah is not happy about this insinuation and smites Micaiah upon the cheek (verse 23). His spiritual pride was obviously hurt. Micaiah's warning was ignored, and he was removed and imprisoned (verse 26). Yet the Lord confirmed his statements.

Today in principle, frequently one encounters the same reactions and a rebellion similar to Zedekiah's response. A person may believe himself to be specially blessed; then is suddenly told he has been deceived. Watchman Nee again:

> Countless saints consider themselves beyond deception because they have had frequent spiritual experiences. This very element of self-confidence betrays the deception they are in already. Unless they are humble enough to acknowledge the possibility of being deceived, they shall be deceived perpetually.... The danger of such false security is to give opportunity for the evil spirits to work or to continue to work.[20]

Unfortunately today more and more people prefer those who are deluding God's people into a false security. But the Word of God has foretold this development (2 Timothy 4:3–4).

There is also the danger today of emphasising the transmitting of blessings by means of laying on of hands. So-called 'services of blessing' are taking place more and more frequently in which such things are practised. But I cannot find this as a doctrine in the New Testament. Sometimes one quotes the Old Testament, for instance, Ephraim's blessing by Jacob (Genesis 48:14) as proof for such actions. It must be said, however, that in those days Israel was in a visible, earthly relationship with God. One became a member of God's people by birth, not by regeneration, and the blessing was transferred in a visible way. On the other hand we read of the believers in the New Testament who were not only raised up and made to sit in heavenly or invisible places through the finished work of the Lord Jesus Christ (Ephesians 2:6) but were also blessed with all spiritual blessings (1:3). This ought not to declare the prayer for blessing as unnecessary (Luke 6:28). I also know, partly from my own experience, of really wonderful interventions of our Lord in services rendered according to James 5:15, and in this respect God's children could call on the elders of the church much more often. Yet I fear that the hasty laying on of hands for the transference of blessings reveals an unconscious self-elevation. (It says in Hebrews 7:7: 'The lesser is blessed by the greater.') According to Philippians 2:3, '...but in lowliness of mind let each esteem others better than themselves', our attitude ought to be exactly the opposite of placing oneself above the other.

According to Hebrews 6:2 the laying on of hands is also part of the basic doctrine of the New Testament. These basic doctrines, though, are repeated and emphasized several times, it should therefore be the case that the New Testament states 'bless by the laying on of hands' at least once. However, one looks for such a command in vain.

It very often pointed out that in the New Testament the Lord Jesus had blessed the children by laying on His hands (Mark 10:6). This is definitely correct: anyone who is touched by the Lord Jesus (also in the spiritual sense) is blessed; it always signifies blessing. Yet for someone to put himself on the same level in this respect with our Lord seems rather a little questionable to me.

2 Corinthians 5:16—'Though we have known Christ after the flesh, yet now henceforth know we him no more'—also shows a transition from the visible to the invisible, from sight to faith (2 Corinthians 5:7). The next verse 17 explains how we are now IN Christ and how everything has become new in the invisible world. Only in this position do we receive the spiritual blessings, for we can only identify ourselves with the Lord Jesus Christ through accepting His cross. I am afraid that with some it is disguised super-spirituality—that those Christians want to be unconsciously and too hastily equal with our Lord Jesus in this area. This form of subtle pride when one exalts oneself clearly contradicts the bearing of the Cross in Philippians 2.

Another widespread mode of action is the practice of laying hands on believers after a counselling session, resulting in the belief that now the counsellee is freed from all bondages. The enemy has completely withdrawn, it is believed, and then the counsellor additionally 'blesses' by means of laying on his hands. I fail to find this practice anywhere in the Bible. Despite the fact that many a person can testify how a spirit was transferred through the sudden laying on of hands, and was cast out only after much wrestling in prayer, this concept of 'blessing' is fairly widespread. I have already personally had cases in counselling where darkness had been transferred to the believer because of this action of the counsellor. The words spoken to the priests in Malachi 2:2 have almost literally been fulfilled: 'I will even send a curse upon you and I will curse your blessings: . . . yea I have cursed them already, because ye do not lay it to heart.'

Infection through Darkness

Somehow the opinion must have been formed that hands have or even emanate a special power. I am afraid that we find the same pride behind that concept as well as the idea that 'the work of my hands' is so very important.

> Thus saith the Lord of hosts: Ask now the priests concerning the law, saying, If one bear holy flesh in the skirt of his garment, and with his skirt do touch bread, or pottage, or wine, or oil, or any meat, shall it be holy? And the priests answered and said, No. Then said Haggai, If one that is unclean by a dead body touch any of these, shall it be unclean? And the priests answered and said, It shall be unclean. Then answered Haggai, and said, So is this people, and so is this nation before me, saith the Lord; and so is every work of their hands; and that which they offer there is unclean (Haggai 2:11–14).

Here we are shown, as an impressive illustration, because Israel was in this visible relationship, how the danger of infection can be present in the case of touching and defilement. An infection can also take place in the unseen world. The exhortation in 2 Corinthians 6:17, 'and touch not the unclean thing,' may be interpreted the same way. At this point we want to remember again Leviticus 7:21–22. If anyone came into contact with anything unclean, he became unclean too. '. . . and eat of the flesh of the sacrifice of peace offerings, which pertain unto the Lord, even that soul shall be cut off from his people.'

At this point I want to mention an event in the history of medicine. Ignaz Semmelweis (1818–1865) is known as the saver of mothers. He recognised the cause of the frequently-occurring puerperal (childbed) fever which took the lives of so many young mothers at that time. In those days one knew practically nothing about micro-organisms. The doctors came directly from the dissecting of the dead and then treated the mothers with unwashed hands and instruments. No wonder that many of them died. Semmelweis introduced strict washing and cleaning instructions in his clinic (the blood of Christ cleanses us) and the number of deaths subsided rapidly. Were they all enthusiastic at this? No. The gynaecologists were shocked. Their academically-trained 'hands'—they believed themselves to be special helpers— could not be the actual source of infection and death! Because of these accusations they started to really persecute this poor man. In many a doctor's eyes this insinuation was going too far. This simply could not be true. Semmelweis was despised and slandered from every direction. He ended up in a mental institution. His successor removed the washing basins, and, again, the mortality-rate of the mothers rose rapidly, and everything returned to the old routine and order.

The adversary of mankind in general and of the Church in particular is very reluctant to allow his best weapons to be taken from him. If we raise the above-mentioned aspects of the laying on of hands, we touch a main nerve of the strategic forces of darkness; accordingly, the reaction is violent. The reason: the conspiracy of the invisible world against the Church of our Lord Jesus Christ should not come to light. People who are warning others about this subject are especially endangered. The enemy of God is trying everything to slander them or to make them appear untrustworthy in some other way. Often the worst resistance comes out of our own ranks. It is alarming to witness how quickly many a child of God can be used by the enemy for that purpose.

God gave His people Israel clear instructions in the Old Testament in order to prevent any physical infections. He warned His people clearly against touching any unclean things, carcasses (Leviticus 5:2) in order that they might not become unclean and guilty. In many churches today spiritual hygiene hardly prevails any more. One lays on hands indiscriminately and at every possible and impossible opportunity; and sometimes even women do it. Instead of coming to the Cross anew, one calls for gifts and experiences. Not repentance or humility, but laying on of hands, should secure the desired fullness of the Spirit. Any evangelist can practically already 'bless' a whole congregation by laying on his hands. We experience a real spiritual mass infection today.

In certain assemblies it is also customary to form a circle by way of holding hands during prayer. It is surely not a coincidence that this forming of a circle is the usual practice of spiritists.

Thus we read along with the spiritist Greber on the subject of holding hands, or forming 'chains' the following:

The 'forming of a chain' is also of highly symbolic significance. For just as those people present are united outwardly by holding hands, so should they also become one heart and one soul with each other. They ought to love one another, help each other, forgive the mistakes of another, and remove anything from the heart which could disturb the inner union or harmony.[21]

In Christian circles today such actions are motivated in a similar 'religious' way. One can be manipulated very quickly in this way, can be seduced. This is the prerequisite for the transference of spirits. An emotional atmosphere is created which opens people for special experiences, particularly for healing miracles and the receiving of the 'baptism of the spirit'. The emotional manipulation of today is alarming. A well-known theologian even believes that the spirit of the group-dynamic, the liberal theology as well as the Charismatic movement move on one and the same plane. Kildahl's investigations point in this same direction too.

From the point of identification, it is clear why the Bible never reports that women have laid on hands. We must beware when woman lay on hands. One can also observe this more and more today. 'Evangelists' who like to lay on hands especially after counselling are to be evaluated with caution.

Such actions cannot be biblically substantiated, but from my own observations in cases of counselling I can only warn against such things. There are no such shortcuts to a spirit-filled life.

In a more favourable case such 'blessed' laying on of hands may not have any negative after-effects. But I know of several cases where the believers were 'blessed' with darkness through these practices. Thus the laying on of hands by a Pentecostal evangelist on a girl turned out to be the reason why evil spirits had invaded her. She had made her decision through the clear message of the same man, but then she still had to be 'blessed'. One almost wants to cry out with James: 'Cleanse your hands, ye sinners and purify your hearts, ye double minded.' (James 4:8b).

Certainly this is hard to digest, McGraw reports similar incidents in his article 'Tongues should be tested', yet here we find a horrible strategy of the enemy. It is always his aim to break into the temple of God (2 Thessalonians 2:4). If he cannot accomplish this through gross sins, then he will just try it as an 'angel of light'. And he very often succeeds by means of the biblically-disguised laying on of hands. Since it does mean to declare oneself one with someone else, it is rather a serious matter in the eyes of God. The Lord does not change His principles. He has promised His fullness by way of brokenness and repentance. If one is not broken and someone lays his hands on, then unfortunately it may happen that another spirit 'fills' him, especially if the motivation is wrong or unbiblical things are prayed for. Then hell does not usually wait long to be asked. Thus a well-known counsellor once stated that the laying on of hands by Pentecostals may have the same effect as an occult enchantment.

The Growing Danger

It is a little-known fact that the enemy of God can use born-again believers as a weapon in his battle, as Francis Schaeffer once literally formulated it according to Romans 6:13. The fact is that the devil used God's people of the Old Covenant to demand the crucifixion of the Messiah. Today he uses believers to strike out against the Church and to do it the most harm. It is a satanic, horrible plan. We have an adversary who very brutally takes advantage of every weakness, whether spiritual, mental or physical, and profits primarily from our ignorance and unawareness. For that reason Peter says that we 'are not to be led away with the error of the wicked' as we 'know these things before' (2 Peter 3:17).

Ernst Modersohn writes in his book, 'Im Banne des Teufels' (*Under the Spell of the Devil*, translated):

> And only where the holy will for a complete surrender to God exists can God bless the laying on of hands. Otherwise the terrible danger persists that one transfers his own spirit of sin into the other person and therewith becomes not the mediator of blessings but the mediator of sin and damnation.... For that reason we must again earnestly refer to the word of Paul: 'Lay hands suddenly on no man.' (1 Timothy 5:22). And the Apostle has certainly added the deliberate exhortation in this connection: 'Neither be partaker of other men's sins.'[22]

The idea that a child of God could transfer darkness into another believer is often rejected in a spontaneous and emotional way. The reaction is as in the case of Semmelweis. Yet here a great need prevails. The thought that a child of God could not have a false spirit is sometimes nurtured (or fostered) by pride, that we are something special, instead of primarily remembering that we are first of all saved sinners and unprofitable servants (Luke 17:10). Was it not precisely spiritual pride which caused the doom of the people of Israel?

Unfortunately one increasingly finds the reaction which Watchman Nee describes in the following way:

Because of his long capitulation a person may easily commit the fatal error of defending the malevolent operation of the evil spirits.... Although he is in distress, nevertheless he is siding with the evil spirits in preserving their ground.... For the sake of saving face or of some other reason, the Christian refuses to believe his mind could possibly be occupied by the devil and objects to hearing anything about him or his works. Such distaste of examination for fear that he may lose his 'spiritual experience' is a great hindrance to deliverance. He may retort in any of a number of ways: 'I don't need deliverance, why should I want to be delivered?' or 'I have overcome through Christ; He has overcome Satan already, so now I need pay no attention to him but just leave him to God. I focus my attention on Christ.' or 'know nothing about satanic matters' or 'I concentrate on preaching the gospel, why should I notice Satan?' With these or many other responses the believer dismisses the actions of evil spirits in him.[23]

Other pleasing arguments are: 'This is too extreme.... You devilise everything.... You see evil spirits everywhere.... You give the devil far too much credit.... You always speak only of him...I cannot listen to this any more....' We can hear these or similar sayings all too often. Now it is correct that one can speak too much about it, yet it does not say: 'Ignore the devil and he will flee from you,' but 'Resist the devil.' (James 4:7). However, it is always easier to justify oneself than to admit that one has been cheated and deceived.

Let us imagine for once we could go to the scribes, elders and Pharisees at the time of Jesus, to the elite of the people therefore and could tell them that they would soon crucify their Messiah; yes, that they were the chosen instruments of the enemy of God to kill their King. We do not need a lot of imagination to depict how they would have reacted to that. If they would not have thrown us straight into jail for blasphemy (today we are accused of 'blasphemy' against the Holy Spirit), then a comprehensive theological justification would in any case have followed why this would simply and plainly be impossible. They would surely not have had any lack of Scripture passages to prove this biblically. After all, they were God's chosen people, God has promised... and so on. The Creator could simply not allow this; it would be blasphemy and absolutely out of the question. Similarly, as we read in Micah 3:11 they would possibly have called upon the presence of God, upon His promises and pledges and upon His temple. Besides, they were surely not the instruments of Satan (this is absolutely the very last imputation), but were privileged servants of God who were serving their Lord with all their hearts and were ready to do anything for their God. In the case of such blessed servants of the Most High our hint is nothing but a blasphemous insinuation and such thoughts could only have originated from a very severe spirit of judgement. In this or a similar way they would have 'refuted' us, and yet the Lord said at that time: '...but this is your hour and the power of darkness.' (Luke 22:53b). What a tragedy! Not by coincidence did the betrayer of Jesus come out of the group of Christ's disciples and the worst enemies of the Church still rise up from within its own ranks today (Acts 20:29–30). The tragedy is that such are very often genuine children of God and consequently we are in danger of quenching Christian love while fighting for purity of doctrine in the Church.

The fact is that a sudden laying on of hands or touching of any part of the body is the distinguishing mark of all people involved in the occult, miracle healers, spiritists and spiritualists. Many believers have allowed themselves to be sucked into a similar trap. It is an old observation that the carriers of such a counterfeit spirit are urged inwardly, one could almost say controlled, to pass on to others this power which they have received themselves. This usually takes place through laying on of hands or by the forming of a chain. One is clearly driven to establishing physical contact. All too often sexual sins follow.

One often feels a tingling sensation during the laying on of hands, or a flowing through of power, like an electric current. One frequently also feels a trembling sensation. These are typical symptoms of the invasion of satanic spirits. Sometimes one gets dizzy, or drunk, or even unconscious. Let us remember the previously mentioned principle of self-control. Watchman Nee writes:

This means that the Holy Spirit who bestows diverse supernatural experiences upon men will not infringe on their rights by manipulating any part of their bodies against their wills. They continue to retain the power of self-control.[24]

At this point I would like to remind you again of the report quoted earlier about the 'Spirit-baptism' of Bishop Burnett in 'Wort und Geist' (*Word and Spirit*). There we read in the second sentence: 'His body prickled, he made strange sounds, and he realised later that he had prayed in a strange language.' With Kathryn Kuhlman we can read the following account of a strange experience:

She trembled so badly that she could hardly take off her splint from her leg. Fire went through her body. She turned to the lady who was helping her and told her she could hardly breathe. She was so hot and then she heard someone say not to touch her for she was under the anointing of the Holy Spirit.[25]

But in fact here again we can recognise the loss of self-control. What Dennis Bennett writes is noteworthy:

When people are praying therefore that they may be filled with the Holy Spirit, they oftentimes experience an involuntary trembling, moving or shaking of their teeth. These are physical reactions in relation to the Holy Spirit which in themselves do not have any significance, except that they can indicate the presence of the Holy Spirit.[26]

In a similar, peculiar way we read in the bestseller, *The Cross and the Switchblade*, where David Wilkerson reports about the 'baptism of the Spirit' of his grandfather:

But then one day, while he was in the pulpit preaching against the Pentecostals, he himself began to tremble and shake, which is one of the things that happens often when people first have this power flow into them. It is something you feel, a little like a shock, except that the sensation is not at all unpleasant. Anyhow, Grandpa was the most surprised person in the world when this happened to him, and he himself received the baptism and began to speak in tongues.[27]

Here we have to determine how this spirit came over this man and obviously caused him to speak in tongues against his will. But the Holy Spirit does not work in this way, as we have illustrated on the basis of 1 Corinthians 12:2. Rather this is a compelling spirit of Satan, whose receipt was experienced as being very pleasant. Unfortunately we find this to be the case so very often today (2 Corinthians 11:4).
John Stott writes:

It is a great mistake to suppose, therefore, that those first Spirit-filled believers were in a kind of drunken stupor, or that such a state is intended to be a pattern for all future experience of the Spirit's fullness. *The opposite is the case.* There is a clear implication in Ephesians 5:18 that drunkenness and the Spirit's fullness are not comparable in this respect, for drunkenness is branded as 'excess' (AV) or 'debauchery' (RSV). The Greek word '*asotia*', which in its two other New Testament occurrences means 'profligacy' (Titus 1:6; 1 Peter 4:4), literally describes a condition in which a person cannot 'save' or *control* himself. It is because drunkenness involves a loss of self-control, Paul writes, that it is to be avoided. It is implied that the contrasting state, the fullness of the Spirit, involves no loss of self-control. On the contrary, we are distinctly told in Galatians 5:23 that a part of the fruit of the Spirit is self-control '(*enkrateia*)'![28]

The above criterion alone would be sufficient to unmask the false spirit. But the accompanying physical symptoms disperse any doubts. Here we find deception to a very great extent. Yet this book of David Wilkerson is really thrilling; surely it has helped many a person or shown him the way to Jesus Christ (I myself have been most deceived by this work)—but unfortunately here we find intermixture. There are two possibilities here: Either I look at the experience and conclude: The experience is rather unusual, but the effects are obviously positive. Therefore it is divine. Unfortunately tests like this are common today. Or I come from the authority of the Word of God and the clear context of the Scriptures; then the matter becomes obvious rather quickly. Here it is often determined whether someone loves the Lord and His Word more than a blissful experience. In connection with John 14:23 one is almost inclined to think of the warning in Deuteronomy 13:2-4, or the words of Jesus Christ in the dark hour of temptation: 'Satan hath desired to have you that he may sift you as wheat' (Luke 22:31).

Of course anyone who claims the experience as the test is unfortunately very often ready to accept many peculiarities uncritically.

But it turns out to be still more peculiar. In the widely-read book *9 o' Clock in the Morning*, by Bennett, after the author had at last experienced the 'Spirit baptism' we read how his wife embraced and kissed him. She told him she could tell by his radiant face what had happened to him. But she had known it already the night before, when something very strange had happened. When he had come home she was fast asleep, yet when he had opened the door a current of power went through the house and woke her up.[29]

We are really faced with the anxious question now: What will become of our dear brothers in the Charismatic movement if they confuse such obvious spiritism with the Holy Spirit? More than that, what great danger arises here for the Church if such intermixture is not recognised any more, if such people start to lay hands on others? Apart from the fact that Dennis Bennett ranks as a key figure of this whole Charismatic renewal.

When Francis Schaeffer in his book, *The New Super-Spirituality*,[30] labels the new superspirituality and new Pentecostalism as 'new Platonic spirituality' then he may not be so wrong after all. Yet such movements are gaining more and more influence, and with a stronger circulation they penetrate into more circles and ranks. Ivar Lundgren, cultural editor of the Pentecostal daily paper, *Dagen*, in Sweden recently expressed his opinion in regard to the spreading of the Charismatic movement to Roman Catholics as well:

Naturally the aim of the leaders of the Charismatic movement revival is that the church will be interwoven with it, until the charismatic wave is not a separate phenomenon any more.[31]

What kind of a spirit is really the driving force for the uniting of the church? Are we really aware of what is going on here?

Let us imagine that the sorcerer Simon had actually succeeded in penetrating the ranks of the believers. A favourite method of the enemy in destroying the local church is to send occultly-bound people among the children of God. Let us assume Simon would have started to lay hands on people. Many a gift would have 'appeared', wonderful signs and miracles, and surely also healings would have occurred. In reality he would have leavened everything (Galatians 3:1; 5:9), infected everyone. Such things happen more and more frequently today: tarrying-meetings 'tarrying in Jerusalem', praying for the Pentecostal blessing, laying on of hands, waiting for the outpouring of the Spirit, etc. Because the sins of sorcery and aspects of spiritism are growing rapidly today, the danger of these 'Simons' is also increasing more and more. And if they may not be acting in such a way themselves, then they are at least open to these things and even promoting them. Does it not say: 'Forbid not or love covers'?... Such or similar, usually twisted, verses provide the biblical stage for the tragedy of deception (or should we say, comedy of darkness?).

The Growing Deception

It is my observation that people with an occult background or after the laying on of hands from Pentecostal circles are especially susceptible to these things. One only has to think of the principles of intermixture. They also may be—if they do not remain alert—unconsciously manipulated very quickly by God's adversary and in extreme cases it goes as far as mediumistic connection with the powers of darkness.

The fact is that today the devil has many spiritualistic mediums whom he tries to bring into the ranks of believers, superspiritually disguised. Then the confusion and the din of voices usually increase. One prophesies, casts out demons, lays on hands, speaks in tongues, etc. And the confusion, as well as the deception, increase (Jeremiah 23:15b).

According to the theology of some faith healers, the Apostle Paul was a considerable failure when he writes to Timothy: 'But use a little wine for thy stomach's sake and thine often infirmities...' (1 Timothy 5:23). Or in another passage: 'but Trophimus have I left at Miletum sick' (2 Timothy 4:20). These healers would have acted much more 'biblically'. They would have busily laid hands on them and tried to cast out the 'demon of sickness' from poor Timothy and Trophimus. How very close we are coming already to the actual conditions described by our Lord Jesus in Matthew 7:22! 'Many will say to me in that day, Lord, Lord, have we not prophesied in Thy name, and in Thy name have cast out devils? and in Thy name done many wonderful works?' Visions, dreams and hasty laying on of hands are again a typical sign. While Detmar Scheunemann, in his lecture in Lausanne, still clearly warns and differentiates:

We ought not to lay hands on a possessed person, but have to command the evil spirits to depart in the name of our Lord Jesus Christ. We see in the Gospels that the Lord Jesus as He met with possessed people commanded the evil spirits (Mark 5:8; Matthew 17:18), but only laid his hands on the physically sick (Matthew 8:15; 9:29; Mark 7:33).[32]

We hear and read today more and more of ministers and healers who lay hands on demon invaded believers and unbelievers. Actually we not only experience a growing deception today but also growing confusion. Unfortunately one must say that many—especially women, of whom many circles are very enthusiastic because of great signs and wonders (Matthew 12:39)—are not the special 'anointed' ones of God, but spiritualistic mediums. They have been completely re-oriented. They do not mediate the Holy Spirit but spirits of the pit. Many 'saints' of the Roman Catholic church were usually the same, namely mediums of Satan. They were fascinated by the visions, appearances of angels and Mary, gifts, ecstacies (Colossians 2:18), by the wonderful 'humility' and devoutness—yes, many a man or woman could even show the stigmata of Christ. It may be mentioned that these are typical symptoms of spiritism. Also frequent visions and hearing of voices usually have the same source.

In psychiatry these phenomena are regarded as symptoms of paranoiac schizophrenia, especially the frequent occurrences of the hearing of voices. This does not say that God cannot speak audibly as well. But this is the extraordinary rather than the everyday occurrence.

If one brings to mind the biblical principles, and then investigates the believers, one finds an alarmingly high percentage of Christians who have already experienced an unbiblical laying on of hands. Such must be brought to light and must be repented over so that it can be forgiven. But one comes- up against growing opposition even here. Many a person believes his moral perfection spares him from cleansing. The believer already feels himself to be sinless and has no need of the fifth petition of the Lord's prayer: 'Forgive us our trespasses.'

This spirit of pride then mediates inspirations and convictions like these: doctrines of Spirit baptism, of the second blessing, of the clean heart, of the higher life, a life of new dimensions, etc.

One enhances oneself into this condition already here on

earth, which has been promised for a latter era, where 'there shall be no more death, neither sorrow, nor crying, neither shall be any more pain' (Revelation 21:4; 7:17).[33]

The still more intensified form of pride where one quickly puts himself into the place of Jesus Himself, as we have mentioned earlier, is also found in the phenomenon of prophecy in the form of 'I-Jesus' or 'I the Lord say'. This obviously contradicts Hebrews 1:2. Here the believers are used as mediums. Thus, for example, Watchman Nee writes:

> These Christians mistake the supernatural for the voice of God. They disregard their reasonings, their conscience and other people's advice. They turn out to be the most stubborn individuals in the world: they refuse to listen to anyone. They picture themselves as obeying a higher law of life than the rest of their spiritual conferees.[34]

People who have experienced this 'blessed' laying on of hands have usually little discernment and often confuse awakenings of the occult with revivals, evil spirits with the Holy Spirit, gifts of familiar spirits with gifts of the Spirit, invasion of evil spirits with baptism of the Spirit, soulish power with the power of God, mediums of Satan with people authorised by the Lord, false prophets with real evangelists, and so on (Jeremiah 28:15–16).

A closer look at 'Prison to Praise'

I would like to illustrate this rather strong statement with the following example. We find a typical case—one could almost say a paradigm or exact example—of the intermixture of occult background in the book *Prison to Praise* by Mervin Carothers. As this manifests itself in such an obvious and consistent way, I would like to go into more details here. Thus we read on page 18 that suddenly a low voice was speaking into his ear. After that: '...but I knew God' (page 21). This is really a rather peculiar conversion. As soon as people hear audible voices it is a sign to me for alarm. Yet it may be real. We really do not want to dictate how God wants to call people, especially with regard to unbelievers. But if we look at the fruit by which we can identify the tree, as we all know, it becomes more questionable indeed. Because his life as a military chaplain and 'Christian' does not comply with the freedom and fullness he so very much desires. We read afterwards how he started to search for spiritual experiences:

A friend gave me a book about an eastern cult claiming to know the method of opening people's minds to the power of God. I learned to lie on a board with my feet elevated and to practise silent meditation. I began to read everything I could find about psychic phenomena, hypnotism, and spiritism, hoping to find a clue to the secret of letting God's Spirit work in and through me.[35]

It is really rather sad, if not a strange thing, that a 'believer' is going in such a direction. Yet it gets worse still. He takes part in spiritistic meetings.

Here I continued studying hypnosis with renewed vigour and got involved in the Spiritual Frontiers movement led by Arthur Ford. I had heard that many ministers were drawn to this movement. In Arthur Ford's home I saw firsthand evidence of the workings of a spirit world completely separate from our known rational world. I was fascinated.[36]

Arthur Ford has been one of the best-known Spiritists in the USA. It must be very clearly stated here that if one takes part in spiritistic seances one comes under the influence of demonic powers—satanic powers take hold of us. The question already arises of how far a person can come under the influence of Satan by reading above-mentioned literature and by opening oneself to these phenomena of eastern meditation and hypnotism. But this behaviour eliminates any doubts concerning demonic influence. Interestingly enough, the author admits this freely. On the following pages we read:

> I had greatly underestimated the powers of the enemy. I did not know it then, but hypnosis is potentially very dangerous spiritually leaving the subject wide open for impulses from the realm of Satan.[37]

It is noteworthy that he states, very correctly, on the same page concerning the 'Spiritual Frontiers' movement:

> Satan can cleverly counterfeit the work of the Holy Spirit. I felt reasonably sure that I wasn't getting myself into a blind alley. These spirits, and the people I met in the movement, did after all, speak very highly of Christ. They certainly recognised Him as the Son of God and a great spiritual leader who worked many miracles.[38]

The author correctly warns us of the dangers of spiritism. What he does not know is the fact that the demons not only reverently speak of the Lord Jesus, but to seize their victims they can also mention the blood of Christ and His Cross which can take away our sin and also speak of the deceitfulness of Satan! (Anyone doubting this may remember the earlier quotation from the *Book of Mormon*.) Moreover, Carothers writes on page 32: 'Satan quoted Scriptures even in Jesus' time.' This reminds me of the statement of a theologian: 'It may even be that a movement which rightly warns us of certain anti-Christian dangers of our times, may itself be the carrier of a different evil danger. It sounds incredible. We may be warned of certain deceptions by people who are themselves deceivers of another kind.'

Mervin Carothers came, as he himself partly recognised and confessed, under strong bondage of the occult. These things such as hypnotism and spiritism are an abomination to the Lord. This man had opened himself to the most severe influences of Satan and became a victim of demonism. The Lord Jesus Christ is victor over these abominations. Through humble submission, genuine repentance, confession and renunciation of these abominations, claiming the victory of the Lord Jesus on the Cross and the cleansing power of His blood, God will free a person from such bondages of darkness.

How is Mervin Carothers set free? How did he come to the recognition of his guilt and sins before God? We read about it in the next chapter. One reads and wonders—He joined a Pentecostal group, 'Camp Farthest Out'. He anticipated the great event—a woman laid hands on him! She did not inquire about his guilt, his attitude to the Cross and so on, but she repeatedly mentioned the baptism of the Holy Spirit (page 35). Instead of bringing his sin into the light, hands were laid on him:

She placed her hands on my head and began to pray softly. I waited for 'it' to hit me. Nothing happened. I didn't feel a thing.[39]

Instead of repentance and confession we find the longing for experiences, for a great feeling. Previously we read:

I felt a twinge of excitement. Could it be that I could experience my own Pentecost? Could I see tongues of fire, hear the rush of wind, and speak in an unknown tongue?[40]

Naturally the emotional man, the old Adam, wants to have experiences, especially when under occult oppression. Only he does not want to repent; and the laying on of hands usually costs little or no repentance. At Pentecost Peter did not say: 'I will lay my hands on you and then you will receive the Holy Spirit,' but 'Repent'. What sort of Gospel is this? Through this 'treatment' he becomes conditioned in such a way that he receives thoughts and words on the basis of spiritistic principles, after the manner of the laws of passivity. If we think of the book, *The Spiritual Man*, we surely still remember how especially hypnotism requires the laws of passivity. In the case of a strong will even the most 'able' hypnotist is pretty powerless. Mervin Carothers has occupied himself very strongly in this area. For this reason he became easily susceptible to the passive phenomena. From this point of view perhaps one can see the connections in a new light, which John P. Kildahl had also confirmed, namely, that the main prerequisite for (false) tongue-speaking is the ability to be hypnotised. People with such a past have a great inclination for such 'gifts'. After all that has been said, we hardly have to state again that tongue-speaking is formulated by evil spirits in an empty, passive mind.

We read further in Mervin Carothers' book:

Again she placed her hands on my head. I felt nothing, saw nothing, heard nothing. When she was through praying, she asked if I could hear or sense any words within me that I didn't understand. I thought for a minute and realised that there were in my mind words that didn't mean anything to me. I felt certain that these strange words were strictly a product of my own imagination, and I told her so. 'If you said them out loud, would you feel as if you were being made a fool of?' she asked. 'I certainly would.' 'Would you be willing to be a fool for Christ's sake?' This put the whole situation in a different perspective.[41]

Now in such situations the question arises as to whether such a thing should be accepted without contradiction.

Now he actually speaks in an unintelligible babbling (which has nothing to do with a language), yet:

> ... Still I felt nothing different.[42]

Do we recognise the difference? Instead of an active and deliberate decision or surrender, one is waiting passively for something to happen, for anything to come upon him. And as we read further on, this is exactly what happened. Unfortunately one verbally fulfils the laws of spiritism and mediumism in this way.

> 'Thank you, Jesus.' I stood up, and as I reached my full height, something hit me. I was suddenly filled and overflowing with a feeling of warmth and love for everybody in the room. It must have happened to Dick simultaneously, for I saw tears coming out of his eyes. Without a word we embraced each other and laughed and cried at the same time.[43]

A Satanic deception and its associated instability, so often found in those oppressed by the occult. Afterwards one is supposed to be 'full of the Holy Spirit' and then begins the 'full-power-life', 'life in abundance'.

Therefore instead of deep submission and real repentance, which guarantees the filling of the Holy Spirit; instead of confessing the abominable sins and acceptance of forgiveness by faith, we find a passive waiting for experiences accompanied by the laying on of hands and, finally, emotional crying and laughter. This would really seem to be another gospel.

One can see in Mervin Carothers' book in the following chapter called 'His power in us' the effect or occurrence of a spiritualistic, mediumistic control. These are strong state-ments, but I would like to explain it by means of particular passages.

First of all, one can read again and again of how an inner voice is speaking to him, which he can obviously hear inwardly, thus:

> I bowed my head. Within me I prayed silently: 'Show me how to pray, God.' I heard: 'Pray in the spirit.' I silently prayed in my new language. 'Now begin to translate what you have said.' 'Lord, forgive this man for his drunken-ness, his dishonesty in business.' I was shocked at my own words.[44]

This means, therefore, that he did not consciously formulate these words himself. He was only the language tool. Watch-man Nee's opinion on this is:

> The Christian must unmistakably understand that all his utterances have to be the result of his own thinking. Any words which bypass the process of thinking are formu-lated by wicked spirits.[45]

When he hears that voice, who is actually speaking? As we will see later, Carothers emphasises that he blocks out his mind.

> All supernatural revelations, visions or other strange occurrences which require the total cessation of the func-tion of the mind, or are obtained only after it has ceased working, are not of God.[46]

Thus writes Watchman Nee. One can recognise just how justified these exhortations are when reading the following in Carothers' book:

The principle of letting go and letting God was valid. All I had to do was relax in the presence of God, letting my mind go blank and opening my mouth in faith to speak whatever God impressed on me.[47]

This is exactly the thing which we are warned of in the book, *The Spiritual Man*, page after page, of becoming a robot, a puppet of an alien will.

The divine Spirit does not directly control man's body either. If man desires to speak he has to engage his own mouth.... The Holy Spirit indwells us to witness that we belong to God, whereas evil spirits manipulate people to reduce them to robots. God's Spirit asks for our co-operation; evil spirits seek direct control.[48]

In another passage Carothers writes how another voice is speaking to him again:

My son, because I love you I am going to teach you to be thankful for everything. You can learn standing right there all the things you are thankful for, or I can let you go back to bed and not let you move, see, or hear until you learn.[49]

This reminds us very much of compulsion and total physical control. But that contradicts the laws of God. Friedrich Nietzsche the great God-hater, who considered himself to be uniquely inspired, said: 'I have never had a choice.'[50]
Watchman Nee even writes:

When the Christian has sunk into such a state he unconsciously may even rely upon the help of the evil spirits. He cannot will anything by himself, hence looks for outside forces to help him.... They delight in enticing a person to follow outside revelation blindly without using either thought or will; they therefore often impart a host of strange and supernatural phenomena to men. The Christian, unaware of the principle of God's working, assumes he is being obedient to God when actually he is a prey to deception.[51]

And this is exactly what we read in the book by Mervin Carothers. Unfortunately there are many believers today who are informing us of or propagating the same or similar experiences.

Should we not be alarmed when Peter Beyerhaus, for instance, reports:

I was in the Calvary Chapel of the Golgotha Church in California. This is the place of origin of the so-called Jesus movement, whose initiator, a certain Chuck Smith, is still working there as leader today. He conducted a Bible study on a chapter in the book of Daniel. During this whole exposition I did not hear one word of the Cross of Christ, not one word of repentance and forgiveness of sin. Chuck Smith had only one theme: We ought to learn how to make ourselves responsive to the voice of God; we ought to learn how to block out the outward impressions and senses. Instead of mixing into the bustle of the world, we have to condition ourselves inwardly to become responsive through meditation. When we have therefore acquired the right sensibility, then God would be able to start really speaking to us. Smith's last sentences were: 'Whatever will happen to you then, I cannot determine for you in particular. You may have dreams, you may receive visions; perhaps God sends you an angel or you hear His own voice.'[52]

Do we recognise the extent of the deception? Here children

of God are taught how to be receptive to spiritualistic impulses.

On a similar doubtful basis may be the following instructions in the booklet of Witness Lee, 'Das Beten-Lesen des Wortes' (*The Prayer-reading of the Word*, translated):

> We would do better to close our minds.

Or:

> If we pray uninterruptedly we do not give our mind any time to form its own opinions.[53]

We have shown above just how dangerous this conscious evasion of the mind is. One thereby satisfies the conditions for the working of deceptive powers, as we read in *The Spiritual Man:*

> If man does not use his intelligence, neither will God, because to do so would be contrary to the principle of God's operation. Evil spirits will do so however; they never hesitate to seize the opportunity to use man's mind. It is therefore most foolish for one to allow his mind to sink into a state of passivity because the enemy spirits are on the prowl seeking whomever they may devour.[54]

And they devour many—very many—right under our eyes. Should one still keep quiet? It is surely more convenient and simpler to keep our mouth shut, not to criticise. But considering these deceptions, should warnings be neglected and these things not called by name? Suggestions to simply block out our minds and to submit ourselves to supernatural experiences are becoming more and more frequent today and they are accepted with enthusiasm. Should one not try at least to erect dams against this flood? Does not Scripture

command us to reprove the unfruitful works of darkness
(Ephesians 5:11)?

With Carothers we read:

In other words, my job was strictly that of being obedient
to the impressions or urgings I felt within me.[55]

This reminds us very strongly of emotional dependence, that
is, control by inner impulses and feelings. One may indeed
feel like 'in a third Heaven', as Witness Lee expresses himself, yet these beautiful feelings and inner enchantments may
likewise have a deceptive source, as Watchman Nee points
out:

Another danger may arise for those who live by sensation
rather than by the spirit through the will: they may be
deceived by Satan...how much more will he play his
tricks on those who desire to follow their feeling. In their
pursuit of emotion they fall directly into the hand of
Satan, for he delights to supply them with all kinds of
feeling which they assume to be from God.... Sometimes
Satan will even induce him to experience supernatural
sensations of shaking, electrifying, freezing, overflowing,
floating in the air, fire burning from head to foot and
consuming all his uncleanness, etc.... At this stage he
follows Satan's will in almost everything, for the enemy
merely needs to supply him with some particular feeling to
goad him to do what he wants him to do. The tragedy is
that the believer is not aware he is being tricked by Satan;
he instead pictures himself as being more spiritual than
others since he enjoys such supernatural experiences.[56]

Indeed, what a tragedy! One believes himself to be serving God in a special way, to be especially spiritual, but in
reality is being deceived in a special way.   •

We find the basic principle of temptation, that is deception by suggestion, already with Adam and Eve. Their motives were pure and sincere (everything was still without sin). Yet this does not protect us from deception (Romans 16:18b). The enemy promised them 'more' ('you shall be as gods') and thus drew them into sight, the opposite to faith. (Eve saw that it would be nice to eat from the tree and a pleasure for the eyes, and so on.) Today it still happens in just the same way: One wants to have or experience more power, influence, 'authority'; signs, wonders, gifts (if possible spectacular visible ones). And one does not want to live by faith, but wants to hear, feel and sense these workings of power, as we have also read in the book of Carothers.

We do not want to create the impression here that our general attitude is against the gifts of the Spirit. There are so many charisms of which one hears little today. For instance the gift of ministering (deacon), of exhorting, of giving (Romans 12:8), of teaching, and several others. We hope with all our hearts that believers are serving each other with such gifts. What we are warning against here is the one-sided emphasis on gifts of sensations and signs and the supernatural manifestations very often accompanied by them, which appeal to sight and not faith. They let one unconsciously slip into sight, therewith causing apostasy.

Supernatural phenomenon such as those described damage the spiritual life of many a Christian most severely today. Countless numbers of God's children have fallen into this pit. They consider these supernatural occurrences—which give them a physical feeling of the spirit and render them happy or sad, hot or cold, laughing or crying and which supply them with visions, dreams, voices, fires and even inexpressible wonderful sensations—as most definitely bestowed by the Holy Spirit, and thus represent the highest attainment of a Christian.

> They are unable to recognise that these are but the works
> of the evil spirit. They would never dream that the evil
> spirit as well as the Holy Spirit could perform such work,[57]

says Watchman Nee. Yet in this book, *Prison to Praise,* we
find things getting stranger still.

> They began to pray, and I suddenly saw in the spirit, Jesus
> kneeling before me. He said: 'I don't want to use you. I
> want you to use me.'[58]

At least here we should be put on our guard. Perhaps it
should further be mentioned that the Greek word for 'kneel'
actually means worship. This vision almost literally reminds
us of 'Jesus' temptation (Matthew 4:9). This is actually a
different Jesus who becomes the puppet of a human being.

One believes in a similar way that one can manipulate or
mediate the Holy Spirit by means of his 'sacred hands'. The
deception is alarming. Mervin Carothers is a deceived person who is unknowingly deceiving others. One naturally
assumes oneself to be a special vessel of grace, filled and
moved by the Holy Spirit. Miracles, healings, 'conversions',
leadings of the Holy Spirit, are taking place continuously,
but in reality one has become an almost perfect example of a
spiritualistic medium.

> Though he conceives himself to be truly dead, entirely
> selfless, and intensely spiritual, his consecration is not
> towards God but is as to the evil spirits.[59]

What a tragedy! Someone has correctly stated once: 'The
end-time is the climax of deception.' When one considers
that this book has an edition of millions in America, has
been a bestseller in England and is recommended and read
with enthusiasm in Germany, one can imagine the spiritual

decline. One ought to cry over such delusion, ignorance and naivity on the part of God's children. Do we realise the extent to which we have already been infiltrated, how far we have already been undermined, how far we have become intermixed and ready for judgement, how far the deception has already progressed?

By now the message should have come across that the devil can also say 'Hallelujah' and 'Jesus'. One could recognise this at least since the rising of the 'Children of God'. And here we find an occult background as well, namely, astrology and palmistry, again connected with super-spirituality and super-religiousness. And how many believers were deceived here in the beginning—were really enthusiastic. They mistook, as it happened so many times before in the history of mankind and church, the Saviour for the criminal. Appropriately G. H. Lang writes:

There is no limit to the folly of a spirit-blinded Christian.[60]

Here I would like to emphasise again, especially since several names were mentioned, I distinguish between personal and theological errors. In order that this may not be misunderstood, I would like to quote, as so often before, Watchman Nee:

We must not fall under the misapprehension that those believers who are deceived by evil spirits must be the most defiled, degenerate and sinful. They are on the contrary often-times fully surrendered Christians spiritually more advanced than ordinary believers. They strive to obey God and are willing to pay any cost.[61]

It is really tragic what is taking place today almost right before our eyes. May many a warning be heard and the blindness be healed.

Religious and Sacramental Intermixture

The basis or the result of deception is delusion. The spiritual blindness also prevents a clear separation between Gospel and mystery religion, from which direction the theory of the laying on of hands is inclined to come. The believer sets himself up as a kind of mediator between God and man, in a similar manner to a Catholic priest. The ritual of the Roman Catholic 'trans-substantiation' alone has taken four elements from the Dionysus cult. The thought of the hasty blessing or mediation of the 'spirit-baptism' by laying on of hands may be founded on the same basis; for here the personal attitude of my heart before God is not the decisive element but the 'position'—the sacramental laying on of hands, as well as the words of the 'mediator' or the 'blessed and anointed' man, ought to produce these blessings. This is the principle of Catholicism and the mystery religions; furthermore of the sacramental acts right down to the religiously-disguised superstitions.

To that extent the laying on of hands has been redirected more and more into a sacramental, mystical ritual. One just indiscriminately lays hands on anyone, regardless of whether that person wants it or not, repents or not or knows what is going on or not. Whoever does not believe this may read it in the books by Bennett. In these movements the 'answer' to spiritual problems seems to be very often tongues and the laying on of hands. Then everything has been 'done'. This becomes increasingly the gospel of our time. Just like so many things today, eg the doctrine of sacraments, it passes by the 'offence' of the Cross. In this connection the following observation in a Catholic magazine is noteworthy:

Experience shows that many Christians because of their Charismatic experience gain a deeper relationship to the sacraments, especially to the Eucharist ('Erneuerung in

Kirche und Gesellschaft,' 'Renewal in Church and Society' translated, No. 10, 1981, p 9).

From this point of view it is not surprising that the New Apostolics have declared the sealing of the Holy Spirit a sacrament which can only be mediated through the laying on of hands by an apostle or his representative. This also is a false doctrine. Some want to seal with the Holy Spirit; others want to 'bestow' the baptism of the Spirit through laying on of hands. But both of these divine actions, the Scriptures teach, God works in us at the moment of repentant submission as a sinner to the Lord Jesus Christ—without any other mediator, for the Lord 'is not worshipped with men's hands... as though He needed anything, seeing He giveth to all life and breath and all things' (Acts 17:25).

A drastic parallel should illustrate these facts: The Church is built on the foundation of the apostles and prophets (Ephesians 2:20). As we know, foundations are only laid once. In order to dig up these 'masses of earth', which have to be removed for the laying of the foundation, special tools (Acts 9:15) and machines are required. Now as explained earlier, the Lord has intervened in a great visible and sometimes wonderful way (Acts 8—10 and so on) especially at the beginning of a new dispensation. People such as the New Apostolics and others who are taking their teachings into the churches with the references to the initial events in the Book of Acts, are really driving their 'bulldozers' and 'excavators' into the top floors, one might almost say, into the roof. They can be very sincere in referring to the history of the first Church and other events in the Scriptures. But it becomes clear that nothing more than ruins remain. Sometimes it results in spiritual casualties.

It is certain that such 'building methods'—in the beginning anyhow—bring a lot of movement into certain 'stories' (speaking of enthusiastic and lively meetings). However if we check on these after some time we find most or very much of it destroyed. One simply observes where the 'Children of God' are heading. Yet it started seemingly biblically and almost looked like a revival.

The Doctrine of Balaam

The Church has a twofold battlefront; it is subject to attack both from outside and from within (Acts 20:28–30). Therefore the Apostle warns us to be watchful especially on the inner front (Acts 20:31). The Book of Acts shows us how the attacks sometimes come from without, but sometimes also come from within the ranks. While the Church usually resisted the outward attacks very quickly, surprise attacks from within inflicted grievous wounds. The danger of an invasion by the enemy through the laying on of hands is either not recognised at all or it is widely under-estimated.

If we neglect to be watchful then this inner frontline makes possible an infiltration and invasion by the enemy. We also see how such literature comes out of the Christian camp. This inner undermining results in the very effective satanic strategy of intermixture and syncretism.

This strategy of intermixture is the 'doctrine of Balaam'. What did this doctrine consist of? We read in Numbers 22—24 that Balaam should have cursed Israel, but could only bless it. Immediately afterwards, in Chapter 25, we read that the people began to commit fornication with the daughters of Moab (verse 1). Moreover the people ate and bowed down to their gods (verse 2). From Numbers 31:16 we learn, as well as from Revelation 2:14, that Balaam suggested this deception to Balak in order to ruin the people after he was unable to curse them. The blessing and power of God's people was in separation. Should they abandon this position and mix, then powerlessness and the curse would follow. The enemy of Israel executed this plan and it resulted in the union with the Gentiles, with the world. In the first verse of

Numbers 25 we see first the carnal, then the spiritual fornication, which is idolatry, fellowship with demons, union with darkness.

> They did not destroy the nations, concerning whom the Lord commanded them; but were mingled among the heathen, and learned their works. And they served their idols: which were a snare unto them. (Psalm 106:34–36).

Similarly, one makes a decision for Jesus, but does not go all the way and does not bring everything into the light. This can result in fellowship with darkness, a mixture by which one becomes defiled (Psalm 106:39). The three elements which Jesus indicates as the doctrine of Balaam (Revelation 2:14) are interestingly also found in the believers in Corinth. This church was, as already shown, very mixed. The three points are: (1) cast a stumbling block (1 Corinthians 8:9), (2) eat things sacrificed unto idols (1 Corinthians 8 and 10) and (3) commit fornication (1 Corinthians 6).

The risen Lord stands before the Church at Pergamos with a sharp, two-edged sword, just as the angel of the Lord confronted Balaam with the sword. This sword speaks of judgement, with which Jesus Christ also threatens the Church, if the believers do not repent (Revelation 2:16). The sword also points to the Word of God (Ephesians 6:12). The Word preached in full power of authority can also reveal mixture. In Revelation 2:17 the Lord Jesus Christ promised to him that overcometh (repenteth)—he that confesses this mixture, abandons it and therefore comes out of it—that He will give him of the hidden manna. Manna is a picture of divine food, the Word of God. There is therefore a 'hidden' food, insight into the hidden meanings in the Word of God, things which are not revealed to everyone.

In Hebrews 4:12 the Word of God is again called, with practically the same words, a sharp, two-edged sword which divides soul and spirit. Here we find, in my opinion, a part of these hidden things, namely the mixing of soul and spirit. Here the main offensive, the invisible strategy, built up. Disguised as an angel of light (2 Corinthians 11:4) the enemy imitates the Holy Spirit in the soulish life of the believer— usually extremely cleverly, cunningly and biblically disguised—as shown so very clearly in the book, *The Spiritual Man*. Only the clear and authoritative Word of God can reveal such mixture or unmask imitation.

> But they fail, according to the command given in the Bible, to test all the spirits to see if they are of truth or of error (1 John 4:1–6). They instead accept as being the Holy Spirit every spirit which comes to them. They think this obedience must be highly pleasing to God.... Should anyone make God the Spirit his object of obedience and forget God the Father he tends to obey the spirit in him and around him instead of obeying through the Holy Spirit the Father Who is in heaven. This will set him on the road to passivity and in addition provide the evil spirits the chance for counterfeit.[62]

This is exactly what is happening more and more today. The Holy Spirit and certain gifts are becoming the central points. Therefore one runs the great risk of being deceived by a very subtle counterfeit.

A passage from the book, 'Verkehr mit der Geisterwelt' (*Communication with the Spirit World*) should show us just how cleverly this can be done.

> In our meetings we started with prayer. Then we spent a few minutes in quiet inner concentration. There followed a reading from the Holy Scriptures and explanation and discussion of the reading, as well as answers to the questions asked by those present. We also considered together

how we could bring help to the poor in our immediate and more distant neighbourhood. I was surprised how especially the three brothers were taking this thing so very seriously (two of them became mediums). Yet I was not the only one who noticed something peculiar; their mother did too. The expression on the faces of these three boys became different, much nobler and fairer. Even strangers noticed this. One of these three also confessed that he did not know what was really going on in him. When he is working out on the field an inner voice is constantly reminding him to praise God and to thank Him. Such thoughts had never come to him before. And if he should give way to a fit of anger with his bad temper then straightaway this would be laid heavily on his soul so that he had to stop immediately with his work and ask forgiveness of God for this mistake. Only then could he continue happily with his work. He would fall into this dozens of times before but had never inwardly felt burdened.[63]

And this we read in a purely spiritistic book where the front is still evident. How much more cunning does the imitation become, than when it is dressed in more biblical expressions and concepts. For it is a fact that one hears reports of almost the same kind of experiences from people who have received the 'baptism of the spirit'. The strategy of Balaam is very successful. However this growing mixture makes us ready for judgement (Revelation 2:16). We are coming to the end.

The Last Battle has begun

Today we are experiencing the concentrated powers of God's adversary on the main offensive attack, literally an invasion from another world, a foreshadowing of Revelation 6:8: '...and his name that sat on him was Death, and Hell followed him.'

In this connection it is also worth mentioning how the very spiritisticly orientated 'Moonsect' or 'Unification Church'...interprets such phenomena. 'Departed spirits in the growing stages come to earth (in our epoch) and look for a union with people in order to be perfected through such mediation and to reach the resurrection stage of their perfection. Therefore we find that some Christians speak in tongues, heal the sick, prophesy and do great works in the name of Jesus. This is mostly done through the assistance of these departed spirits of paradise' ('Die Göttlichen Prinzipien', 'The divine principles' translated, from Hutten, 'Seher, Gruebler, Enthusiasten', a book on Sects, Quell Verlag, Stuttgart, p 769). Many groups and believers think that these signs and wonders are happening today through the help of the Holy Spirit. No, it is the invasion of Death and Hell (familiar spirits), just as the Scriptures have prophesied it for these last days.

A terrible danger is threatening the Church. Before he writes about the new Pentecostalism, Dr Francis Schaeffer states:

If I analyse it correctly, we are in the midst of another titanic struggle. ('The New Super-Spirituality', Telos, p 24).

The adversary of God and of mankind has devised a special weapon in the counterfeit Pentecostal spirit and in the laying on of hands which is controlled from below. He will see to it that all this does not come to light too quickly. Usually a storm of anger arises, one is accused of lack of love and exaggeration, of judging and of over-estimation of the power of the enemy (unfortunately the holiness of God is underestimated and thanks to this profanity the enemy is able to interfere to such an extent). Many behave as those doctors during the time of Semmelweis. The devil does not like to have these weapons revealed.

If we are not watchful and resisting, then the evil one will undermine our spirit through deception and counterfeit.[64]

The Apostle Peter does not write: 'The devil can hardly do anything. Nothing can happen to you.' No, he says clearly and distinctly:

Be sober, be vigilant; because your adversary the devil, as a roaring lion, walketh about, seeking whom he may devour. (1 Peter 5:8).

And as I have said already: He devours many. Today we see the occult on the offensive. And not only in the world, in my opinion the enemy is extending his spiritistic empire— his kingdom—within the Church. He bestows crossless experiences and gifts to a crossless Christianity; a crossless and bloodless gospel, full of wonders, signs and sensations. This is the gospel of the last days. According to 16:8–11, as has been said earlier, the working of the Holy Spirit manifests itself primarily through the acknowledgement of our own grave sin and the holiness of God, and less as an 'awakening' of gifts. However, people are increasingly yearning for these gifts today, and believers see in them the true power of God (Acts 8:10). Obviously P. A. Dubois does not unjustly state:

The Charismatic movement appears to be on the whole an emanation of the world-wide wave of the irrational, the occult and the mysticism upon the life of the Church.[65]

On page 130 of the previously-quoted book by the spiritist Greber we also read:

The closer a person comes to his god inwardly the greater is his portion of power coming from God. But so much the greater and more wonderful are the gifts as well which he receives from God for the good of his fellowman.[66]

Should it not make us thoughtful that today we hear so much about gifts and experiences and so little about obedience and brokenness? No wonder, therefore, that Conrad Murrell states in his booklet, *True and False Tongues*:

The thing that makes this task so difficult is the close resemblance much of the present supernatural phenomena bears to that of the scriptural record. Coupling that with the fact that multitudes are wearing broad 'happy' smiles, talking much about Jesus, leaving previous sinful bondages such as drugs, crime and immorality, and becoming devoutly religious, the person who dares suggest that it all might not be what it appears is going to be marked as suspicious, unkind and prejudiced. But we must bear this in mind: the most dangerous error in the world is the one closest to the truth: and the deadliest counterfeit, the one which most closely resembles the real.[67]

What a true word! The acceptance of such imitations of the enemy provides room for the seducing powers (1 Timothy 4:1). It results in such a terrible mixture of the doctrine of devils and the doctrine of God, of psychic and spiritual manifestation, of biblical and unbiblical views (sometimes even parallel and simultaneously), of the spirit of darkness and the Holy Spirit, that it could hardly be worse. The possibility of this mixture is hidden to many; they believe that if someone is a child of God, then everything must henceforth come from God. They think that if supernatural abilities appear, then these must also be of God. This intermingling together opens two completely different channels through which the Lord, but also at the same time the devil, 'bless'. Many turn off at this point; it is simply unbelievable to them.

The power of the enemy should not be exaggerated or even overestimated in this book. But to ignore or underestimate this highly gifted adversary and his cunning attacks (Ephesians 6:11) is a deadly danger. Again the Bible does not teach to ignore the devil and he will flee from you, but to resist the devil and he will flee from you (James 4:7). We should also never forget that we read of Satan in Revelation 12:9 that 'he deceiveth the whole world'. He was with God face to face and therefore we can hardly imagine how cleverly demons can imitate the Holy Spirit. In *War on the Saints* it says:

> This illuminates the condition of the mixture, for instance, into which the Church had slipped since the Welsh revival; for almost in every country without any exceptions, where new life had come through, a seducing spirit had mixed with the true one after a short time. And just so the false spirit was accepted along with the genuine Spirit, almost without exception, because the believers did not imagine such a competing influence possible.[68]

It reminds me of a statement that the late Dr Grattan Guinness, the founder of the Regions Beyond Missionary Union, made:

> The cleverest counterfeit of the devil in the closing days of this dispensation would be that he would put into the soul of man what God wants in the spirit.[69]

Therefore we have these alarming conditions that children of God can simultaneously be instruments of darkness.

Unsuspectingly, and because of the attitude that this is absolutely impossible for believers, one opens one self to a false spirit.

In the Old Testament we read about Gideon, that he liberated Israel from the bondage of the Midianites (Judges 7). The same man who was blessed in such a way put up an ephod (idol) (Judges 8:27) with which *all* Israel committed idolatry. This may be hard to accept, but we read it in the Bible. The story of Samson is a similar one. Although sin and compromise were obviously prevalent, one could almost say a union with the enemy was the case, still he acted in the power of God. The Lord confronts this mixture with His sharp two-edged sword. Only when we let ourselves be judged by the two-edged sword of the Bible and we renounce any alien influence in the name of our Lord Jesus Christ can the Lord stop the judgement.

The enemy knows the reason why a kingdom or a house divided against itself shall not stand (Matthew 12:25). Here we find his strategy. He causes the churches to disagree, to quarrel, and therewith robs them of their power. Actually nothing has split the Church so much, torn it apart and caused so many divisions, than this satanic counterfeit of the Pentecostal Spirit. Anyone who opens himself to this spirit subtly slips into the devil's workshop, accentuated with gifts and laying on of hands. Anyone who can speak of blessing here has become the victim of spiritual blindness in these last days. May the Lord give us open eyes (Revelation 3:18). May the Lord give grace to a Church ready for judgement. Should the believers know how far the infiltration has already progressed they would have to deliberately refuse to acknowledge this or they would finally have to wake up. Many prefer to remain in these strong errors. If the Lord does not continue to be merciful, everything shall collapse much sooner than we can imagine in our most distant dreams.

Tozer once said, that the Lord Jesus Christ had practically no authority in the circles which are calling themselves by His name. This book should not give glory to God's greatest adversary; but I am afraid that a great portion of Christendom today, at least in the Western world, lives so far away—miles away—from the standards of the New Testament and from the holiness of God, that any amount of darkness can be retained in the hearts of the believers. If we would truly repent, really be broken, much would be different and the Lord could reveal many a deception (2 Timothy 2:25–26). But if one lives constantly in the twilight, and it actually does get darker and darker, then one will consider even a weak candle as the normal light. It is the distance from the Cross which makes this deception possible and it is the unpreparedness to bow ourselves down which blinds us in such a way.

Let us take two informative examples from the Old Testament. In Joshua 7:4–6 we read how Israel was conquered by its enemies. Joshua knew that only sin could be the cause of it and he humbled himself with the elders before God (verse 6). He repented and the Lord revealed the true reason. After they had thoroughly removed this impediment, victory returned. In 1 Samuel 4 we are told of another defeat of Israel (verse 2). But this time we find a completely different reaction in the people responsible. The elders suggested the ark of the covenant of the Lord should be fetched. Therefore, instead of repentance they asked for a visible sign of God's presence, the power of God. This is the common trend today as well. Instead of coming to the Cross, the source of all power, one wants to disguise his lack of power and authority and unspirituality with 'spirit-baptism' and other visible signs. The people of Israel shouted so strongly about the ark that the earth rang (verse 5). The shout of 'Hallelujah' is also very impressive and loud today. One speaks of 'Jesus is in' and 'Full-power'. We find deafening music, people radiant with emotional enthusiasm and that joy is so great that one could really believe that revival was just around the corner. Yet it is highly dangerous to offer strange fire before the Lord (Leviticus 10:1). The emotional high is used more and more as a measure of evaluation. Thus Francis Schaeffer writes in his book concerning the new Pentecostal movement:

> ...and they make these external signs the test for fellow-ship and acceptance. In other words, as long as you have the signs, you are accepted as one of 'us'. You are 'in'. The rub, of course, is this: There are Unitarian groups and Buddhist groups who have these external signs. Furthermore any external sign can be easily duplicated or counterfeited by the devil.... One can also see a parallel between the new Pentecostals and the liberals.... A dismissal or lessening of content has occurred in the new Pentecostalism...content does not matter as long as there are external signs and religious emotions.... Everything is experience—emotion (or emotionalism) is the base.... But when we come to those who are caught up in this brand of Christian Platonism, we find that we talk to them and ask them how they know they are Christians, so very often they speak solely about their own experience and their own emotions and not about truth.[70]

The emphasis moves more and more away from the Bible and towards human experiences, as John Stott, quoted earlier, explained. Finally the human being again becomes the standard for all things and is exalted as god. It is not repentance and obedience to the Bible which unite any more but religious experiences. As a mission leader believes, this is one of the most subtle as well as the most dangerous developments of the last days and great is the number of those who fall prey to this deadly danger.

In the book, *War on the Saints*, we also read:

One can definitely say that it is always a dangerous thing, to try to feel God with the senses. In such cases it is fairly certain that it is a case of an imitated presence of God, a clever trap of the enemy who wants to get entrance into the heart of a person. For this reason we find many who have forced this idea of a 'God-felt presence' on other believers and to their dismay and distress have lost their own 'experience' and sunk into darkness and apathy. These believers did not know that all supernatural manifestations perceived through their senses end in such a way, soon or even years later. The victim is then trying to explain this 'breakdown' or this 'mental derangement' by overexertion, sin, or outward circumstances, but not that all this is the true nature of his earlier 'inspired' experiences.[71]

Going back to the passage in Samuel, Israel was also conquered then and the defeat was greater than before (1 Samuel 4:10). Many a person who was formerly floating in a spiritual enthusiasm is further away from Jesus today than ever before.

A Short Look at the World

Thus one dreams of great outpourings of the Spirit and revivals today, but one look at the world ought to make us sober. Have we not noticed that right in front of our eyes it is going downhill in one country after another, and dictatorship is increasing? This is but a sign of defeat and judgement. The terror, the confusion, the chaos, the brutality and the sexual liberation right down to the demonic perversion are all growing like a torrent. Anarchism is spreading. A human life is worth less and less. Inconsiderate and thoughtless murders, kidnappings, blackmails, yes, satanism are increasing alarmingly. And the believers speak of great acts of God. Something is wrong with our authority and our signs and wonders.

1975 was called the year of terror. Even the people of the world are horrified by the 'animal in us', as we literally read in one of the magazines. The condition of the world is in a certain sense the barometer for the spiritual effectiveness of the believers who are the salt of the earth, as we know. Anyone who can speak of revival here would seem to be sadly blinded (Revelation 3:17–18). But this blindness is partly already the judgement of God (Isaiah 29:9–10; Psalm 69:23, etc).

We do not have a world-wide revival before us, but, as the principal of a Bible School has written, we have a satanic Pentecost before us which is being prepared by the powers of anarchy and confusion. Let us think for a moment of the conflicts in the visible world: One fights wars without official declarations of war, conquers countries without official battles, one undermines and sabotages the enemy, infiltrates the battle lines which are becoming more and more confused, one smiles friendly at a conference and then kills in an ambush, ideologically intersperses the armies in such a way that one does not know who is friend or enemy any more. In my opinion all this shows us to a certain degree in the visible world what is going on in the invisible battlefronts. A horrible infiltration strategy which brings the enemy into the ranks of God's children, which is intended to stir them up, divide them and turn them against each other. And the sin of lukewarmness, as well as compromise, successfully opens the doors for our enemies. The people of Israel believed themselves to be very spiritual, yet the prophets compared them with Sodom and Gomorrah (Isaiah 1:10).

May the Lord bring His Church to the Cross anew, for without repentance there is no victory. Watchman Nee writes in his book, *The Latent Power of the Soul*:

All who have spiritual insight and sensitivity know the reality of this statement. Soul power is rushing towards us like a torrent. Making use of science (psychology and parapsychology), religion, and even an ignorant church (in her seeking excessively supernatural manifestations and in her not controlling supernatural gifts according to the guidance of the Bible), Satan is causing this world to be filled with the power of darkness. Yet this is but Satan's last and final preparation for the manifestation of the Antichrist. Those who are truly spiritual (that is, those who reject soul power) sense all around them the acceleration of opposition from the evil spirits. The whole atmosphere is so darkened that they find it hard to advance.[72]

The praying believers alone are still able to hold back the judgement.

Epilogue

I am aware of the fact that not everyone will be happy about my interpretation of this subject. But it is the result of many years of confrontation, often right at the front. There was a time in my Christian life when I esteemed all these warnings lightly and reached out after these experiences and gifts with all my heart. As I have already mentioned, I prayed with a very nice brother who was at that time a tongue-speaker, with laying on of hands for the 'spirit baptism' for almost half a night. The immediate time afterwards was simply magnificent. Joy, power, wonderful 'spiritual' experiences, more prayer and inner certainty, were simply so overpowering and beautiful that there could be no doubt that this was from God. Only after months did I realise my dependence on spiritual experiences and feelings.

Yet these doubts were driven back again by the 'evidence' of the positive success in the beginning, for people had even been saved. In addition I would like to casually mention an illustration which history has brought us, which is a perfect paradigm. Taken from the visible historic world we find a typical example of satanic deception in the rise and following downfall of Hitler.

Unemployment and corruption decreased a great deal, the uncertainty became less and confidence grew. There were great diplomatic successes and at the beginning of the war the amazing 'Blitz' victories. Who can doubt this? Through these impressive economic and military successes at the beginning, one man won the confidence of almost a whole nation, and finally on this basis, the enemy steered them towards the abyss, and millions were pulled into a Christless eternity. Anyone who thinks the working of evil spirits has to be always negative outwardly, is greatly mistaken.

At the beginning, just for the sake of winning our confidence, the enemy works an imitation of God's presence in us and thus produces the most positive effects and results. Anyhow, my dependency on the feeling of a spiritual high grew. Looking back I can only say that I literally fulfilled those principles of passivity of which God's Word warns us. I could simply let myself passively glide in prayer for hours. I felt myself carried away as by an invisible power. It was a pleasant floating feeling. I only had to close my eyes and to open myself to this inner force. If I pressed my hands against my face the feeling of this inward floating would become distinctly stronger. Besides, this is a typical spiritistic symptom. Here we find that power is mediated through hands. Sometimes I could meditate in this inner state of passivity for hours. Many suggestions for prayer which I have found in certain literature—and such suggestions and books are increasing steadily—are exactly in accord with these phenomena. The believer thinks because he is a child of God this spiritual reality and experience must unquestionably come from the Holy Spirit. This is how I thought—at least for some time. After such meditations and 'quiet times' I was often enormously happy, enthusiastic, simply blessed. One really depends on these experiences. Today I know that what I practised had more resemblances to transcendental meditation than to biblical prayer. But I did not realise this at that time. This is how badly blinded I was: the Lord needed more than a year—thanks be to Him for His unfathomable patience and love—before He could open my eyes to this cunning snare of Satan. Only after I repented was I allowed to see the truth (2 Timothy 2:26). It is almost an unbelievable deception.

However, today I understand much better the reason why our Lord Jesus admonishes us in the Lord's Prayer to pray that we may be delivered from evil (Matthew 6:13). I believe that anyone who has not experienced this deception 'in their own body' and had his eyes opened through God's grace can hardly form an idea of how subtle this deception really is. Since then, my counselling experiences have proved dozens of times, sometimes in an amazingly impressive way, the deceptions and the deceit of believers, especially in the charismatic field. If I had not experienced it so clearly in the case of God's children, and had I not been confronted with these manifestations I would not be able to warn of these things so distinctly, or try to speak in such a decisive way. I would like to cry out with all my heart: please let yourselves be warned. We are dealing with a wave of deception of the worst degree. If we do not really accept the Bible accurately and let ourselves be corrected, we expose ourselves to unbelievable dangers of deceit.

When I must watch today, how God's children stumble into the same traps and snares in which I was once caught, then I am filled with the desire to help them and to pull them out of these snares. Yet this cannot be done in one's own strength. I believe, even if one has only a little love and a burden for the Church, one ought to warn of these deceptions. One should find the courage to call these crucial issues by name.

I would like to emphasise again here, even though I have cited names, it does not mean that these are not God's children. We shall not judge, but we are commanded to test the spirits. I do, however, have certain doubts about some people, but the Lord knows them that are His (2 Timothy 2:19). In closing it should also be said that many Pentecostals are not aware of these things. Many serve the Lord with true dedication. For that reason we are united with many in the love of Jesus Christ and in the desire after fruit and blessing.

Yet sometimes it is very sad to see how, on the other hand, many do not allow themselves to be warned and will not take advice. They believe it is impossible for God to allow deception.

Many will wonder why God does not protect them. Is not their motive pure? How can God permit such faithful seekers of His to be deceived by evil spirits? Many people will contend that He ought to safeguard His own children under any circumstances.... Should a person fulfil the conditions for the working of the evil spirits God cannot forbid the latter to work, for He is a law-abiding One. Because the Christian intentionally or unintentionally has surrendered himself to the evil spirits God will not hinder them from the right to control that one. How many hold to the idea that a pure motive safeguards them from deception. Little do they realise that the people most deceived in the world are those with good intentions. Honesty is no condition for not being deceived; but *knowledge* is. Should the believer neglect the teaching of the Bible, failing to watch and pray even though trusting his pure motive to keep him from deception, he may be deceived,[73] says the oft-quoted Watchman Nee.

Yet honesty can cause us to be set free from these bond-ages. This book was written with the honest desire to warn of a great danger, especially because I have made the frequent observation, how otherwise sincere believers are confronted with these most subtle of all deceptions in a strangely de-fenceless way. May this book prevent or reveal many a deception.

But because I know of my own weaknesses and failures, I am thankful for prayers and intercessions.

APPENDIX
TO THE FIFTH (GERMAN)
EDITION

I have tried to show in my book how genuine children of God can also be infiltrated by false spirits. Just here we find the greatest ignorance and lack of awareness. Therefore another argument should be brought up here. Everyone knows that even a child of God (unfortunately) can make himself visibly one with another person in an ungodly relationship. This is a rather awkward definition of fornication. Now if this is possible in a visible way, and no one can argue about that, let us think of Corinth for example, how much more valid is this then in the invisible world, for we all know as believers that the satanic spirits are, in reality, personal beings. After all the events are always taking place first in the invisible world or prior to the visible world. We only have to think of the fall of man. The spiritual death took place instantly; the visible death followed hundreds of years later. And today we have so much fornication and prostitution, unfortunately not only in the world, but also too often in circles of believers, for we already find such a high degree of infiltration of seducing spirits within the unseen world.

Thus we read in Revelation 2:22:

Notwithstanding I have a few things against thee, because thou sufferest that woman Jezebel, which calleth herself a prophetess, to teach and to seduce my servants to commit fornication, and to eat things sacrificed unto idols.

Here we also find visible and invisible identification. Those two aspects were expounded in detail in the chapter on First Corinthians. May the believers at last wake up to these facts and become more careful in their walk and not accept everything without discernment even if it comes from the Christian side. May the believers take God's Word and its warnings, especially discipleship, much more seriously.

We also want to express our view about another book here which unfortunately has also been receiving a big distribution lately, namely: *The Happiest People on Earth*. It deals with the life story of the founder of the 'Full Gospel Business Men's Fellowship International', Demos Shakarian. First of all, it is very informative to read the account of the 'spirit baptism'.

> As I sat there on a rear bench with the other boys, I felt something like a heavy woollen blanket settle over my shoulders. I looked around, startled, but no one had touched me. I tried to move my arms, but they met resistance, like I was pulling them through water. Suddenly my jaw began to shake as if I were shivering with cold, although the 'blanket' felt warm. The muscles in the back of my throat tightened. I had a sudden yearning to tell Jesus that I loved Him, but when I opened my mouth to say so, out came words I couldn't understand.... Even hours later, driving home in the car, anyone who spoke to me was answered in tongues.... It was as if the invisible mantle which had remained on my shoulders all evening had become irresistibly heavy—though not unpleasantly so. I sank to the floor and lay there on the rug absolutely helpless, unable to get up and get into bed.[1]

We want to mention again here that the characteristic of a Spirit-filled life is self-control. Again we find the exact opposite in this report. Let us remember the chapter on 'Compulsion by the powers of darkness'.

In this connection we find a most interesting letter of

Jung-Stilling, about the evangelist Rock, who was the leader of the so-called 'Inspired Ones' who settled in the German-speaking areas in the 17th and 18th centuries. These people believed God would reveal Himself, besides in the Bible, constantly in His favoured ones through inspirations of the Spirit. In this letter we read:

> I have read Rock's writings and I am wholeheartedly convinced that he had truly and sincerely meant well. But dearest brethren, the Holy Spirit does not use fainting fits, convulsions and loss of consciousness when He cares to have His testimonies proclaimed. I know of many men and women who have also had such twitchings then fell into a rapture and thus spoke of the most beautiful and holiest truths of the Bible in the nicest and holiest way, even prophesied of things to come, which also happened promptly. But gradually and at the end it finished sadly and often shamefully and now it became clear that a false spirit had disguised himself as an angel of light.... Dearest brethren, let us only stick to the Bible. There we find that everything has been sufficiently made known to us. I think of Rock as a devout and honest man but I am firmly convinced that the Holy Spirit did not speak through him but that it was his own overstrained spirit, developed through his ability of presentment, and will be convinced of it, till you my dear brother, can prove other-wise to me. Dear brother in the Lord, nothing in the world is more dangerous than inspiration; it is an open door for false spirits. The Bible alone is our guiding star which leads us to Jesus Christ. He is and may remain our all in all.[2]

Another passage is highly informative in Demos Shakarian's book, about an 'anointed' evangelist called Bob Smith.

The strange thing about the fellow was that in spite of his over-concern for money, he was an anointed, God-inspired speaker. We never had bigger crowds than we had that summer, never more people coming forward to the altar, never more wonderful healings.[3]

But later this man came to a sad end.

This was the first—but by no means the last—time that Rose and I encountered the phenomenon of a man with a tremendous ministry of God for others, whose own personal life was a shambles. Sometimes as with Smith, the problem was money. Sometimes it was alcohol. Sometimes women, or drugs, or sexual perversion. Why did God honour the ministry of men like this? Was it the power of Scripture, working independently of the man who quoted it? Was it the faith of the hearers? I didn't know.[4]

Yet this is exactly the biblical mark of the false servants and prophets of God. Not by their great speeches, acts, gifts, signs and wonders do we recognise them, but, as we know, by their fruits. These are frightening, as Shakarian himself admits. It could hardly be clearer.

But because one argues from the pure visible point of view and is so very impressed by the wonderful gifts and miracles, and not from the invisible things, using the Word of God therefore as guide, we find such bad spiritual delusions. Notably, the Bible is rarely mentioned in this book, but more frequently words such as Holy Spirit and power.

This biography is filled with visions, dreams, angels, voices, etc. It is just plain spiritualism that one could almost despair for the lack of discernment of those Christians who are still recommending such writings. Surely we are in the last days.

Naturally they believe those supernatural voices to be God's directions. Yet we read in Demos Shakarian's book the following:

> Even as I spoke a voice answered me. An inner voice, yet as unmistakable as though I heard it with my ears. 'Demos, you are to abandon this Fresno campaign...'[5]

The whole night through he torments himself whether he should finish the evangelisation or not, whereby he hears this warning voice continuously. Suddenly he comes to the amazing conclusion:

> I recognised that voice. 'It was Satan', I told them.[6]

By now, even as an unsuspecting reader, one ought to face those voices and inspirations of Shakarian sceptically. Why are the other voices suddenly of divine origin? Perhaps, because they fit better into the concept?

In this connection a letter of Zinzendorf to the same man called Rock is again worth mentioning. As already pointed out, Rock was the leader of the so-called 'Inspired Ones' who likewise had experienced inner voices and visions in connection with all kinds of physical concomitant symptoms. If asked about the source of this 'inner voice' they reacted in a most upset fashion. Zinzendorf therefore wrote:

> We are not afraid of the 'inspiration' because it wants to correct us in our things, for we like to see that; but we are only concerned that this inspiration could fail in the application and therefore we are apprehensive. Therewith I am convinced that a child of God need not necessarily be a wise and experienced servant of God and that his intellect and imagination can be misled. Would I believe the latter to be impossible then I could err in the judgement of

the most precious souls; for I have countless proofs of their heedlessness in history, their wrong concepts, who have been burned, but they themselves were saved, yet as through fire.... That I should accept your word of inspiration—a word which can fail and has failed—as the Word of the living God itself, yes, as you call it as the independent word in tongue and heart, I cannot, and you must be patient with me. And you know that I have criticised from the beginning that one had used the expression 'Thus saith the Lord'.[7]

But just these precise words are so popular in Pentecostal and Charismatic circles. The Pentecostal church actually starts with such words and prophecies. We should consider that we do not find the words 'Thus says the Lord' in the New Testament at all. It is an Old Testament phrase and thereby shows another dogmatic weakness of these groups. John Stott is of a similar opinion:

Moreover, 'prophets' come second to apostles in the Ephesian and Corinthian lists mentioned above, and 'apostles and prophets' are bracketed in several texts and said to be the foundation (because of their teaching) on which the church is built (Ephesians 2:20; 3:5). Now the simplest knowledge of architectural construction is enough to tell us that once the foundation of a building is laid and the superstructure is being built, the foundation cannot be laid again. So in the primary sense of 'prophets', as vehicles of direct and fresh revelation, it seems we must say that this chàrisma is no longer given. There is no longer anyone in the church who may dare to say 'The Word of the Lord came to me saying...' or 'Thus says the Lord'.[8]

Rev Cochlovius points out a further aspect which is worth mentioning.

> The esteem for so-called prophecies (often in 'I'-form) has consequences for the understanding of the Bible in the Charismatic movement. The word of the Bible becomes the 'past Word' and the 'present Word', namely prophecies, visions, etc are placed on a par with it. Thus the principle of the Reformation 'by the Word alone' (that is, the word of the Bible) is abandoned. The openness for the historical-critical interpretation of the Bible is also remarkable.[9]

These are interesting comments. Thus we may expect an unprecedented, refined and biblically disguised attack on the Word of God. By means of such charismata it is gradually reduced to the status of an old book. It is in the enemy's interest that we become powerless and that the Holy Scriptures are not our primary spiritual nourishment (Matthew 4:4). So we are to be perfect, but not by emphasising certain gifts, but rather through the Word of God (2 Timothy 3:16–17).

Is this perhaps the reason why David du Plessis, Mr Pentecost, had to make the following confession about the Charismatic Movement:

> The most remarkable thing is that this revival is found in the so-called liberal societies and much less in the evangelical and not at all in the fundamentalist segments of Protestantism. The last-mentioned are now the most vehement opponents of this glorious revival because it is in the Pentecostal Movement and in the modernist World Council Movements that we find the most powerful manifestations of the Spirit. This seems to be true almost

without exception in most parts of the world, as far as I know.[10]

The vision of Shakarian which is responsible for the formation of 'Full Gospel Business Men's Fellowship International' is described to us on pages 133 and 134. Shakarian floats high above the earth, sees millions of people. First the faces seem to be dead but obviously after a tremendous outpouring of the spirit they are filled with joy and life. Afterwards:

> And then the vision was over. I felt myself returning to earth. Below me was Downey, California. There was our house. I could see myself, kneeling, and Rose seated at the organ.[11]

This is the so-called phenomenon of the excursion of the soul or 'out-of-the-body experience', a highly spiritistic manifestation. If one considers that this movement has stimulated (also financially) the Charismatic renewal to a high degree, then one asks oneself, what is approaching us in this movement, what is threatening to undermine the Church?

With regard to the Charismatic movement it very often comes to heated discussions about the value or not of tongue-speaking, as if this were the only characteristic. There are almost as many opinions about tongue-speaking as there are people who write books about it. Yet the Charismatic movement has still other accompanying symptoms.

In zoology we know of the so-called mimicry. A harmless insect imitates a dangerous one in his appearance. Thus we have butterflies which look like wasps. The layman cannot usually distinguish between the two. Now let us assume, the course of this comparison, that tongue-speaking complied with one of the physical marks of this insect, for instance the feelers. Even the experts cannot agree if this form of feelers are like the one of the wasp or the butterfly. Yet such an insect does not only consist of feelers. Thus the Charismatic movement has still other characteristics, 'physical' marks as well.

Firstly, one of these marks is, with a few exceptions, the exegetically untenable interpretation of Spirit baptism as an experience separated from conversion.

This doctrine is practically the basis of this whole movement. Again the simplest architectural information is sufficient for us to realise that the most beautiful and impressive building cannot stand on the wrong foundation. The inconsistency of some believers concerning this point has often astonished me. Many are shown to be dazzled by the growing superstructure.

The Scriptures do not teach anywhere to ask God or the Lord Jesus for a Spirit baptism. The apostles do not encourage or exhort us in any of their letters to seek a Spirit baptism or a 'second experience'.

This main doctrine of the Pentecostal movement unmasks itself because the passage in 1 Corinthians 12:13 teaches the unity of the body of Christ as a result of Spirit baptism and the emphasis lies on the word 'all'. That, which is the basis for the unity of all believers in the Scriptures, is used as the ground for distinction, discrimination and separation. No wonder that the body of Christ suffers so many outward divisions.

Secondly, we always find the arbitrary and hasty laying on of hands for all kinds of possible and impossible, biblical and unbiblical purposes. Just as we receive the Holy Spirit by faith in the Lord Jesus Christ in an invisible way here the false spirit is mediated by the laying on of hands in a visible contrary demonstration.

Today it has really become the main source of infection. Yet we do not have any commandment in the New Testament to lay hands on anyone, but only one exhortation to be cautious. He that lays on hands frequently, demonstrates not his great faith, but rather his lack of faith.

Perhaps it is useful to call to mind a warning made by the evangelist Elias Schrenk who was blessed by God:

> Today more than ever we need a moderate position in the whole truth of Scriptures. It will keep us from the sensational, from dangerous and risky strivings after the equipping by the Spirit. It causes that spiritual moderation which recoils from laying on hands by people from California, Norway, England and Holland. *I have known various people who through the laying on of hands permanently came under the influence of evil spirits*. A moderate position in the Scriptures will keep us from seeking after signs and wonders.[12]

Thirdly, we find the phenomenon of passiveness, that is, simply giving oneself to the spirit. Often enough one is requested to do just that. But these are, as shown, the laws of the demonic world and mediumism.

How far eastern mysticism has already infiltrated, is shown by the following example from Charismatic literature. Under the title, 'Now the time has come for you to receive the Holy Ghost' (translated), A. G. Dornfeld writes:

> Firstly: Please close your eyes, lift up your head and look at Jesus.... Secondly: Open your mouth wide! The Bible says: 'Open thy mouth wide, and I will fill it', Psalm 81:10. Is this not exactly what you want to do? You want to be filled with the Holy Spirit. Just open your mouth like a small hungry robin. Thirdly: Now breathe in and out— your mouth wide open—as deep as you can. Continue to do so until you can feel the presence of God.[13]

I think this passage needs no further comment.

Fourthly, we find it an exegetically untenable interpretation that the prophecy of Joel is an event to be expected for the closing of the Church age.

Fifthly, the wrong emphasis on signs and wonders as proof of genuine spiritual power, although the Scriptures warn us against it. What we see today is primarily a preliminary fulfilment of Revelation 16:14: 'For they are the spirits of devils, working miracles...'

Where this passion for signs and wonders leads one can very emphatically recognise in the book *Face Up With a Miracle*, by Don W. Basham. We read there, for instance:

> A young lady named Irma Grace told us afterwards, what she had been blessed to see during this holy moment. During the worship, at the beginning of our service, Jesus appeared in our midst. When Alice started to pray for the young people, Jesus kneeled down beside her and wept. He even stretched forth his hand and touched the knee of our daughter Cindy who was sitting next to her mother.[14]

The Lord Jesus states explicitly about the coming of the true Spirit: '...because I go to my Father, and ye see me no more' (John 16:10). Although we know that there have been exceptions, especially during the time of the apostles, these 'blessed Charismatics' see 'Jesus' with increasing frequency. Usually 'Jesus' appears in such meetings after the descending of the 'Spirit'. This, however, contradicts the Word of God. Here again some things have been upturned, as so often happens today. Besides this, how a kneeling Christ is to be understood, I have mentioned before.

The beginning and further development of the Pentecostal movement was marked by visions and messages, that the coming of Jesus, the day of the Son of Man, is at hand. Here the Lord Jesus warns appropriately: '...The days will come, when ye shall desire to see one of the days of the Son of Man, and ye shall not see it. And they shall say to you, see here; or, see there: go not after them, nor follow them.' (Luke 17:22–23).

Because of the grave misuse of the book of Acts for such visions and manifestations I would like to let two men speak on this subject. First Alfred Kuen:

Since this was the time of the official commencement, the Lord made sure that the founding of the Church was accompanied by certain wonderful acts.... 'Since the Jews required a sign' (1 Corinthians 1:22), God exceptionally granted them such, in order to show, that from now on His blessing would be on those, who acknowledge the Lord Jesus as their Saviour.... Just as the beginning of the Old Covenant was accompanied by unique signs, so the time of the apostles was enjoying special blessings from God too. This was necessary, as they did not have the New Testament yet.[15]

Again John Stott writes:

Large tracts of Biblical history contain no record of any miracle. John the Baptist, who Jesus said was the greatest man of the Old dispensation, is specifically said to have performed no miracles (John 10:41). In fact when we seek to discover where the Biblical miracles are, we find that they cluster in Scripture like stars in the night sky. There are four main constellations. They cluster first around Moses, next around Elijah, Elisha and the prophets, thirdly around the Lord Jesus Himself and fourthly around the apostles. Now these are the four main epochs of revelation—the Law, the prophets, the Lord and the apostles. And the major purpose of miracles was to authenticate each fresh stage of revelation...while God also bore witness to the message of the apostolic eye witness 'by signs and wonders and various miracles and by gifts of the Holy Spirit distributed according to His own will' (Hebrews 2:3–4). It is correct, therefore, to refer to the Book of Acts as 'the Acts of the Apostles', for all the miracles Luke records in this book were performed by apostles (Acts 2:43; 5:12, etc) and the only exceptions were by men whom the apostles had personally commissioned by the laying on of hands (6:8; 8:6,7). Paul's miracles, too, were described by him as 'signs of a true apostle' (2 Corinthians 12:12).[16]

We have already stated how 2 Corinthians 5:16 shows a change from the visible to the invisible, as we read literally in 2 Corinthians 4:18. This verse ('Wherefore henceforth know we no man after the flesh...' 2 Corinthians 5:16) is for me the clearest indication that there can no longer be apostles in the true sense of the word. John Stott also points this out. By definition, the apostles knew Christ 'after the flesh' (see 1 John 1:1–3) and Paul declares explicitly that he is an apostle because he has seen the Lord Jesus (1 Corinthians 9:1).

Now it can be argued that other disciples who did not belong to the Twelve are also called apostles. Barnabas is called an apostle (Acts 14:4) and some translations also allow this conclusion in the case of Andronicus and Junias (Romans 16:7). But it is to be assumed that this still refers to eye-witnesses. After all, the Bible plainly states that there were more than only twelve apostles.

For instance we read in 1 Corinthians 15:5 that Jesus was seen by the *Twelve* and then by *all the apostles* (verse 7). In theory there could have been 500 of them (verse 6), but still they were eye-witnesses. This time is definitely past. Hence the transition from the visible (2 Peter 1:16–18) to the Word (2 Peter 1:19), which took place long ago, and which is therefore not repeatable today, for example by referring to the Book of Acts for support.

The apostle, which really means 'sent', would today in the widest sense be the missionary (the Latin word for 'sent') who founds churches or does pioneer work. But he can no longer lay claim to the signs and authority of the apostles, just as he cannot add to the Word of God (which according to Colossians 1:25 was the prerogative of the apostles), nor can he claim that he knows Christ after the flesh. Otherwise the judgement of Revelation 2:2b applies to him.

Similarly, when we compare Matthew 12 with Matthew 13, we see such transitions from signs (Matthew 12:39 regarding Israel) to the nations and therewith Word (Matthew 13:3 and 19). After the clear rejection of Israel, the Lord mentions the blasphemy of the Holy Spirit (Matthew 12:32) and the condemnation of this generation (Matthew 12:41–45), there follows the first parable of Jesus in this gospel (Matthew 13:3). Now we see mysteries (Matthew 13:11) and parables (Matthew 13:10) for the nations and Church age. This age is allegorically fore-shadowed by this transition, and we no longer see the visible signs now.

Matthew 12:46–50 also suggests the same thing. The Lord's mother and His brothers want to talk to him. That is those who according to the flesh, as Jesus' most direct relatives, represent the people of God in the strongest possible way. But this visible relationship is not valid anymore (2 Corinthians 5:16), and He turns away. Not the physical or visible relationship (Matthew 12:47) is decisive any longer (Israel), but the spiritual (Matthew 12:50, John 1:12–13, Church). After all, in the New Covenant we are born of God, Israel relates to the Angels, signs and the Law; the Church is under the Holy Spirit, the Word and Grace. It is impossible to put God's plan of salvation for Israel onto the same plane as the Church.

In a similar way, as the Galatians mixed Law and Grace and Paul speaks of bewitchment (Galatians 3:1) and leaven (Galatians 5:9), the Old Testament prophet Joel, who according to Matthew 11:13 prophesied for the Old Covenant, is today mixed with the period of grace by the Pentecostal movement. We have already sufficiently treated the 'bewitching' mystical background of this movement and also the destructive effect of the leaven (1 Corinthians 5:7). It is an almost classical mixed movement. Because of this mixture of Law and Grace the fiercest fights and arguments took place in the First Church (Acts 15). Today, because of this Charismatic mixture, we find a similarly intense battlefield.

Exegetically Hebrews 2:3–4 is probably the clearest passage which shows why those signs were only an initial phase. The writer shows the three witnesses of the New Covenant, with whom God confirmed His Word once and for all. It is well known that in the Bible an issue is affirmed on the testimony of two or three witnesses (eg Hebrews 10:28).

Now the first witness is the Lord Jesus ('at the first began to be spoken by the Lord'). Then follow the apostles, the eyewitnesses who confirm the Word ('confirmed unto us by them that heard him', verse 3). God is mentioned as the third witness ('God also bearing them witness...' is a present participle in the original text), who bore witness to His Word with signs, wonders and deeds (verse 4). Does God also work in this way today?

Now the predicate of the main clause (the 'was confirmed' of the eyewitnesses in verse 3) is Aorist Passive Indicative. That is clearly a past tense. Although verse 4 has a present tense form, it is a so-called Genitive Absolute, and as such it is temporally subordinate to the time, set by the predicate in the previous main clause.

This explains why God worked through so many signs only at the beginning (for example, if we call to mind God's judgement on Ananias and Sapphira in the days of the early Church). For this reason some translations render the participle in Hebrews 2:4 quite correctly with a past tense form.

Mark 16:17–18–20b also leads chronologically into this statement of Hebrews 2:3–4.

In this connection the following is worth mentioning. The same concepts which are mentioned in Hebrews 2:4 (*semeion*—signs, *teras*—wonders, *dunamis*—divers miracles) we find again in 2 Thessalonians 2:9. In this letter the second coming of our Lord Jesus Christ and the preceding events are mentioned. Thus the signs and wonders with which God had confirmed His Word in the beginning are going to appear again prior to the second coming of the Lord. This Charismatic movement fulfills, so to speak, God's Word. Had I never heard of such a movement, I would have to assume according to biblical prophecy that something just like this must emerge and spread before the end of the Church age. Yet this time the source is not from God, as Hebrews explains, but Satan, as we read very clearly in 2 Thessalonians 2:9. Especially the history of the Pentecostal as well as the Charismatic movement shows this quite clearly. It looks like the early church, the same terms are used, but behind it is concealed something completely different. This explains why counsellors who look behind the scenes of something, that at first sight seems so biblically conducted and disguised, usually find an occult source. This also explains why the followers of this movement usually refer to the initial events in Acts (Chapters 2,8,10 and 19), historic breakthroughs, therefore, which God still confirmed with signs.

These relations also explain why these movements grow so rapidly, why the number of the followers of the Charismatic movement steadily increases. The closer the second coming of Christ draws nigh, the more tongue-speaking, miracles, healings and great signs will spread. The massive spiritualism of the 'Full Gospel Business Men's Fellowship International' will widen. These people will have 'success', do great things and will win many to themselves. Yet it is unfortunately a consequent fulfilment in a negative respect, the manifestation of strong delusions which are named significantly almost straight after verse 9.

It is clearly shown to us on the basis of the story of the rich man and Lazarus, in Luke 16:23–31, that the suggestions to bring people to repentance by means of signs and wonders comes literally out of hell (verse 23), which are spreading more and more today. According to Matthew 16:18 the confrontation will lead as far as to the gates of hell. Gates, which have, thanks to the Charismatic breakthrough, already opened wide, and in the same measure these suggestions are growing: 'Nay, father Abraham: but if one went unto them from the dead, they will repent.' (Luke 16:30). This means in other words: 'The Bible is alright, but not sufficient. We need the signs and wonders, then something is really going to happen.' This is why the rich man was in hell. He despised the Word of God. He put signs and wonders above the Scriptures. This is the mark of fallen mankind and the carnal Christian.

Such a way is the way of deception because the authority of the Word of God is reduced. For that reason God answers through Abraham, showing that His Word is completely sufficient: 'If they hear not Moses and the prophets, neither will be persuaded, though one rose from the dead.' (Luke 16:31).

Sixthly, another wrong emphasis on certain gifts, especially regarding these charismata with sign character—foremost the tongues. Here the last biblical gift has been put first. Spiros Zodhiates writes concerning this:

> We also note that the term 'Holy Spirit' does not occur at all in connection with tongues in 1 Corinthians 14. Whenever the words 'spirit' or 'spirits' occur in this chapter, they always refer to man's spirit.... We have no record that this phenomenon occurred in any other New Testa-

ment church, nor did Paul ever seek to introduce it to them in his epistles. If this were the indispensable evidence of spirituality and the infilling of the Holy Spirit, we could certainly expect him to urge all believers to pray for this gift. Instead, he seeks to play it down among the Corinthians as much as possible.[17]

The Holy Spirit motivates the believer to seek the abiding fruit, the false spirit causes him to reach for the extraordinary gifts.

John Wesley also remarks on Acts 4:31:

Here we do not find any visible sign, as on the first occasion. Neither are we told that these unique gifts of the Holy Spirit were then given to all or only some disciples, like the gift of healing, working miracles, prophecy, or discernment of spirits, to speak in tongues or to interpret. Whether these gifts were to remain with the Church through the ages or whether they will be given again to the Church at the 'times of restitution of all things' (Acts 3:21), these are questions we do not have to decide. But we should notice that they were distributed by a thrifty hand even at the beginning of the Church age. Were all disciples prophets then, were all workers of miracles? Did all have the gifts of healing, did all speak with tongues? Not at all. Perhaps not even one in a thousand. Perhaps no one, apart from the teachers in the Church, and only a few of those. But it was through a much more excellent gift that they 'were all filled with the Holy Spirit'.... Let us not be concerned with these hypercritical or idle questions any more, regarding these extraordinary gifts, but rather let us look at the ordinary fruits of the Spirit about which we definitely know that they will abide for all ages.[18]

Seventh, the false anthropology of the Pentecostal and Charismatic movement is also connected with the phenomenon of passivity and the point mentioned in the paragraph above. Dave Hunt writes:

> Sir John Eccles, winner of the Nobel Prize for his research on the brain, has described the brain as 'a machine that a "ghost" can operate'. In the normal state of consciousness, the human spirit or mind is the 'ghost' that operates the brain.... In an altered state of consciousness, however—achieved through drugs, hypnosis, yoga, TM, or other similar means—this normal connection is loosened, allowing an alien mind to operate the brain. This alien mind could be a human who has hypnotized the subject, or it could be a spirit being, such as a demon.... The altered state of consciousness is a perfect setup. Having gained control of the mind left passive and open to its entrance through hypnosis or any of the other means of achieving 'higher' consciousness, a demon may then begin to activate the neurons of the brain. In this manner an entire universe of illusion could be created.... An 'inner experience' will be transmitted that will seemingly validate the claims and teachings of the guru or cult leader.[19]

The Holy Spirit enables me to utilise this 'machinery' increasingly well. He produces the result that my 'self or ghost' (in biblical anthropology, my soul, Greek *psyche*) can operate this 'machine' efficiently. But the Holy Spirit will never interfere or use my brain directly, because God respects the order of His creation. He has restricted Himself here and does not manipulate man, because He loves him. But the false spirit will try everything to use man's brain directly. Sometimes it even takes place against the will or as a surprise to the person, when we think of the phenomenon of compulsive thoughts.

I would like to place these fundamental facts in juxtaposition. The Holy Spirit causes self-control. The false (demon) spirit seeks direct control. The Holy Spirit illuminates the understanding, while the false spirit switches it off. The Holy Spirit makes one watchful and active, the false spirit makes one passive. The Holy Spirit influences my heart through my will and obedience. The false spirit uses my body directly.

Because of that false understanding, the Charismatic and Pentecostal circles proclaim the Holy Spirit's direct use of the human body and mind, and therefore all too often begin their prophecies with: 'Thus says the Lord.' However, we do not find this formulation anywhere in the New Testament, it is limited solely to the Old Testament.

It is believed, usually by quoting verses of 1 Corinthians 14 that the Holy Spirit speaks or prays directly through or in a person. But as already pointed out earlier, the Holy Spirit is not mentioned in this passage. 1 Corinthians 14:14, 'For if I pray in an unknown tongue, *my spirit* prayeth...', makes it clear that Paul talks of the human spirit. To confuse the spirits in this case, is surely not a matter of secondary importance.

Arnold Bittlinger, who could be called the father of the Charismatic movement in Germany, writes in his book 'Glossolalia':

Many Christians have experienced that 'it' is constantly praying in them—even when they are silent or their thoughts are occupied with work.[20]

These are typical laws of a false spirit. The Holy Spirit works it out that I myself pray and I myself speak. He will not do that for me, because God never encourages laziness or passiveness.

The above mentioned quotation by Arnold Bittlinger

became very real to me while counselling a young man entangled in autogenic training, who later became converted. He described his basic teaching from autogenic training as expressed in the sentence, 'I am breathed' or 'it breathes me'.

In this context it should be interesting to note what G. H. Lang writes about the beginning of the Pentecostal movement:

> A woman rose in a meeting and moved toward the piano. Her husband, knowing she could not play, shut the piano to avoid a fiasco. But she, though walking among the seats with her eyes tightly closed, reached the piano safely, opened it and played musically.[21]

This is a classical example of the working of counterfeit spirits. The 'biological machine' of the woman served as a tool of the seductive spirit which played the piano through her. In this sense she only acted as a medium.

We mentioned the case of Bennett, whose tongue and jaw was worked by an unseen power, and several others. We sadly meet these phenomena of mediumism and passivity throughout these whole movements. Completely disregarding the biblical teaching about man's personality the Pentecostal and Charismatic circles proclaim the Holy Spirit's direct use of the human body and mind—such as speaking out of him as if he were a medium. Therefore all movements of this kind—be it the Pentecostal movement of Los Angeles 1906, the Charismatic movement with its beginning about 1960 or the Catholic Charismatic movement which joined in 1967—in every case started off with prophecies introduced with these words: 'Thus says the Lord.' It has already been stated that we do not find this formulation anywhere in the New Testament.

We must keep in mind that the New Testament inspiration works on a different line. Even admitting the fact that the inspiration will remain a mystery which cannot be completely unfolded, we may maintain that the Holy Spirit never eliminates the human mind and personality. Rather we observe a wonderful harmony between the Holy Spirit and the human personality.

As the direct speaking of the Holy Spirit through human beings is believed in these circles, this will explain the occasional strong feeling of self-importance which often results in pride and stubbornness against sound doctrine. If anyone doubts the origin and biblical basis of these prophecies or even 'I-Jesus or I-the Lord-messages', the doubter will often be accused of having blasphemed the Holy Spirit, a statement which only belongs to the living God, our Lord Jesus Christ. Otherwise one judges a person and just this is forbidden in the Word of God. But we are commanded to try the spirits.

A. E. Ruark writes:

Those who speak in tongues under the power of a spirit without testing it do so in disobedience to God's positive command. They throw themselves open to Satanic deception.[22]

Any uncertainty as to whether the Spirit had directly spoken is frequently considered wrong. The biblical attitude of alertness is even taken as sin against the Holy Spirit. Again these wrong views arise from a completely wrong understanding of the biblical teaching of the Holy Spirit (pneumatology) and of human personality (anthropology).

Depending on the intensity of infiltration, these evil powers will gradually gain control of the human brain, soon being able to operate or manipulate it like a machine, as Dave Hunt has pointed out. As a result, we see an increasing number of reports of people hearing voices, having dreams, visions, appearances of angels and so on. Some even claim that they have seen Jesus himself. Again we must call this the work of a counterfeit spirit, following the laws of mediumism and passiveness.

While stating this, I do not mean that each supernatural dream or each miraculous event (I do believe in divine healing) must be false or demonic. What I want to point out is that this increasing emphasis of supernatural phenomena, particularly healings, as predicted for these last days, have a false source driving them.

By gaining control over the brain, these evil powers attack the nervous system of their victims. Many who have spoken in tongues, after seemingly having experienced wonderful 'blessings', end up with nervous break-downs, uncontrolled emotionalism, or worse, in psychiatric hospitals or even gross immorality.

G. H. Lang, by quoting a letter, has made a similar observation:

This will end, you will see, either in immorality or insanity. It has ended in both ways already in many, many cases.[23]

This relationship also explains, why the Charismatic movement has such an attraction for emotionally unstable people and why the majority of those, who were entangled in drugs before their conversion, are in such circles where tongue-speaking is practised. Some of them thought they could compensate for an inferiority-complex by aspiring to and striving after extraordinary manifestations and gifts. They are all the more susceptible to emotions, signs and miracles and the totally blissful experience.

A. E. Ruark mentions the following:

The body is the easiest point of entrance for demon

spirits.... For this reason demons insist on the person seeking tongues. When an entrance is once gained, they take steps towards their further evil designs, which lead to nervous troubles and even insanity. Statistics of two large mental institutions in the United States show that between eighty and ninety percent of the inmates are from branches of the Christian Church which practise speaking in tongues.[24]

With the growing intensity of the influence of darkness, such believers are sometimes partly or even fully controlled by counterfeit spirits. This can result in being thrown to the floor, 'slain in the spirit', fainting, strong physical reactions, etc. This grave, serious word, demon possession, means that someone else is in possession of me so that I am not able to do what I want to do. I lose control of my brain or parts of my body, etc. The Scripture declares: 'The spirits of the prophets are subject to the prophets' (1 Corinthians 14:32).

In the Pentecostal magazine 'Wort + Geist' ('Word + Spirit') Yonggi Cho relates his conversion and subsequent healing from tuberculosis. After stating how Jesus stood beside him wearing a crown of thorns and blood running down his temples, he continues:

My tongue and my lips began to speak. I tried to stop, but it appeared as if another person controlled my tongue and wanted to express himself forcefully. I did not know what it was, but I realized that the more I spoke the better I felt.' ('Wort + Geist', December 1973, p 13, translated).

Similar phenomena, where people lose self-control and allow themselves to be controlled, take place at meetings with John Wimber. So he reports with his own words about the history of his work in a message given in 1980 at Yorba Linda:

The Holy Spirit fell on us.... I walked up to a woman to pray for her and I raised my hand and she went flying...bam! against the wall she went, over a couch, knocked over a table and a lamp and hit the corner. Now she had a bad neck she wanted to be prayed for.... Another guy fell against me and hit me in the chest speaking in tongues like a machine gun.... I thought what have we released here? This is weird. The moment they touched me, we both went down and there was the sense, the presence of something in the room. God!...I went home and I was sort of drunken.... I said to Carol (his wife, author's note), 'I think we are in for something,' and when I said that I went right to the floor!...One girl fell so hard, I thought oh no, she is gonna die. She hit her head on a chair and on a table and on the floor. Bam! bam! bam!...Then I heard about catchers. So we got a catcher.' (verbatim quotations from a tape).

In one of the highest forms of control, according to my understanding, these evil powers can even remove the inner self of a man out of his body for an extended time. This is called 'out-of-the-body experience' (OBE) and a known phenomenon of high grade spiritism, as mentioned before.

In the same category belong the death experiences, referring to 'Kubler-Rose' reports and Raymond Moody's bestseller, *Life after Life*, in which people gave the account of having the sensation of being outside their own body sitting or lying somewhere in distance. I mention this, because this phenomenon is found more and more in Christian literature, as will be shown later.

Eighth, it is not the Lord Jesus who is spoken of first, but the Spirit. But He just does not want to speak of Himself very much according to God's Word. The Holy Spirit works like a searchlight, who illuminates the person of the Lord Jesus and is not visible Himself. Only in the presence of 'spiritual' fog does the source of light manifest itself increasingly, whilst one can hardly recognise the illuminated person. And when the best man puts himself in the place of the bridegroom, then there is utter confusion.

Ninth, a completely false view of eschatology is taught. During the time just prior to the second coming of Christ, the Bible does not teach a world wide revival, but a world wide deception and falling away (2 Thessalonians 2:3). Some enthusiasts even think we are standing before a 'world revival'. As a matter of fact, we are standing before a world disaster.

If we summarise all these points and consider all the distinctive marks, then one easily and clearly recognises that the Charismatic movement is a mimicry, the most dangerous and cleverest imitation of Satan; right from the beginning a spiritualistic, mediumistic movement which is seen in a positive way by those who are (to a certain extent) infiltrated themselves by such deceiving spirits. Thanks to the enormous occult revival of our days, a regular Pentecost of hell, the number of sympathisers and members of this movement is growing steadily, and this movement is going to run right into the superchurch of the world dictator; moreover a movement which also fits perfectly into the picture of the last days drawn in the Bible.

Let us quickly summarise: In Matthew 24 the Lord Jesus speaks about His return sounding a warning of deception (verse 4). He speaks of false prophets and falling away from the faith (verses 11–12). For there shall arise false Christs, and false prophets and shall give great signs and wonders so as to mislead, if possible, even the elect. (verse 24). Besides, He compares the time of His return with the time of Noah (verses 37–39). If we read in Genesis 6, then we learn that the sons of God had united themselves with the daughters of men. Whichever way one interprets this passage, it definitely reveals an ungodly mixture. And this is exactly what is taking place right in front of our eyes today.

It should not surprise us therefore that a leading man of this movement, Larry Christenson, suggests prayer practices which are common in the occult tenets of Christian Science.

In this sect both sickness and death are brought forth as unreal and are the result of false teaching. If anyone really gets sick, then he will be healed by the others concentrating on the patient, and seeing him healthy through mental powers. They really have remarkable success, right down to the healing of cancer. They themselves call it 'mind-healing'—mental concentration on a sick person.

Almost identically to this, Larry Christenson recommends:

> ...For example, you have a person who is sick and you are praying for him to get well. Don't see him in the hospital bed with that broken leg up in a sling, or all yellow and under-nourished, or whatever else his condition might be. See him well. Or, if that's a little too difficult for you, see a picture of light around him and see a picture of Jesus standing by the bedside and ministering to that person, so that you are bringing the activity of God into the situation through your active imagination.[25]

These mediumistic instructions concerning prayer should not surprise us, since Larry Christenson is strongly influenced by Agnes Sanford. Perhaps her most famous book is called 'Healing Light'. In the preface (page 5) Larry Christenson reports how a new world was opened to him through this work. He basically owes his Charismatic impulses to Agnes Sanford.

Now this woman writes, how the dead work through us and how we receive an influx of power thereby. This is sometimes so strong that one can actually feel it going up one's spine.

> His angels and spiritual messengers also work through us, and perhaps we are often allowed to become aware of their assistance and support. Even the 'spirits of just men made perfect', for whom we perhaps prayed while they were on earth, are present (Hebrews 12) and work through us, for the bridges which were built from spirit to spirit last beyond the gulf of death.... When we pray for His coming and when we work with the other 'saints', we experience an influx of power. Many of us experience it as a current, full of life, which penetrates in the innermost part of our body, rising upwards through our spine. It is so powerful that we are forced to stand quite straight and to breathe quite lightly and calmly. Perhaps for a short time we are unable to speak.... This fullness must be passed on.[26]

But these are the classical phenomena and symptoms of spiritism, which is defined as contact with the dead. Is it really so misleading and extreme to call these movements mediumistic and spiritualistic?

Now Agnes Sanford is by no means a minor figure, but was decisive in introducing the healing services into the large churches in America, as Francis MacNutt, a Catholic priest, points out in his book *Healing*:

> Although her husband died some years ago, Mrs Sanford has carried on the work of teaching and is perhaps more responsible than anyone else for renewing the healing ministry in the main-line churches.[27]

In this book (*Healing*) we also learn that Agnes Sanford was one of the main speakers at meetings of 'Camp Farthest

Out', a movement which she has also influenced. In this group Mervin Carothers received his 'baptism of the Spirit', and Ruth Stapelton Carter, sister of the ex-President, was in the group for some time. From this movement, which among other things suggests and practises prayer on the plane of telepathy, many impulses have gone out and are still going out. The international director of 'Camp Farthest Out' was Roland Brown. We have already mentioned his guidance for passive and meditative prayer.

In fact it is shocking what a wave of deception, what a current of mysticism and spiritualism is sweeping over the churches!

The Cup of Drunkenness in the End Times

The Bible states several times how the judgement of God is accompanied by intoxication: 'Thus saith the LORD God of Israel, Every bottle shall be filled with wine and they shall say unto thee, Do we not certainly know that every bottle shall be filled with wine? Then shalt thou say unto them, Thus saith the LORD, Behold I will fill all the inhabitants of this land, even the kings that sit upon David's throne, and the priests and the prophets, and all the inhabitants of Jerusalem, with drunkenness.... I will not...pity...but destroy them.' (Jeremiah 13:12–14). 'Thou hast shewed thy people hard things, thou hast made us to drink the wine of astonishment.' (Psalm 60:3).

The false spirit acts like a cup of drunkenness and leads to a state of intoxication, linked with a lack of self-control. 'Stay yourselves, and wonder: Cry ye out and cry: they are drunken, but not with wine; they stagger, but not with strong drink. For the LORD hath poured out upon you the spirit of deep sleep...' (Isaiah 29:9–10). When the Lord Jesus speaks of His second coming He exhorts us to be especially vigilant.

When we think of the spiritualistic prayer practised by Agnes Sanford, Isaiah 29:4 assumes a most amazing topicality in regard to the end times: 'And thou shalt be brought down (as we know, judgement begins at the house of God— Author), and shall speak out of the ground, and thy speech shall be low out of the dust, and thy voice shall be, as of one that hath a familiar spirit out of the ground, and thy speech shall whisper out of the dust.'

'Thus saith the LORD God of Israel unto me; Take the wine cup of this fury at my hand, and cause all the nations, to whom I send thee, to drink it. And they shall drink, and be moved, and be mad because of the sword that I will send among them.... Drink ye...and fall and rise no more, because of the sword which I will send among you.' (Jeremiah 25:15,16,27).

Reinhard Bonnke describes in his paper 'Revival Report', how in a stadium in South Africa 3,500 people come forward to receive the 'baptism of the Spirit'. Within five seconds they are struck to the ground by a power which is sadly, as so often today, mistaken for God, and they speak in tongues. Characteristically, most of them lie on their backs (Isaiah 28:13) and some can only get up again when they have touched Reinhard Bonnke's fellow-counsellors. What a depressing, anticipatory fulfilment of Jeremiah 25:27 this is already! It is true that we are living in the last days.

'Make ye him drunken: for he magnified himself against the LORD.' (Jeremiah 48:26). Hardly a generation in the Western World has suppressed the commandments and rebelled against God as much as the present one. It should come as no surprise that we are intoxicated.

The Campaign 'Youth Protection in Baden-Württemberg' has published a book entitled *Youth in a Trance?* It is clearly shown how this generation is increasingly falling a victim to intoxication and it is stated:

A trance is what we call the state in which a person no longer possesses complete control over himself. To fall into a trance, it is enough to stare into a glass ball filled with water, or to concentrate on looking at a white chalk circle on a black floor. The presence of a hypnotist is by no means necessary for this. The effect of auto-suggestion or self-hypnosis is generally known.... What does this mean for the discotheque? There at least the exterior conditions for a trance or a slight hypnosis are present: ecstatic dancing, helpful group atmosphere and music with a steady, stamping, deafening rhythm. Let us consider the remarks made by young people: 'Some time after I have left the disco, I have the feeling as if I were awakening from some dream or other.'[29]

An intoxicated or drunk person usually does not recognise the danger confronting him, he overestimates himself and is no longer in a position to assess his own condition properly. Often there is a rude awakening.

'The cup also shall pass through unto thee: thou shalt be drunken, and shalt make thyself naked.' (Lamentations 4:21). Group dynamics lead to the exposure of the soul. However, the sex-revolution and lack of restraint in our day have led to an exposure of the body, which is virtually unparalleled in the history of the world.

In the Book of the Revelation we see then how Babylon the Great has offered the cup of drunkenness to all the nations (17:2). It has been briefly mentioned how the Roman Church bears many features of Babylon. Therefore it should not surprise us that charismatics are increasingly sympathising with this church and feel themselves drawn towards Rome. David du Plessis, the so-called Mr Pentecost, gives the following report in *Christian News*:

The Catholic Church has become a tremendous interest to me and I sometimes wonder if I'm not more Catholic than some Catholics are.[30]

People have drunk from the bewitching, befuddling cup of drunkenness of the Church of Rome in the form of these spirits of tongues. David du Plessis reports concerning his 'baptism of the Spirit':

> But before I knew it, I began to laugh as never before in my life. No one stopped me. I held my side and said, 'Lord, I can't take any more. Help me...help me to express what I feel!' And again I wanted to begin to shout 'Hallelujah', but I could only articulate the 'Hal-'...instead I began to speak in new tongues, words that I had never heard before. The 'Hal-' had opened my mouth and the Lord filled it with a new language. This language sounded funny to me.[31]

In fact this reminds us more of an emotional, spiritual intoxication than of the serious holiness of the Spirit of God.

Today we are being increasingly intoxicated by sex, drugs, loud music (especially heavy rock music has the same physiological effect as drugs), alcohol, television, astrology, occultism and mysticism. In the German periodical *Der Spiegel* there was an editorial about astrology with the title 'Astrology—the 'in' drug', and it is reported that 54% of the Germans read their horoscope regularly.[32]

Babylon the Great, to whose ancient wisdom astrology belonged, is in fact arising again. We hear of experiences of 'Close encounters of the third kind', UFO's, star-wars, PSI, clairvoyance, Yoga, hovering caused by TM, acupuncture, autogenic training. Palmistry is recommended just as the magic power of the black arts, levitation, hypnosis and summoning in a séance, a spirit pretending to be the spirit of a deceased relative, or of a person who was, when alive, famous, have become popular party-games in America and elsewhere.

In the wake of this downward trend into mysticism in the

end times, we should not be surprised to read the following in a secular newspaper under the title 'The Occult: Truth and Deceit':

A current American bestseller named *Shaman's Doorway* lists the following among the modern cults and trips: Zen, macrobiotics, space-travel, sorcery, 'Tarot', Yoga, voodoo, astrology, palmistry, 'speaking in tongues' and others.[33]

The evangelical author George Tarleton reports in his booklet, *The Occult Mushroom*, about the situation in England:

Our preoccupation with the whole gamut of occult is seen in a survey carried out by a youth worker. He questioned 80,000 school children between the ages of 13 and 15. He found that 80% of them had a working knowledge of either ouija or levitation.[34]

Seen from this perspective it is not surprising that speaking in tongues is very widespread in the churches there. Such spiritualistic practices are the ideal cultural medium for the tongues movement.

On the same page of his book he complains that his country (England) is about to go on a psychic trip. One should be aware that he wrote this as early as 1973. In the meantime the intoxication has not diminished, but has grown even worse.

A secular magazine complains:

Everyone has heard of 'Yoga', Transcendental Meditation, 'Yin and Yang', sufism and such cults; many have come into direct contact with them somehow. We hear and read about bio-rhythms, telepathy, extra-sensory perception, telekinesis, astrology, UFO's, time-travelling and other crazes. Everyone knows from the mass media or from his friends' cases where someone is striving for 'cosmic experiences' and an expansion of the consciousness by means of the most varied chemical substances. And no one can fail to have noticed that the world is currently experiencing the worst epidemic of drugs.[35]

'And I will tread down the people in mine anger, and will make them drunk in my fury...' (Isaiah 63:6), says the living God.

The mystic trend is uncanny and it is alarming how much it has already caught hold of believers. Someone once stated that we are living in a post-literary age. Formerly, the greatest instrument of influence was the word, today by means of television it has become the emotion conveying picture. A similar development is occurring in the church. Formerly, believers used to say: It is written, today more and more: I have experienced.

We hear of visions, voices, healings, signs, miracles, appearances of angels and Jesus, prophecies, messages in tongues, and experiences of death; believers now have their own intoxicating music—when music is supposed to have a neutral value, there is no objection to bringing these hot beats into the church—we read of people being raised from the dead, people claim to have come back from Paradise, we are invited to passive meditation and contemplations of an image, to the creative depiction of prayers, etc. In fact, this generation of the last days, believers and unbelievers alike, has drunk deeply from God's cup of wrath, as the increasing Charismatic wave shows so strikingly.

John MacArthur, Jr states:

...washing machines are 'healed'; empty gas tanks are supernaturally filled; people are 'slain' (knocked flat) by the Holy Spirit. One lady reports being given a new 'belly button'. A man named Marvin Ford testifies that he has actually been to heaven and back. Amazing experiences like these seem to be the order of the day as God, in an apparent hyperkinetic out-burst, puts on a supernatural performance rivalled only by the six days of Creation and the Egyptians plagues![36]

Our spiritual fathers erected defences and sought to dam up these tides of deception. Martin Luther even declared:

Those who talk about and look for revelations and dreams are despisers of God, since they are not satisfied with His Word. In spiritual things I expect neither a revelation nor dreams; I have the clear word, that is why Paul exhorts us to adhere to it, even if an angel from heaven (Gal 1:8) teaches differently.[37]

In the course of the spiritual 'policy of detente' today, it is normal to pull down clear fronts. The spirit of the age demands pluralism and as a result it is orientated towards ecumenism and syncretism. People talk about balance and broad-mindedness.

In 2 Corinthians 6:13, Paul exhorts the believers to be enlarged. Be filled with Christ and His Word. And then to be narrow for the world (verse 14) and come out from amongst them (verse 17), although on the other hand, we should be balanced. (1 Cor 5:9–13).

These who accuse others of being narrow-minded are often lacking in obedience to Christ and His Word, if we just remember the parallels between liberalism, ecumenism and Charismatic movement, as pointed out before. Then, like the Corinthians, one is wide open to the world and soon yoked together unbiblically. This seems to be the real secret of our present 'broad-mindedness'.

Many churches and believers today are like Samson, who peacefully fell asleep and who loved the person who was his worst enemy. Today Christians defend movements and phenomena, which in reality are making them ripe for judgement.

So Dave Hunt states:

Until very recently, most church leaders classified clairvoyance, psychokinesis, out-of-body experiences, and other psychic phenomena as occult. *That attitude is changing rapidly.* In 1977, Morton Kelsey, a prominent Episcopal priest who teaches at Notre Dame University, came out openly in favour of cultivating psychic experiences. In his book *The Christian and the Supernatural*, Kelsey described Jesus as comparable to a 'shaman' (psychic) and encouraged Christians to develop psychic powers such as clairvoyance, precognition and telepathy. While acknowledging that there are some dangers, Kelsey believes that development of ESP within the Christian church would help to validate the miracles claimed in the Bible.[38]

With this background it is naturally not surprising that Kelsey is strongly in favour of speaking in tongues.

In fact, as stated earlier, in Christian books excursions of the soul or out-of-body experiences (OBE) are increasingly offered as the work of God. We have already mentioned it with regard to Demos Shakarian. Roland Buck, whose life story is told by Charles and Francis Hunter, experiences it:

The whole time I was in the throne room, I felt very much at ease, but the experience was over too quickly. Suddenly I came back to my office and could see myself sitting bowed in prayer.[39]

Bilquis Sheikh had a similar experience, as we can read in her book *I dared to call Him Father*:

I was resting one afternoon and thinking of my Lord, when I suddenly felt myself floating out of the window. I was sure that I was not asleep; I floated through the filigree wood work of the window and saw the earth beneath me. I was so afraid that I cried out in terror and suddenly I found myself back in my bed. I was dizzy and hardly dared to breathe.[40]

George Richie's *Return from Tomorrow* and other alleged experiences of death and paradise in a Christian disguise, belong in this category. It is uncanny how much this cup of drunkenness has already caught hold of Christendom.

In this decline in the end times, where man is developing more and more supernatural characteristics and usurping apostolic powers as divine—and thereby he is increasingly making himself into a god and he thinks arrogantly that he can control the sovereign God—we find that the pantheistic magic teachings of Yonggi Cho are not out of place. His book *The Fourth Dimension* is full of instructions which through the power of positive thinking ultimately lead to self-deliverance.

Therefore speaking in tongues is the initial sign of baptism in the Holy Spirit. . . . So think that Christ is dependent on you and on your spoken word to release His presence. What will you do with this Jesus on your tongue? Will you set Him free to bless others, or will you imprison Him with Your silent tongue and your closed mouth?[41]

When we read such statements it reminds us of the first twisting of truth in the history of mankind: 'You will be like God!'

Whereas the Holy Spirit creates a dependence on the personal God, which usually works through brokenness, in these movements the so-called spirit becomes an impersonal force which is only too often perceived psychically, which the 'Charismatic' can have at his disposal and which he usually passes on through the laying on of hands. Of course, this is not true of every member of this movement, but these tendencies can be identified.

It is true that there is a lot of talk today about the gift of discernment of spirits, but Paul apparently did not think too much of this charisma in the Corinthians, who are supposed to have had all the gifts. After all, he had to say to them: 'For if he that cometh preacheth another Jesus, whom we have not preached, or if ye receive another spirit, which ye have not received...ye might well bear with him.' (2 Corinthians 11:4).

Such a reproach can hardly be made of someone who has kept some discernment. But sadly today the situation basically looks similar, especially among the circles where people like to make reference to the Epistle to the Corinthians.

We have already mentioned, how the 'Moon sect' sees this revival of gifts as the working of the departed spirits from paradise. A partly spiritually blinded Christianity sees in this the working of the Holy Spirit.

Anyone who is still guided by the Word of God and has not allowed his view to be obscured by the spirit of the world can recognise just what is really taking place here and what we can actually think of this charismatic 'revival'.

After all, these movements are amazingly in accordance with the spirit of the world. The Corinthians were limited in their growth (children), immoral in their way of life, they tolerated evil, they were charismatic in their practices and heretical in their teachings. This is so similar to the spirit of the modern age in these days in which the church is being increasingly influenced by the attitude of the world, that we find the same state of affairs today:

George Gardiner writes:

> But not only was the city tragically like our civilization, the church of Corinth was tragically like a large segment of Christendom in our days.... It has been said that the letters to the Corinthians are the most relevant books of the New Testament for the last half of the twentieth century. Truer words were never spoken.[42]

Someone who is guided by the Scriptures will have little difficulty in seeing through this spirit.

Conclusion

The question now arises, whether in the face of all the advancing mysticism and spiritualism we should remain silent or not. As I have already mentioned, in Christendom today the trend towards the policy of spiritual detente is prevalent. People talk of being well-balanced, and this strategy is already so successful that soon everyone who clearly opposes the charismatic wave and mysticism will be branded as an extremist.

However, in these discussions and struggles there is naturally the great danger that one falls into the flesh and becomes unloving. Here I would also like to express my regret that in the past I did not say many a thing with more love and patience. We are commanded to love our neighbour even though we are to object to and reject his false teachings and messages (Revelation 2:6). I would like to emphasise again that these brothers and sisters often have the best intentions and are well-meaning and sincere.

However, I can in no way change my opinion on the subject. In fact my wish to warn people becomes greater the more I look behind the scenes, the more I come across literature from this movement, the more I see how these trends are maturing. When the Lord in His mercy has opened one's eyes to this adulteration, it is a heavy burden. Often I have written my statements with deep anxiety, and one should really express these warnings with tears in one's eyes (Acts 20:31). In certain questions of doctrine one may afford to be generous, but is this permitted also in the case of false spirits?

Here I would like to quote H. E. Alexander: 'It would be easier to keep silent in the face of the different kinds of Pentecostal movements. Tolerance as it is practised in our day is less costly than the warning-cry of the watchman. However, we can see what tolerance is in reality when we place it opposite the destructive doctrines in the balance of times and facts. Tolerance is cowardice, the religious spirit of the world, vagueness and goes hand in hand with unwillingness to suffer for the truth. Love acts differently. Truth proceeds more honestly, it does not keep silent when so many members of our heavenly Father's family are threatened by dangers.'[43]

Another argument says: "But in these movements people are saved." Therefore we ought to look positively at this. Some people even think that the Charismatics partly fulfil the commission to world mission.

Now we must stress that it is in fact true that people in these movements come to a saving faith in the Lord Jesus. But in this connection I would like to quote H. E. Alexander again: 'The Charismatic movement owes its existence to two facts: it embellishes itself with truths which it takes from Christianity, and also uses negative psychic and spiritual powers which support its fallacies, its false concepts and interpretations of the human and the divine. Thanks to the first-mentioned fact, God in His boundless mercy works to a certain extent even in circles in the Pentecostal movement to the salvation of souls. However, due to the second fact, the enemy is able to creep in under the guise of holy, divine things, to lead souls astray, to harass and agitate them so that he can enslave them. This leads to the sad results which we have already described. The cases we meet in all the countries where the Pentecostal movement has found an entrance confirm it; there are cases of disillusionment, divisions, fanatical proselytism, slandering and the like.'[44]

Recently in all these questions and discussions I have been increasingly stressing the following: Many Christians, also in these movements and often especially there, long for more power and authority. Who does not feel affected by the statement that we really lack something, that there is much which is not as it should be according to the Word of God?

Now does the answer lie in seeking and striving after these gifts? Is this the shortcut? Here others have already raised their voices in warning. For instance, Carlton Long writes: 'Perhaps the greatest danger of all is to seek a short-cut to spiritual power and victory. Whether we believe in tongues or not let us state that there is no short-cut to spiritual joy, power and effectiveness in the service of the Lord. There is no experience which could suddenly solve all our problems as Christians once and for all. God wants us to depend on Him and to rely on Him every moment of every day. Jesus says, "...let him take up his cross DAILY and follow me." In an excellent and fair writing about speaking in tongues titled "concerning spiritual short-cuts" Raymond W. Frame revealed that the temptations of the Lord Jesus were all temptations to a short-cut.'

Satan recommended that instead of waiting for the Father to send His angels to satisfy His hunger after 40 days of fasting, our Lord should quickly satisfy His hunger through a miracle, by turning stones into bread.

In a second temptation Satan tempted Jesus to avoid the three long years, during which He taught, healed and performed miracles under steadily increasing, malicious opposi-

APPENDIX TO THE FIFTH EDITION (GERMAN)   265

tion, and which finally ended in the Crucifixion. Why would He not instead use a far more pleasant and simpler expedient to win the Jews over to Himself, by dramatically jumping from a pinnacle of the temple during a great festival?

And finally, why would He not, instead of allowing Himself to be delivered into the hands of Gentiles and to be crucified as a criminal, rather simply bend His knee in worship before Satan, and thereby accept 'all the kingdoms of the world, and glory of them which were offered to Him by the "Prince of this world"?'[45]

In this offer of a short-cut to spiritual power lies perhaps the most dazzling temptation of the Charismatic movement. Furthermore, it sometimes presents quite astonishing results and successes in a short time, at least at first glance.

Let us not forget one thing. Only once in the Bible does it say that the Father runs, that the Creator hastens towards His creature with giant steps, i.e. that the presence, authority, fullness and blessing of God is imparted to us almost at the speed of lightning. It is the story of the prodigal son (Luke 15:20).

In this connection, a blessed evangelist once asked the question: Whom does the Father run towards? The great people in this world? The saints? The Churchgoers? Or, if we apply the question to our subject, those who reach out for more power, gifts, experience or even the 'baptism of the Spirit'? No! But to the sinner who cries for mercy.

In the letters to the churches in Revelation grave defects are mentioned. All the churches except two are rebuked. The Lord Jesus does not reproach any church for striving too little after gifts or for not having received the 'baptism of the Spirit', but He says five times: Repent!

And so I would like to reiterate this message to all, myself included, that there is no other way to power and authority but the old way of the Cross where man is judged and everything of which we can possibly be proud and which gives us self-confidence, must be broken.

May God grant that His children humble themselves before Him and repent—we have every reason to. May He bestow on us a great love for Himself and for His word (2 Chronicles 7:14).

FOOTNOTE REFERENCES

Chapter One

1. Ivar Lissner, 'Rätselhafte Kulturen, Heyne Verlag, p 118, 1966, translated.
2. Zahn, Commentary to the New Testament.
3. Johannes Greber, 'Der Verkehr mit der Geisterwelt' ('Communication with the Spirit World'), Brunner Verlag, p 133, 1937, translated.
4. Watchman Nee, 'The Spiritual Man', Christian Fellowship Publishers, Inc., New York, 1968, Vol. 3, pp 92–93.
5. Larry Christenson, 'The Christian Family', p 184, Bethany Fellowship, Inc., Minneapolis, Minnesota, 1970.
6. Watchman Nee, 'The Spiritual Man', Vol. 2, p 64, 1968.
7. Larry Christenson, 'The Christian Family', pp 186 and 191.
8. Watchman Nee, 'The Spiritual Man', Vol 3, p 21, 1968.
9. Wilhard Becker, 'Nicht Plappern wie die Heiden' ('Not babbling as the Heathen'), translated, Rolf-Kuehne-Verlag, p 146, 1967.
10. Watchman Nee, 'The Spiritual Man', Vol. 3, p 31, 1968.
11. Larry Christenson, 'The Christian Family', p 187.

12. Watchman Nee, 'The Latent Power of the Soul', p 46, 1972, Christian Fellowship Publishers, Inc., New York.
13. Roland Brown, 'Beten lernen' ('Learn to pray'), translated, Rolf-Kuehne-Verlag, pp 24–25, 1972.
14. Watchman Nee, 'The Spiritual Man', Vol. 3, p 31, 1968.
15. Ibid, p 119.
16. Johannes Greber, 'Der Verkehr mit der Geisterwelt', 1937, pp 29–30 ('Communication with the Spirit World'), translated.
17. 'Wort und Geist' ('Word and Spirit', translated), Nr. 6 June 1973, p 5.
18. G. H. Lang, 'The Earlier Years of the Modern Tongues Movement', pp 28–29, 1958.
19. Watchman Nee, 'The Spiritual Man', Vol. 3, p 119, 1968.
20. Kathryn Kuhlman, 'Nothing is impossible with God', Prentice Hall, The Englewood Cliffs, New Jersey, USA, p 192, translated.
21. Hans Brandenburg, 'Kinderkrankheiten des Glaubens' ('Childhood Diseases of Faith', translated), Brockhaus Verlag, 1975, pp 80 and 52–53.
22. Kathryn Kuhlman, 'God can do it again', Prentice Hall, pp 170–171, translated.
23. John Kildahl, 'Psychology of Speaking in Tongues', p 59, Hodder and Stoughton, 1972.
24. Michael Griffiths, 'Three Men filled with the Spirit', pp 28–29, Overseas Missionary Fellowship, 1969.
25. G. H. Lang, 'The Earlier Years of the Modern Tongues Movement', p 57, 1958.
26. John MacArthur, Jr, 'What's Wrong in the Charismatic Movement?', quoted from a series of tapes, Msg. 3.
27. Watchman Nee, 'The Spiritual Man', Vol. 3, p 53, 1968.
28. William MacDonald, '1.Korintherbrief' ('1 Corinthians', translated) Emmaus Bible School, p 131, 1971.
29. Ibid, p 132, translated.
30. Hans Brandenburg, 'Kinderkrankheiten des Glaubens'

('Childhood Diseases of Faith'), Brockhaus Verlag, 1975, p 86, translated.

31. Ibid, p 87, translated.

32. Michael Griffiths, 'Three Men filled with the Spirit', Overseas Missionary Fellowship, pp 38–39, 1969.

33. Spiros Zodhiatos, 'Tongues', Ridgefield AMG Press, p 70.

34. John Stott, 'Baptism and Fullness', pp 114–115, Inter Varsity Press, 1977.

35. Hans Brandenburg, 'Kinderkrankheiten des Glaubens' ('Childhood Diseases of Faith', translated), p 49.

36. William MacDonald, '1.Korintherbrief' ('1 Corinthians', translated), 1971, pp 150–151.

37. Michael Griffiths, 'Three Men filled with the Spirit', 1969, p 41.

38. Ibid, p 39.

39. John Stott, 'Your Mind Matters', Inter Varsity Fellowship, 1972, pp 27–28.

40. Ibid, p 10.

41. Michael Griffiths, 'Three Men filled with the Spirit', p 21.

42. William MacDonald, '1.Korintherbrief', p 154, translated.

43. Ibid, p 132, translated.

44. Michael Griffiths, 'Three Men filled with the Spirit', p 21.

45. W. Schlatter, 'Gesunder Glaube und Schwarmgeist' ('Sound Faith and Enthusiasm', translated), Buchhandlung der Evangelischen Gesellschaft, 1929, pp 72–73.

46. Paul Yonggi Cho, 'The Evangelist and the life of Faith', Publication from the 'International Conference for Itinerant Evangelists', July 17, 1983, Amsterdam, pp 7–8.

47. William Welmers, 'Christianity Today', November 8, 1963, pp 127–128.

48. John Kildahl, 'The Psychology of Speaking in Tongues', p 47.

49. Ibid, p 63.

50. Michael Griffiths, 'Three Men filled with the Spirit', p 31.

51. Merrill F. Unger, 'What Demons Can Do To Saints', pp 164 and 168.

52. Watchman Nee, 'The Spiritual Man', Vol. 3, p 123.

53. Gerald McGraw, 'Tongues should be tested', 'The Alliance Witness', June 5, 1974, p 6.

54. Ibid, p 5.

55. Watchman Nee, 'The Spiritual Man', Vol. 2, pp 57–58.

56. John Kildahl, 'The Psychology of Speaking in Tongues', p 50.

57. A. Schuetz, 'Bibel und Gemeinde' ('Bible and Church', translated), April–June 1975, pp 172–173.

58. Watchman Nee, 'The Spiritual Man', Vol 1, pp 95 and 193.

59. Ibid, Vol. 3, p 30.

60. Gerald McGraw, 'Tongues should be tested', p 6.

61. Ibid, p 4.

62. 'Wort und Geist' ('Word and Spirit', translated), August 1975, pp 7 and 13, translated.

63. G. H. Lang, 'The Earlier Years of the Modern Tongues Movement', pp 25–26.

64. Arnold Bittlinger, 'Glossolalia, Wert und Problematik des Sprachenredens', Rolf-Kuhne-Verlag, 1966, 22–23, translated.

65. Ibid, p 22, translated.

66. Robert Ruegg, 'Bücherrundschau über Geistesgaben und Gemeindedienste', 1976, translated.

67. Watchman Nee, 'The Spiritual Man', Vol. 3, p 121.

68. Arnold Bittlinger, 'Glossolalia', p 52, translated.

69. Roland Buck, 'Angels on Assignment', by Charles & Frances Hunter, Leuchter-Verlag, 1980, p 61, translated.

70. John Stott, 'Your Mind Matters', pp 10–11.
71. Watchman Nee, 'The Spiritual Man', Vol. 3, p 109.
72. Francis Schaeffer, 'The New Super-Spirituality', Hodder & Stoughton, 1973, p 25.

FOOTNOTE REFERENCES

Chapter Two

1. Watchman Nee, 'The Spiritual Man', Vol. 3, p 106, Christian Fellowship Publications, New York, 1968.
2. Ibid, Vol. 2, p 60.
3. Watchman Nee, 'The Spiritual Man', Vol. 3, pp 126, 129.
4. Ibid, Vol. 1, p 130.
5. Lindsay and Carlson, 'Satan is Alive and Well on Planet Earth', Zondervan, 1973.
6. Gerald McGraw, 'Tongues should be tested', The Alliance Witness, June 5, 1974, p 5.
7. Merril F. Unger, Unger's Bible Handbook, Moody Press, 1966, translated.
8. Alexander Seibel, 'Relativitätstheorie und Bibel' ('The Theory of Relativity and the Bible', translated), 1974.
9. Watchman Nee, 'The Spiritual Man', Vol. 2, p 2, p 191, 1968.
10. Otto Riecker, 'Ruf aus Indonesien' ('Call from Indonesia', translated), Telos, p 186, 1971.

FOOTNOTE REFERENCES

Chapter Three

1. F. Rienecker, 'Lexikon zur Bibel' ('Bible Commentary', translated), Brockhaus Verlag, Wuppertal, 1960.
2. Peter Mayer . . . 'dass sie los sein sollen' ('That they may be free', translated), Verlag Bibelschule Beatenberg, 1974, pp 68–69.
3. John Stott, 'Baptism and Fullness', Inter-Varsity Press, p 34, 1977.
4. Gertrud Wasserzug, 'Mitternachtsruf' ('Midnight Call', translated), May 1975, pp 21–22.
5. F. Rienecker, 'Lexikon zur Bibel' ('Bible Commentary', translated), p 1407.
6. Watchman Nee, 'The Spiritual Man', Vol. 3, p 11, 1968.
7. Peter Mayer, 'Dienstgaben für Gottes Volk' ('Service-Gifts for God's People', translated), Bibelschule Beatenberg, p 63.
8. John Stott, 'Baptism and Fullness', p 15, Inter-Varsity Press, 1977.
9. Michael Griffiths, 'Three Men filled with the Spirit', p 18, Overseas Missionary Fellowship, 1969.
10. F. W. Bautz, 'Die Neuapostolische Kirche' ('The New

Apostolic Church', translated), Schriftenmissions-Verlag Gladbeck, p 4.

11. Gertrud Wasserzug, 'Mitternachtsruf', June 1975, p 20.
12. Alfred Kuen, 'Die Charismatische Bewegung' ('Charismatic movement', translated), Brockhaus Verlag, Wuppertal, p 54.
13. Hans Brandenburg, 'Kinderkrankheiten des Glaubens' ('Childhood Diseases of Faith', translated), p 85.
14. The Book of Mormon, Mormon 9:6–9.
15. R. C. Trench, Synonyms of the New Testament, p 342.
16. Watchman Nee, 'The Spiritual Man', Vol. 3, p 18, 1968.
17. John P. Kildahl, 'The Psychology of Speaking in Tongues', p 55, Hodder & Stoughton, 1972.
18. Watchman Nee, 'The Spiritual Man', Vol. 2, p 60.
19. John P. Kildahl, 'The Psychology of Speaking in Tongues', pp 60–61.
20. Watchman Nee, 'The Spiritual Man', Vol. 2, p 103.
21. Johannes Greber, 'Verkehr mit der Geisterwalt' ('Communication with Spirit World', translated), Brunner Verlag, p 125, 1937.
22. Ernst Modersohn, 'Im Banne des Teufels' ('Under the Spell of the Devil', translated), Telos, pp 103–104.
23. Watchman Nee, 'The Spiritual Man', Vol. 3, pp 47–48.
24. Ibid, Vol. 3, p 122.
25. Kathryn Kuhlman, 'Nothing is impossible with God', Verlag Johannes Fix, 1974, p 192, translated.
26. Dennis Bennett, 'The Holy Spirit and You', Leuchter-Verlag, 1973, p 71, translated.
27. David Wilkerson, 'The Cross and the Switchblade', Leuchter-Verlag, p 208, translated.
28. John Stott, 'Baptism and Fullness', p 56, Inter Varsity Press, p 56, 1977.
29. Dennis Bennett, '9 o'clock in the Morning', Leuchter-Verlag, 1972, p 37, translated.

30. Francis Schaeffer, 'The New Super-Spirituality', Telos, 1973, p 24.
31. 'Bible und Gebet' ('Bible and Prayer', translated), September 1975, p 13.
32. Detmar Scheunemann, 'Alle Welt soll sein Wort hören' ('Let the Earth hear His Voice'), Telos, Vol. 2, p 1186, translated.
33. Hans Brandenburg, 'Kinderkrankheiten des Glaubens', p 41, translated.
34. Watchman Nee, 'The Spiritual Man', Vol. 2, p 65, 1968.
35. Mevlin Carothers, 'Prison to Praise', p 29, Hodder & Stoughton, 1970.
36. Ibid, p 30.
37. Ibid, p 31.
38. Ibid, p 31.
39. Ibid, p 35.
40. Ibid, p 35.
41. Ibid, p 36.
42. Ibid, p 36.
43. Ibid, p 37.
44. Ibid, p 42.
45. Watchman Nee, 'The Spiritual Man', Vol. 3, p 42, 1968.
46. Ibid, Vol. 3, p 27.
47. Mervin Carothers, 'Prison to Praise', p 44.
48. Watchman Nee, 'The Spiritual Man', Vol. 3, p 110.
49. Mervin Carothers, 'Prison to Praise', p 65.
50. Schmidt-Schischkoff, 'Philosophisches Wörterbuch' ('Dictionary of Philosophy', translated), Stuttgart, 1974, p 300.
51. Watchman Nee, 'The Spiritual Man', Vol. 3, pp 100–101.
52. Peter Beyerhaus, 'Geisteserfüllung und Geistesunterscheidung' ('Fullness of Spirit and Discernment of Spirits', translated), pp 18–19.
53. Witness Lee, 'Das Beten-Lesen des Wortes' ('The Prayer-reading of the Word', translated), Verlag der Strom, p 8.

54. Watchman Nee, 'The Spiritual Man', Vol. 3, p 25.

55. Mervin Carothers, 'Prison to Praise', p 42.

56. Watchman Nee, 'The Spiritual Man', Vol. 2, pp 237–238.

57. Ibid, Vol. 2, p 238.

58. Mervin Carothers, 'Prison to Praise', p 49.

59. Watchman Nee, 'The Spiritual Man', Vol. 3, p 107.

60. G. H. Lang, 'The Earlier Years of the Modern Tongues Movement', p 50, 1958.

61. Watchman Nee, 'The Spiritual Man', Vol. 3, p 102.

62. Ibid, Vol. 3, p 109.

63. Johannes Greber, 'Verkehr mit der Geisterwelt' ('Communication with the Spirit World', translated), Brunner Verlag, 1937, p 29.

64. Watchman Nee, 'The Spiritual Man', Vol. 3, p 46, 1968.

65. P. A. Dubois, 'Das Gesicht der heutigen Christenheit' ('The Face of Christianity today', translated), Verlag: Das Haus der Bibel, pp 20–21.

66. Johannes Greber, 'Der Verkehr mit der Geisterwelt', p 130, translated.

67. Conrad Murrel, 'True and False Tongues', Saber Publications, pp 4–5.

68. Jessie Penn-Lewis and Evan Roberts, 'War on the Saints', translated from the German Edition, p 111.

69. Grattan Guinness, quoted by Stan Motherwell in an unpublished treatise, 'The Modern Tongues Movement, where is it headed?', p 7.

70. Francis Schaeffer, 'The New Super-Spirituality', Telos, pp 26–28.

71. Jessie Penn-Lewis and Evan Roberts, 'War on the Saints', p 111, translated.

72. Watchman Nee, 'The Latent Power of the Soul', Christian Fellowship Publications, p 34.

73. Watchman Nee, 'The Spiritual Man', Vol. 3, pp 102–103.

FOOTNOTE REFERENCES

Appendix

1. Demos Shakarian, 'The Happiest People on Earth', by John and Elizabeth Sherill, Chosen Books, Old Tapp. N.J., pp 35–36.
2. Jakob Schmitt, 'Die Gnade bricht durch' ('The Grace Breaks Through', translated), Brunnen-Verlag, pp 123–124.
3. Demos Shakarian, 'The Happiest People on Earth', p 92.
4. Ibid, p 96.
5. Ibid, p 106.
6. Ibid, pp 108–109.
7. Jakob Schmitt, 'Die Gnade bricht durch', pp 125–126, translated.
8. John Stott, 'Baptism and Fullness', Inter-Varsity Press, 1977, pp 100–101.
9. Cochlovius, 'Die charismatische Bewegung' ('The Charismatic Movement', translated), Erweckliche Stimme, September 1981, p 4.
10. David du Plessis, 'The Spirit Bade Me Go', published by du Plessis, p 28.

11. Demos Shakarian, 'The Happiest People on Earth', p 134.

12. Elias Schrenk, 'The need of the Church of God for greater equipping of the power of the Spirit, and the conditions for a biblical fulfilment of the same.' Discussions of the Gnadauer Pentecostal Conference, Lecture given by Elias Schrenk, 1910, translated.

13. A. G. Dornfeld, 'Habt ihr den Heiligen Geist empfangen?' ('Have ye received the Holy Ghost?', translated), Leuchter-Verlag, pp 91–92.

14. Don W. Basham, 'Face Up With a Miracle', Leuchter-Verlag, p 158, translated.

15. Alfred Kuen, 'Gemeinde nach Gottes Bauplan' ('The Church according to God's Plan', translated), Telos, 1975, pp 110–111.

16. John Stott, 'Baptism and Fullness', pp 97–98.

17. Spiros Zodhiates, 'Tongues!', AMG Publishers, 1978, pp 22–23.

18. John Wesley, 'Wesley = Predigten' ('Wesley = Sermons', translated), published by Dr Ernst Sommer, Anker-Verlag, 1950, pp 84–85.

19 Dave Hunt, 'The Cult Explosion', Harvest House Publishers, 1980, pp 35–36.

20. Arnold Bittlinger, 'Glossolalia', Rolf-Kuehne-Verlag, 1966, p 26, translated.

21. G. H. Lang, 'The Earlier Years of the Modern Tongues Movement', 1958, p 9.

22. A. E. Ruark, 'Falsities of Modern Tongues', Prairie Bible Institute, p 1.

23. G. H. Lang, 'The Earlier Years of the Modern Tongues Movement', p 45.

24. A. E. Ruark, 'Falsities of Modern tongues', pp 3–4.

25. Larry Christenson, 'The Christian Family', Bethany Fellowship, Inc., p 178.

26. Agnes Sanford, 'Heilendes Licht' ('The Healing Light'),

Oekumenischer Verlag, Dr R. F. Edel, pp 150–151, translated.

27. Francis MacNutt, 'Healing', Ave Maria Press, Notre Dame, Indiana, 1975, p 13.

28. Reinhard Bonnke, 'Revival Report', Vol. 11, Nr. 3/4, 1981.

29. 'Jugend in Trance?', ('Youth in a Trance?', translated), Quelle & Meyer, Heidelberg, 1979, pp 77–78.

30. 'Christian News', quoted by Stan Motherwell in an unpublished treatise, 'The Modern Tongues Movement, where is it headed?', p 4.

31. Bob Slosser, 'Man nennt ihn Mr Pentecost' ('They call him Mr Pentecost', translated), Rhema Verlag, p 37.

32. 'Der Spiegel', November 30, 1981, Nr. 49, p 232.

33. Thomas Molnar, 'Zeitbühne', 'Das Okkulte: Wahrheit und Schwindel' ('The Occult: Truth and Deceit', translated).

34. George Tarleton, 'The Occult Mushroom', Revelation Press, 1973, p 14.

35. 'Kommt jetzt das Zeitalter des Wassermanns?' ('Is the age of Aquarius coming now?', translated), 'War on Drugs', August 1980.

36. John MacArthur, Jr, 'The Charismatics', Zondervan Publishing House, 1978, p 11.

37. Martin Luther, 'Tischreden 5' ('Table Talks', translated), 6211, Fause, Vol. II, p 195.

38. Dave Hunt, 'The Cult Explosion', pp 7–8.

39. Roland Buck, 'Begegnungen mit Engeln' ('Angels on Assignment'), by Charles & Frances Hunter, Leuchter-Verlag, 1980, pp 56–57, translated.

40. Bilquis Sheikh, 'Allah mein Vater?' ('I dared to call him Father'), Special edition of the Orient-Service, Wiesbaden, 1980, p 62, translated.

41. Paul Yonggi Cho, 'Die vierte Dimension' ('The Fourth

Dimension'), Missionswerk Der Weg Zur Freude, 1978, pp 75–76, translated.

42. George E. Gardiner, 'The Corinthian Catastrophe', Kregel Publication, Grand Rapids, 1976, p 11.

43. H. E. Alexander, 'Pfingstbewegung oder Christentum?' ('Pentecostal movement or Christianity?', translated), Haus der Bibel, 1954, p 10.

44. Ibid, p 46.

45. Carlton Long, 'Glossolalie—Zungenreden' ('Glossolalia—Speaking in Tongues', translated), unpublished manuscript, p 29.

Note: The titles in Brackets have been translated literally from magazines and books, originally printed in the German language, it is not always known if they have been published in English.

Other *CHAPTER TWO* Publications

Georges André	*More Fruit*
John Blackburn	*The True Worship*
Cor. Bruins	*Even So Send I You*
William Kelly	*The Prospect*
	(facsimile of magazine)
Jan Rouw	*Gems tell their Secret*
Jan Rouw	*House of Gold*
Jan Rouw	*Shalom & Israel*
W. G. Turner	*John Nelson Darby*